POSITIVE OBLIGATIONS IN CRIMINAL LAW

This book offers a set of essays, old and new, examining the positive obligations of individuals and the state in matters of criminal law. The centrepiece is a new, extended essay on the criminalisation of omissions – examining the duties to act imposed on individuals and organisations by the criminal law, and assessing their moral and social foundations. Alongside this is another new essay on the state's positive obligations to put in place criminal laws to protect certain individual rights.

Introducing the volume is the author's much-cited essay on criminalisation, 'Is the Criminal Law a Lost Cause?'. The book sets out to shed new light on contemporary arguments about the proper boundaries of the criminal law, not least by exploring the justifications for imposing positive duties (reinforced by the criminal law) on individuals and their relation to the positive obligations of the state.

Positive Obligations in Criminal Law

Andrew Ashworth

·HART·
PUBLISHING
OXFORD AND PORTLAND, OREGON
2013

Published in the United Kingdom by Hart Publishing Ltd
16C Worcester Place, Oxford, OX1 2JW
Telephone: +44 (0)1865 517530
Fax: +44 (0)1865 510710
E-mail: mail@hartpub.co.uk
Website: http://www.hartpub.co.uk

Published in North America (US and Canada) by
Hart Publishing
c/o International Specialized Book Services
920 NE 58th Avenue, Suite 300
Portland, OR 97213-3786
USA
Tel: +1 503 287 3093 or toll-free: (1) 800 944 6190
Fax: +1 503 280 8832
E-mail: orders@isbs.com
Website: http://www.isbs.com

British Library Cataloguing in Publication Data
Data Available

ISBN: 978-1-84946-505-2

Typeset by Hope Services, Abingdon
Printed and bound in Great Britain by
TJ International Ltd, Padstow

Preface

Two types of positive obligation are explored in the essays that make up this volume. First, there are positive obligations laid on individuals, companies and other organisations by the criminal law. While the predominant form of criminal laws is the prohibition, most legal systems contain some offences of omission. The failure to fulfil a certain duty is criminalised, sometimes at common law (eg misconduct is a public office; manslaughter by gross negligence), more commonly by statute. Criminal liability for omissions is typically understood by common lawyers to be 'exceptional' or 'special,' and one of the objectives of this volume (in particular, Chapters 2 and 3) is to re-assess the justifications for, and proper limits of, omissions offences.

The second type of positive obligation is one that rests upon the state. It will be argued that the state is under various positive obligations in relation to criminal liability, sometimes as a concomitant of the obligations imposed on subjects. The State's positive obligations include its (international) duty to have in place laws that give adequate protection to the rights of subjects (Chapter 8), not least to children (Chapter 7); and its duty of justice, which applies so as to require the drafting of its criminal laws in a way that respects its subjects as autonomous members of society and enables them to factor the law into their practical deliberations (Chapters 4, 5 and 6); and this includes a particular duty to publicise and communicate its criminal laws (Chapters 2 and 3).

The nine chapters below are designed to throw different shafts of light on these various positive obligations. Chapter 1, 'Is the Criminal Law a Lost Cause?', is a foundational essay on criminalisation, examining the relationship between the criminal law and other forms of legal regulation. This chapter makes the case for a principled approach to the decision to create a criminal offence, equality in its enforcement, and proportionality in sentencing. As is soon evident in Chapter 2, 'Criminalising Omissions', the approach advocated in the first chapter has a particular resonance with omissions liability, in relation to which the decision to criminalise is a little-discussed issue. The new essay that forms Chapter 2 aims to raise normative questions about the basis for and extent of criminal liability for omissions, paying special attention to the neglected issue of the appropriateness of recognising certain civic duties and reinforcing them with criminal offences. The content of Chapter 3 is well captured by its title, 'Ignorance of the Criminal Law, and Duties to Avoid it'. As well as critically re-assessing the common law doctrine that ignorance of the criminal law is no excuse, the essay develops the argument that citizens should have a duty to make reasonable efforts to know the criminal law, and that this should be the concomitant of an obligation on the state to ensure that criminal laws are duly publicised and communicated to all those in the country.

Chapter 4 asks, 'Should Strict Criminal Liability be Removed from All Imprisonable Offences?' This essay examines the reasons why the state should recognise an obligation to ensure that its criminal laws require fault as a condition of liability. It assesses the counter-arguments in favour of strict liability, but then argues that where the deprivation of a person's liberty is a potential sanction, strict liability has no place at all. Chapter 5 explores the connected issue of justifying constructive criminal liability, under the title 'A Change of Normative Position: Determining the Contours of Culpability in Criminal Law'. The argument is that respect for the autonomy of citizens indicates that criminal liability should in principle be based on intention, recklessness or knowledge, and moreover that this subjective element should be linked to any consequence, result or circumstances specified in the crime. Thus the essay attacks common arguments in favour of even a moderate amount of constructive criminal liability, while recognising that there is room for debate on the place of (gross) negligence as a standard of criminal liability. In Chapter 6, on 'The Unfairness of Risk-Based Possession Offences', it is argued the possession offences based on risk tend to be inconsistent with core doctrines of the criminal law. This raises the question of the justifications for criminalising risk-based possession of, for example, firearms or other weapons. A key issue, discussed in this chapter, is the extent to which there should be a positive obligation on citizens to safeguard potentially dangerous objects and, if there is such an obligation, how seriously a failure to carry it out should be treated.

In Chapter 7, on 'Child Defendants and the Doctrines of the Criminal Law', the discussion turns to a sphere in which the state has clear positive obligations under the UN Convention on the Rights of the Child. This chapter considers what the criminal law should expect of young children, and what provisions should be made in the criminal law to reflect the fact that, being under the age of majority, children cannot properly be held to the same standards as adults. Chapter 8 is a new essay which explores the nature and extent of the state's positive obligations under the European Convention on Human Rights to have certain criminal laws in place. It conducts a critical examination of the developing jurisprudence of the European Court of Human Rights, in order to probe its logic and its limits, and to assess the extent to which the United Kingdom can expect to find that this is a further source of pressure to legislate on the criminal law. Chapter 9 is a short Epilogue.

My academic acknowledgements in relation to each essay are printed below. Here, it remains for me to record my deep thanks to Richard Hart and his team for giving me the opportunity to publish with them, and for the smooth publication process. Finally, my warm thanks to Von for her support in this and other academic endeavours: I am very fortunate.

All Souls College, University of Oxford
February 2013.

Acknowledgements

Chapter 1 is a revised version of my inaugural lecture as the 14th Vinerian Professor of English Law in the University of Oxford, and was first published at (2000) 116 *Law Quarterly Review* 225. I am grateful to the Editor, Francis Reynolds, for his acceptance (even, encouragement) of my decision to re-publish. I am indebted to Jeremy Horder, Nicola Lacey, Andrew von Hirsch and Karen Yeung for their comments on an earlier version.

Chapter 2 is a new essay, although there is a small overlap with my article on 'Public Duties and Criminal Omissions: Some Unresolved Questions' [2011] 1 *Journal of Commonwealth Criminal Law* 1, and some continuity with my earlier article on 'The Scope of Criminal Liability for Omissions' at (1989) 105 *Law Quarterly Review* 424. For comments on versions of the new essay I am grateful to Rick Lippke, Stuart Green, Jennifer Collins, Brenda Midson, Julia Tolmie, Lucia Zedner, Antony Duff and Sandra Marshall, and to members of the Law Faculty at the University of Minnesota, members of the Criminal Law Discussion Group at the University of Oxford, and members of the law schools at the University of Canterbury, Victoria University of Wellington, the University of Otago, the University of Waikato, the University of Auckland and Auckland University of Technology who attended and responded to my various talks.

Chapter 3 is a revised version of my Chorley Lecture, delivered at the London School of Economics in June 2010. It was first published at (2011) 74 *Modern Law Review* 1, and I am grateful to the General Editor, Hugh Collins, for responding enthusiastically to my enquiry about re-publication. I am indebted to Beatrice Krebs for research assistance, and, for contributions and comments on drafts, to Petter Asp, James Chalmers, James Edwards, Jeremy Horder, Douglas Husak, Nicola Lacey, Andrew von Hirsch and Lucia Zedner.

Chapter 4 is a revised version of the 16th John Maurice Kelly Memorial Lecture, delivered at University College, Dublin in October 2010. It was first published at (2010) 45 *Irish Jurist* 1, and Thomson Reuters are content for me to re-publish here. I am grateful for comments on drafts to Mark Coen, Caroline Fennell, Shane Kilcommins, Tom O'Malley, Andrew Simester and Lucia Zedner.

Chapter 5 was first published at (2008) 11 *New Criminal Law Review* 232, and the University of California Press is content for me to re-publish here. I am indebted to Grant Lamond, Bob Sullivan and Victor Tadros for their comments on an earlier draft. I am grateful to John Gardner for the inspiration, and some observations on my arguments are to be found in the 'Reply to Critics' at the end of his *Offences and Defences* (2007), 246–48.

Chapter 6 is a revised version of the 2010 Lockhart lecture, delivered at the University of Minnesota Law School in September 2010. It was first published at

(2011) 5 *Criminal Law and Philosophy* 237, and I am grateful to Doug Husak, co-editor of that journal, for enthusiastically endorsing re-publication here. I am indebted to Richard Frase, Fionnuala ni Aolain, Darryl Brown, Andrew Simester, Patrick Tomlin and Lucia Zedner for comments on drafts, and also to members of the Oxford Criminal Law Discussion Group. This chapter stemmed from research which formed part of the three-year AHRC project described below.

Chapter 7 was first published as a contribution to James Chalmers, Fiona Leverick and Lindsay Farmer (eds), *Essays in Criminal Law in Honour of Sir Gerald Gordon* (Edinburgh University Press, 2010). It is reprinted here with the full support of the editors. I am grateful to Heather Keating, Jonathan Herring, Ronnie Mackay and Clare McDiarmid for their comments and suggestions.

Chapter 8 is a new essay, but it derives from research originally carried out in order to write and later to revise parts of what is now chapter 19 of B Emmerson, A Ashworth and A Macdonald (eds), *Human Rights and Criminal Justice* (3rd edn, 2012).

Between 2010 and 2013 I have been co-holder, with Lucia Zedner, of a grant from the Arts and Humanities Research Council (AH/H015655/1) for research into preventive justice. The principal fruits of that research are to be published in a forthcoming monograph entitled *Preventive Justice*, but that project has dominated my intellectual processes in recent years, and has been considerably influential in the development of Chapters 2, 6 and 9 of the present volume. I therefore record my gratitude to the AHRC for their support, and to my colleague Lucia Zedner for her generous involvement in the essays that form this book, particularly her readiness to comment on drafts and to discuss ideas.

Contents

1

Is the Criminal Law a Lost Cause?

T
HE NUMBER OF offences in English criminal law continues to grow year by year. Politicians, pressure groups, journalists and others often express themselves as if the creation of a new criminal offence is the natural, or the only appropriate, response to a particular event or series of events giving rise to social concern. At the same time, criminal offences are tacked on to diverse statutes by various government departments, and then enacted (or, often, re-enacted) by Parliament without demur. There is little sense that the decision to introduce a new offence should only be made after certain conditions have been satisfied, little sense that making conduct criminal is a step of considerable social significance. It is this unprincipled and chaotic construction of the criminal law that prompts the question whether it is a lost cause. From the point of view of governments it is clearly not a lost cause: it is a multipurpose tool, often creating the favourable impression that certain misconduct has been taken seriously and dealt with appropriately. But from any principled viewpoint there are important issues – of how the criminal law ought to be shaped, of what its social significance should be, of when it should be used and when not – which are simply not being addressed in the majority of instances.

This chapter[1] begins by examining the prospects for distinguishing criminal offences from other provisions by reference to their content. Having demonstrated the difficulties of that approach, we move from the descriptive to the normative, in search of features for a model of criminal laws that is more principled, conceptually more coherent, and constitutionally and politically more appropriate. These all turn on value judgements, of course, but that does not diminish the importance of grappling with them. Thus, some of the procedural and functional distinctions between crimes and other wrongs are explored, and the concomitants of that classification (notably the minimum standards of protection for those accused of crimes) are drawn into the discussion. In all of this, detail is sacrificed in favour of a more programmatic presentation so as to demonstrate the procedural implications of decisions to criminalise. We then examine the interplay among factors relating to the seriousness of the wrong, in the light of the principles of proportionality and of equal treatment. This takes us towards the enforcement of the criminal law, and sentencing: once again, the

---

[1] This chapter is derived from my inaugural lecture given at the University of Oxford in May 1999.

aim is to demonstrate the close connection, at the level of principle and policy, between the criminal law and its penal context.

What emerges is nothing so concrete as a formula for determining whether or not certain conduct should be criminalised. Rather, arguments are presented in favour of a more principled development of the criminal law, recognising the essential links between procedure, enforcement and sentence. Without a principled approach of this kind, the criminal law is likely to remain something of a lost cause.

1.1 DISTINGUISHING CRIMINAL OFFENCES BY REFERENCE TO THEIR CONTENT

The sheer bulk of English criminal law makes it highly unlikely that the substantive content of the offences conforms to a single test or set of related tests. There are probably around 8,000 offences now,[2] mostly created over the last 150 years, under the varying influences of governments of different political hues, movements towards criminal law reform, the expansion of regulatory mechanisms, and so forth. It is therefore hardly surprising that, in his classic article on the subject, Glanville Williams concluded that there is no workable definition of a crime in English law that is content-based: only the different procedures of criminal, as distinct from civil, cases can serve as a reliable distinguishing mark.[3] In the realm of description, then, we can affirm that the contours of English criminal law are 'historically contingent' – not the product of any principled inquiry or consistent application of certain criteria, but largely dependent on the fortunes of successive governments, on campaigns in the mass media, on the activities of various pressure groups, and so forth.[4]

This is not to deny that there have been elements of principle in debates on criminalisation in spheres such as abortion, prostitution, homosexual acts, and now drugs.[5] However, those debates are noteworthy for a degree of attention to the proper boundaries of the criminal law which is conspicuously absent from most other decisions to criminalise. The implementation of the Human Rights

---

[2] This is a conservative revision of the estimate produced over 30 years ago by JUSTICE, *Breaking the Rules* (1980), suggesting that there were then about 7,000 offences known to English law.

[3] G Williams, 'The Definition of a Crime' [1955] *Current Legal Problems* 107.

[4] A prime example of this is the Dangerous Dogs Act 1991, pushed through Parliament very rapidly in response to media pressure arising from some well-publicised incidents in which dogs of certain breeds had inflicted injury on children. This sudden invocation of the criminal law did not pass without comment in Parliament, even from those on the government side. For example, Nicholas Budgen MP decried the 'constant appeals to public opinion' and accused the government of legislating 'simply as a result of pressure from popular newspapers' (HC Deb vol 192, col 610 (10 June, 1991)).

[5] The leading essay is by N Lacey, 'Contingency and Criminalisation' in I Loveland (ed), *The Frontiers of Criminality* (1995). See further A Ashworth, *Principles of Criminal Law* (3rd edn, 1999), Ch 2; N Lacey and C Wells, *Reconstructing Criminal Law* (2nd edn, 1998), Ch 4; W Wilson, *Criminal Law: Theory and Doctrine* (1998), Ch 2.

Act 1998 should bring some improvements in this respect. Indeed section 19 of the Act, already in force, requires the Minister introducing a Bill to certify that the terms of the Bill comply with the European Convention on Human Rights (or to announce that no such statement can be made).[6] It is well known that Articles 8 to 11 of the Convention declare rights that must be respected, subject to certain exceptions – the right to respect for private and family life, the right to freedom of thought, conscience and religion, the right to freedom of expression, and the right to freedom of assembly and association. There are also other parts of the Convention that may have an impact on substantive criminal law, such as Article 2 on the justifiable use of force, Article 3 on chastisement of children, Article 5 on the insanity defence, and so on. It would be unwise to overestimate the impact of these Convention rights on the general shape of the criminal law:[7] they are likely to exert some influence on the substance of offences and defences, but this is unlikely to falsify the proposition that the varying content of English offences cannot be captured by any general definition of crime.

In descriptive terms, then, the contours of English criminal law are indeed historically contingent. To cast some light on this, let us examine all the statutes passed in 1997, leaving aside those applying only to Scotland or to Northern Ireland. What we find are at least 39 crimes,[8] most of which take one of four different forms. Some 13 of them are defined so as to require the prosecution to prove either intention or recklessness, which many regard as, in principle, the most appropriate culpability standard if criminal liability is to be imposed, and certainly if a significant sanction is to be imposed.[9] Most of these offences penalise the giving of false information. Then there are nine strict liability offences, subject to exceptions which the defendant bears the burden of proving, a familiar legislative device.[10] Eight further offences take a somewhat similar form, except that they penalise omissions (typically, failing to comply with a statutory requirement), but they too place on the defendant the burden of establishing an excuse or exception. Finally there are six strict liability offences, some of them penalising omissions, which include no specific provision for any defences.

In terms of function, several of the offences of making false statements are designed to underpin a regulatory scheme – for example, those established by the Architects Act 1997, the Nurses, Midwives and Health Visitors Act 1997, the Sex Offenders Act 1997, the Sexual Offences (Protected Material) Act 1997, the Plant Varieties Act 1997, and the Social Security Administration (Fraud) Act

---

[6] Strictly speaking, compatibility with those parts of the Convention that are set out in the Schedule to the Act, notably Articles 2–12 and 14, and Protocols 1 and 6.

[7] For analysis, see B Emmerson, A Ashworth and A Macdonald (eds), *Human Rights and Criminal Justice* (2nd edn, 2007), Ch 3.

[8] This means 39 crimes under separate provisions. If one were to analyse those provisions under the law as established in *R v Courtie* [1984] AC 463, the number of discrete offences would be much higher.

[9] For argument and further references. A Ashworth, *Principles of Criminal Law* (above n 5), Ch 5.

[10] Ashworth, 'Article 6 and the Fairness of Trials' [1999] *Crim LR* 261, at 265–67.

1997.[11] The last-mentioned statute, it may be noted, also provides various strict liability offences of failing to give information as required, crimes of omission which may or may not allow the defendant to establish 'reasonable excuse' in order to avoid conviction. That statute is about the prevention and punishment of fraud, and so criminal offences would be expected. Similar expectations arise, and a similar formula is to be found, in the Firearms (Amendment) Act 1997, a statute designed to tighten the control of firearms following the shootings at Dunblane. It creates several offences of omission, some of them providing that the defendant may prove reasonable excuse or due diligence in order to avoid conviction. Lastly, the Merchant Shipping and Maritime Security Act 1997 introduces various new offences concerned with non-observance of exclusion zones by the masters or owners of ships. Again, the predominant formula is to create an offence of omission, or another strict liability offence, with the proviso that the defendant may prove reasonable excuse or due diligence.

Although 1997 was thus a year in which there were relatively few additions to the criminal law as it applies generally, the Protection from Harassment Act and the Firearms (Amendment) Act being the main exceptions, this small survey highlights some noteworthy features of the existing criminal law. First, the bulk of new offences may be described as 'regulatory', in the sense that they form part of statutory schemes for the regulation of certain spheres of social or commercial activity, and are generally enforced by the regulatory authority rather than by the police.[12] Secondly, the bulk of new offences are characterised by three features – strict liability, omissions liability, and reverse onus provisions for exculpation. All those features lie a considerable distance from the conception of criminal laws held by many university teachers and criminal practitioners. Indeed, they are inconsistent with prominent elements of the rhetoric of English criminal law – that there is a presumption that *mens rea* is a prerequisite of criminal liability,[13] that liability for omissions is exceptional,[14] and that 'one golden thread' running through English criminal law is that the prosecution bears the burden of proving guilt.[15] It would be possible to interpret this dissonance between rhetoric and reality as a deliberate part of the architecture of social control, with the judges declaiming great principles whilst Parliament continues to depart from them. The reality is probably much less orderly than that. Parliament and the judges would be unlikely bedfellows in such an enter-

---

[11] This statute also provides (s 15) for the levying of a penalty, up to 30 per cent of money overpaid to the claimant, as an alternative to prosecution.

[12] This loose description of the regulatory sphere should suffice for the purpose of this chapter. When reference is made below to a 'regulatory offence', this is intended to signify that its origin lies in a regulatory statute rather than in a statute devoted chiefly to the creation of criminal offences. Most importantly, reference to an offence as 'regulatory' should not be taken to imply that it is a non-serious offence or a strict liability offence.

[13] Eg per Lord Goddard CJ in *Brend v Wood* (1946) LT 306, Lord Diplock in *Sweet v Parsley* [1970] AC 132, and Lord Scarman in *Gammon v Attorney-General for Hong Kong* [1985] 1 AC 1.

[14] Eg James J in *Fagan v Metropolitan Police Commissioner* [1969] 1 QB 439.

[15] Per Viscount Sankey LC, in *Woolmington v DPP* [1935] AC 462.

prise, and in any event the judges themselves often qualify a principle soon after declaring it so resoundingly.[16]

Despite the disorderly state of English criminal law, it appears that the Government does profess some principles for criminalisation. In response to a parliamentary question, Lord Williams of Mostyn has stated that offences 'should be created only when absolutely necessary', and that

> 'In considering whether new offences should be created, factors taken into account include whether:
>
> - the behaviour in question is sufficiently serious to warrant intervention by the criminal law;
> - the mischief could be dealt with under existing legislation or by using other remedies;
> - the proposed offence is enforceable in practice;
> - the proposed offence is tightly drawn and legally sound; and
> - the proposed penalty is commensurate with the seriousness of the offence.
>
> The Government also takes into account the need to ensure, as far as practicable, that there is consistency across the sentencing framework'.[17]

We will return to these professed principles at later points in the chapter. For the present, it suffices to say that our brief examination of the criminal laws of 1997 confirms the 'historical contingency' thesis and suggests that the laws being enacted bear little relation to the Government's supposed principles. However, adoption of the 'historical contingency' thesis should not lead us to abandon discussion of principle, even if it warns us to scrutinise rhetoric with care. It is worth recalling the warning of Nelken that 'the corrosive force of insisting that law is no more than a social construction can also undermine objective criticism of its injustices and delegitimate attempts to shape it in supposedly more progressive directions'.[18] With this in mind, we begin to move from the descriptive to the normative, and to consider whether it is possible to identify criteria or standards that ought to be satisfied before it is decided to criminalise certain conduct – some of which may be similar to the principles which, according to Lord Williams, inform current practice.

1.2 THE PROCEDURAL DISTINCTION

Glanville Williams ended his search for a definition of crime with the conclusion that only a formal definition is sustainable: 'in short, a crime is an act capable of being followed by criminal proceedings having a criminal outcome'.[19] The key procedural elements that distinguish criminal from civil proceedings are

---

[16] As in almost all the cases listed in the three previous notes.

[17] Lord Williams of Mostyn (then Minister of State at the Home Office), in a written reply to a question by Lord Dholakia, HL Deb, vol 602, col WA57 (18 June, 1999).

[18] D Nelken, 'Reflexive Criminology?' in D Nelken (ed), *The Futures of Criminology* (1994), 7.

[19] [1955] *Current Legal Problems* 107, at 130.

that criminal proceedings are generally brought by a public official as prosecutor, and that they can result in the conviction of the defendant and in the passing of a sentence. These elements are close to the criteria adopted by the European Court of Human Rights when it has had to determine whether or not certain proceedings should be labelled as 'criminal' rather than 'civil'.[20] Thus if the proceedings (a) are brought by a public authority, and either (b) have culpability requirements[21] (eg in requiring a finding of 'culpable neglect' or 'wilful default', or (c) have potentially severe consequences (such as imprisonment), the court has not hesitated to declare that they should be regarded as 'criminal' for the purposes of the European Convention on Human Rights even if they are labelled 'civil' in the domestic law of a Member State.[22]

It is well known that many offences, in the United Kingdom and in other countries, are offences of strict liability which require little or no fault element. Thus condition (b) is simply a factor that assists in determining whether an ostensibly civil action should be characterised as criminal, and is an alternative to condition (c). As for (c) itself, it is possible to offer many examples of civil judgments which may be far more onerous than criminal sentences – a simple case might be a moderate fine imposed by a criminal court for a driving offence, compared with a substantial award of civil damages for negligence arising out of the same incident. But it is generally true that civil courts cannot impose imprisonment, whereas criminal courts can do so (where the maximum penalty permits it). Civil courts certainly cannot order defendants to perform positive acts of the kinds required by a community service order or probation order, which can amount to severe restrictions on a person's liberty. Injunctions in civil proceedings have a much more limited ambit. Recent decisions of the European Court of Human Rights show that, even if the penalty is a fine, the possibility of imprisonment may be sufficient to justify classifying the proceedings as 'criminal'.[23]

The role of public authorities in bringing proceedings (a) provides a good example of the blurring of boundaries in modern legal systems. It is true that the vast majority of criminal cases are prosecuted by a public authority: the Crown Prosecution Service brings proceedings in most cases of any seriousness, with other authorities such as HM Customs and Excise, the Environment Agency and local trading standards officers accounting for many more. A right of private prosecution remains in England and Wales, but it is used relatively

---

[20] As we will see in part 4 below, a person who is 'charged with a criminal offence' has a much more extensive set of rights under Article 6 than participants in other proceedings; moreover, the European Court of Human Rights regards the term 'criminal' as having an autonomous meaning, ie one that cannot be dictated by domestic law but is determined in Strasbourg on principle.

[21] Somewhat confusingly, the European Court tends to refer to these as 'punitive elements', even though the application of this second criterion demonstrates that it is concerned with culpability and the third criterion might more aptly be described as 'punitive': see *Benham v United Kingdom* (1996) 22 EHRR 293, para 56.

[22] See *Benham v United Kingdom*, ibid, following *Engel v Netherlands*, A 22 (1976) 1 EHRR 647.

[23] Eg *Schmautzer v Austria* (1996) 21 EHRR 511; *Garyfallou AEBE v Greece* (1999) 28 EHRR 344.

rarely and (more significantly in doctrinal terms) the Attorney-General and Director of Public Prosecutions have ample powers to control private prosecutions – for example, by taking over a case and then discontinuing it.[24] Rather more important than this small exception to the principle that criminal proceedings are brought by public authorities is the expanding role of public authorities in bringing civil proceedings. This refers, not so much to the increasing powers of public and quasi-public bodies[25] in regulatory spheres such as competition and financial services, as to the emergence of forms of hybrid procedure which rely on public authorities to initiate 'ordinary' civil actions against individuals.

One recent example of a hybrid procedure is provided by the anti-social behaviour order, introduced by section 1 of the Crime and Disorder Act 1998. Proceedings may be initiated by the police or by the local authority, who must prove to the civil standard (a balance of probabilities) that the defendant has acted 'in a manner that caused or was likely to cause harassment, alarm or distress to one or more persons not of the same household as himself'. The magistrates may then make an anti-social behaviour order, prohibiting a person from 'doing anything described in the order' for a minimum of two years. A defendant who breaches the terms of the order without reasonable excuse is liable to conviction of an offence for which the maximum penalty is five years' imprisonment, and for which a magistrates' court is not allowed to grant a conditional discharge. What is significant about this procedure in the present context is the role of a public authority in bringing civil proceedings, which may then provide the substantive foundation for a later criminal prosecution.

This is not the only hybrid of its kind,[26] but it raises questions about the overall classification of the proceedings. The European Convention on Human Rights has a twofold classification: criminal and other (ie non-criminal). It emerges from the earlier discussion that the third criterion for recognising proceedings as 'criminal' is the most powerful, so that the possibility of loss of liberty may be determinative. Thus in relation to hybrids of the kind introduced by section 1 of the Crime and Disorder Act the question is whether the two processes are regarded as separate (a civil action, possibly followed by a criminal prosecution) or may be viewed as parts of linked proceedings which should then be given an overall classification – in which event it might be concluded that they are brought by a public authority and have potentially severe consequences.

[24] Prosecution of Offences Act 1985, s 3; JLlJ Edwards, *The Law Officers of the Crown* (1964).

[25] The adjective 'quasi-public' is a gesture towards the trends to privatisation and to the creation of independent regulatory bodies, which cannot be explored further in the present context. An example might be the Occupational Pensions Regulatory Authority, which has powers to inflict penalties and 'fines' on those who deviate from the framework established by the Pensions Act 1995 (see ss 10 and 155(4)), broadly following the recommendations of the Goode Report, *Pension Law Reform* (Cm 2342, 1993).

[26] See also s 3 of the Protection from Harassment Act 1997, which allows the victim to bring an initial civil action that may lead the court to make an order prohibiting a person from harassing the victim. Breach of that order is a strict liability offence carrying a maximum penalty of five years' imprisonment: s 3(6).

This, however, is to stray into the realm of the next two topics, the function of proceedings and the concomitant protections, and so the question of the hybrid procedure for anti-social behaviour orders will be revisited below. For the moment, we may conclude that one way of distinguishing criminal cases from civil is generally, and subject to exceptions and to various hybrids, by reference to the procedure adopted – public prosecutor, conviction and sentence – rather than by reference to the content of the law itself.[27]

1.3 THE FUNCTIONAL DISTINCTION

Perhaps the principal function of the criminal law is to censure persons for wrongdoing. The censuring elements consist of the conviction itself, together with the sentence of the court (which usually constitutes a punishment).[28] Thus, to revert to a familiar jurisprudential point, both a fine and a tax require a person to make a payment to the state, but the difference is that the former is a sentence that implies 'should not do' (ie it censures the person for wrongdoing) whereas a tax does not carry the implication of 'should not do'. One might argue that this implication is somewhat diluted in the many offences with low penalties which fill the English statute book, of which we saw examples in the brief survey of 1997 offences earlier. But it is still possible to say, in principle, that the use of the criminal law to penalise such acts and omissions has the function of censuring persons for non-compliance with the commands of the law.

There are, however, other branches of the law that proclaim the function of discouraging wrongdoing, notably those civil wrongs that constitute the law of tort. Is it possible to draw a satisfactory functional distinction between crimes and torts? One obvious preliminary point is that conduct may be both a civil wrong and a criminal offence: sometimes one slips into talking as if there is a choice between making conduct a crime or a civil wrong, whereas in fact some conduct is both a civil wrong and a crime. This is perfectly acceptable, even in an ideal world, since the functions of the various branches of law may differ. Indeed, where there is a question whether to criminalise conduct that is already a civil wrong, this draws particular attention to the justifications for criminal liability.

If we focus on the law of tort, we find that few tort lawyers represent tort law as a system designed merely to secure compensation for people who have been wronged. In the first place there are those non-instrumentalists or essentialists,

---

[27] Cf EJ Weinrib, *The Idea of Private Law* (1995), 10–11, who describes 'an ensemble of institutional and conceptual features' that serve to identify private law, eg that private law involves 'an action by a plaintiff, adjudication culminating in a judgment that retroactively affirms the rights and duties of the parties, and an entitlement to specific relief or to damages for the violation of those rights or the breach of those duties'.

[28] Without elaborating at inappropriate length, it may be noted that at least two of the orders that a court may make as the only order after conviction may be considered non-punitive, the discharge (absolute or conditional) and the compensation order.

such as Weinrib, who regard tort law as a system of responsibility for human conduct, based on corrective justice.[29] But then many would describe tort law in instrumental terms, suggesting that it has the social function of discouraging certain forms of behaviour. Tort liability, as its very name suggests, marks out the defendant's conduct as wrongful (in a way that, say, schemes for the regulation or licensing of certain conduct may not do). As Honoré has expressed it:

'The technique of tort law is therefore to label things as not to be done or omitted or brought about, though in a less stigmatic way than criminal law . . . A supporter of the rule of law . . . will think the state justified in trying to minimize undesirable behaviour by a technique that treats some interests as rights and gives those who have the rights the power to avert or redress the unwanted conduct'.[30]

More will be said about the alleged preventive function of the criminal law later,[31] but it is relevant to note here that it is reflected in tort law to a degree. However, the central function of tort law is surely not censure or prevention but to provide a remedy to the victim for the invasion of protected interests, usually damages but sometimes injunctive or other relief.[32] In most cases the primary function of damages is to compensate the victim for the loss, whereas the primary functions of sentencing are punitive and preventive. Thus in principle there might be instances where, dealing with essentially the same set of facts, a civil court would award substantial damages when a criminal court might impose a relatively light sentence on conviction (eg manslaughter by gross negligence), and where a civil court might award no damages or a modest sum when a criminal court would impose a severe sentence (eg attempted murder causing no actual injury). However, in practice the interrelationship of punishment and compensation is more complex and the boundaries are becoming blurred, especially in criminal cases.[33] Thus criminal courts have a *prima facie* duty to order the offender to pay compensation to a victim who has suffered loss or damage, injury or death.[34] In practice, however, it is rare for them to do so if the offender is unemployed or is sent to prison, which means that criminal compensation orders are not frequently used.[35] It is also perfectly possible for a

---

[29] EJ Weinrib, *The Idea of Private Law* (above n 27) esp Chs 6 and 7; cf P Cane, *The Anatomy of Tort Law* (1997), Ch 7, who adopts a mixed approach that regards tort law as partly an embodiment of sound ethical principles of personal responsibility and partly a system that furthers certain social goals.

[30] T Honoré, 'The Morality of Tort Law' in D Owen (ed), *Philosophical Foundations of Tort Law* (1995), 77.

[31] In part 8, below.

[32] Cf the argument of Birks against those who identify these responses (especially compensatory damages) as part of the very idea of a tort, and pointing out the other forms of response that might be provided for, such as restitutionary and punitive damages: P Birks, 'The Concept of a Civil Wrong' in D Owen (ed), *Philosophical Foundations of Tort Law* (1995), 35–36.

[33] See L Zedner, 'Reparation and Retribution: Are They Reconcilable?' (1994) 57 *MLR* 228.

[34] Powers of Criminal Courts Act 1973, s 35A.

[35] Also noteworthy is the increasing interest in what is known as 'restorative justice'. Various initiatives march behind this banner, and many of them raise the possibility of compensation for the victim. See, eg the essays in A Crawford and J Goodey (eds), *Integrating a Victim Perspective in Criminal Justice* (2000).

victim to sue the offender for damages, whether or not there has been a conviction or even a prosecution, but the better view now is that it would be wrong for a civil court to award punitive damages against a defendant who has already been convicted by a criminal court in respect of the same conduct.[36] Thus, whilst the possibility of awarding punitive damages is consistent with the underlying censuring function that tort law is supposed to have, the restrictions on making such awards demonstrate that tort law has to play second fiddle, in this respect, to the criminal law.

Without straying too far from the themes of this chapter, it may be opportune to give two further examples of the interweaving and blurring of legal forms. The first occurs in intellectual property law, where the civil remedies sit alongside some criminal offences. Cornish states that

> 'most claimants make use of the civil process, partly because its technique and atmosphere are appropriate to the assertion of private property rights among businessmen, and partly because the types of remedy – in particular the injunction (interlocutory and permanent) and damages – are more useful than punishment in the name of the state'.[37]

The technique of the criminal law is most evident in the sphere of trademarks and copyright, with offences triable summarily or on indictment, for which trading standards officers not infrequently prosecute alleged counterfeiters. It is therefore not left to the individuals or companies affected by the activities of the 'pirates' to pursue them, but is rather thought to warrant the intervention of a public prosecuting authority. However, if an affected party decides to bring a criminal prosecution, with or without an accompanying civil action, this is permissible: Parliament has created criminal offences, and there is a right of private prosecution, so it is not an abuse of process if one party to a copyright dispute decides to prosecute the other.[38]

A second example of blurring may be found in competition law, where the Competition Act 1998 was intended to introduce a dual regime for the regulation of trade competition – civil financial penalties levied by the Director-General of Fair Trading, and court actions brought by private parties in order to recover damages for loss through unfair competition.[39] The former is not a criminal-civil hybrid, since the power to levy financial penalties is not intended

---

[36] See, eg Law Com No 247, *Aggravated, Exemplary and Restitutionary Damages* (1997); the New Zealand Court of Appeal in *Daniels v Thompson* [1998] 2 NZLR 22; the High Court of Australia in *Gray v Motor Accident Commission* (1998) 158 ALR 485; and J Stapleton, 'Civil Prosecutions – Part 1: Double Jeopardy and Abuse of Process' (1999) 7 *Torts Law Journal* 244.

[37] WR Cornish, *Intellectual Property Law* (4th edn, 1999), paras 2–19; cf A Firth, 'The Criminalisation of Offences against Intellectual Property' in I Loveland (ed), *The Frontiers of Criminality* (1995).

[38] *Thames and Hudson v Design and Artists Copyright Society Ltd* [1995] FSR 153, where the Chancery judge found no abuse of process but did state that the matters in dispute were more suitable for a civil court than for magistrates at a summary trial.

[39] For analysis, see K Yeung, 'Privatizing Competition Regulation' (1998) 18 *OJLS* 581. The statute as enacted contains no express provision enabling companies and individuals to recover damages for breach, but the Government's view was that this flows from European Community law: cf Yeung, ibid, at 611, with HC Deb vol 312, col 35 (11 May, 1998).

to form part of the criminal law and (unless there are periods of imprisonment in default) it would be unlikely to be held by the European Court of Human Rights to be criminal in substance.[40] Rather, it is a public-private hybrid within the fields of civil and regulatory law. In many countries the enforcement of competition laws has been chiefly the business of public regulators, but private enforcement has now become possible in several jurisdictions.[41] The main advantages of permitting private enforcement in addition to public enforcement are that the private enforcer has a distinct interest in pursuing the action, and may be subject to fewer fiscal or other restrictions than public regulators. Private enforcement can be regarded as right in principle, since it serves the aim of corrective justice if the injured party is able to recover compensation for the losses caused by the anti-competitive practice; also, from a broader perspective the activities of private enforcers may enhance the deterrent effect of the regulatory law by increasing the probability that unfair competitors will be brought to book. There are obvious drawbacks of allowing private enforcement – the possibility of excessive litigation by powerful companies, and the fact that private enforcers cannot be expected to defer to any broad public policies that might conflict with their own interests – but problems of this kind can be minimised by providing the public regulator with the power to take over and (if appropriate) drop any private action that is not thought to be in the public interest.[42] Public regulators may also be expected to pursue some cases in which the incentives to pursue a private action arc weak – eg where only small companies are affected, or where the loss inflicted on each individual or company is too modest to justify the expense of prosecuting. The many questions of principle raised by such arrangements cannot be pursued here.

These mutations of legal form demonstrate that the functional distinction between criminal law and various fields of civil law is less sharp than doctrine, or at least common assumptions, would sometimes have it. And yet the tendency to blur, and the proliferation of hybrids,[43] does not obscure some key differences between criminal and civil liability. The distinction between public and private enforcement remains dominant, although it is certainly not absolute and we have noted various examples (right of private prosecution; civil actions by local authorities; combined public and private enforcement of competition laws) of erosion. The element of public censure remains a central feature of criminal liability, echoed in many social and professional spheres by the tendency to place significance on criminal convictions but not even to inquire about civil judgments

---

[40] Cf *Ravnsborg v Sweden* (1994) 18 EHRR 38, at 52–53 with the decisions in *Schmautzer* and in *Garyfallou* (above n 23).

[41] Cf K Roach and MJ Trebilcock, 'Private Enforcement of Competition Laws' (1997) 34 *Osgoode Hall Law Journal* 461.

[42] Roach and Trebilcock, ibid, at 489 and 503.

[43] One further example is the range of civil disqualifications that a criminal court is empowered to make on conviction, some of which are unrelated to any risk disclosed by the conviction and are therefore difficult to justify. For analysis, see A von Hirsch and M Wasik, 'Civil Disqualifications Attending Conviction: a Suggested Conceptual Framework' [1997] *CLJ* 599.

against a person; yet, again, this is not an absolute distinction, since there are many criminal offences (especially strict liability crimes) that carry such low penalties and low stigma as to have no greater social or professional significance than an injunction or award of damages.

Despite this general significance of censure and punishment, it is sometimes suggested that civil actions can be more apposite and further-reaching, particularly when the unlawful activity is of an ongoing nature. We noted, in the field of intellectual property law, the view that the criminal law may need to be supplemented (or even supplanted) by a civil action in order to deal adequately with continuing wrongdoing.[44] However, there are two issues that must not be overlooked. First, although the criminal law is rarely able to enforce significant positive obligations (other than those required by the terms of a community sentence), it can deal with continuing unlawfulness by means of negative obligations. The criminal courts have a range of conditional sentences available to them in many cases (not merely the conditional discharge, but also probation orders, community service orders and all the other forms of community sentence), and the commission of a further offence during the operational period of a conditional order may give the court the power to revoke the conditional order and to pass sentence for the two offences together. This may amount to a powerful sanction.

Secondly, if the criminal law is not thought to provide adequate protection, then there must be vigilance about the consequences of any blurring of legal forms. Where a civil law mechanism is adopted, the key issue is what happens if the injunction or other restraining order is breached. The general answer is that this amounts to a civil contempt of court, for which a judge may make various orders including imprisonment of up to two years.[45] Anyone sentenced to prison for contempt is classified as a civil prisoner, but nonetheless the deprivation of liberty and the hardships of prison life are present. The European Court of Human Rights would doubtless insist that all the Article 6 safeguards should be maintained, and in most respects this is now true of contempt proceedings.[46] The present government relies on what might be termed 'the contempt model' in order to justify the anti-social behaviour order introduced by section 1 of the Crime and Disorder Act 1998. One of the reasons for adopting this hybrid approach was said to be the inability of the criminal law alone to deal adequately with continuing wrongdoing.[47] However, as we saw earlier, breach of the civil order constitutes a criminal offence, of strict liability, carrying a maxi-

---

[44]   There is a growing number of orders that criminal courts can make (eg forfeiture, confiscation, deprivation of property) which may have the effect of depriving an offender of the means of repeating the offence; but there is no criminal injunction as such.

[45]   *Arlidge, Eady and Smith on Contempt* (3rd edn, 2011), Ch 3.

[46]   Ibid, Chs 2 and 3.

[47]   See the two papers issued by the Labour Party in opposition, *A Quiet Life* (July 1995) and *Protecting our Communities* (September 1996), and then the Consultation Paper on *Community Safety Orders* (Home Office, 1997). Critiques of the proposals may be found in two short papers by A Ashworth, J Gardner, R Morgan, ATH Smith, A von Hirsch and M Wasik, 'Overtaking on the Right' (1995) 145 *NLJ* 933 and 'Neighbouring on the Oppressive' (1998) 16 *Criminal Justice* (1)7.

mum of five years' imprisonment. The European Court might well consider the civil and criminal stages of the process together, in view of the swingeing maximum penalty and the uncertain concepts on which the order depends.[48] This would be particularly appropriate since a major consequence of this hybrid process, indeed one of its purposes, is that it effectively by-passes the normal protections of criminal procedure. It is to that topic that we now pass.

1.4 PROCEEDINGS AND PROTECTIONS

It has already been argued that censure and punishment are two leading and defining features of criminal liability. It is largely because of the social significance of censure and the restrictions on, or even deprivation of, liberty that may be imposed by the sentence of the court that it is thought proper to provide at least certain minimum safeguards for defendants in criminal proceedings, over and above those which apply to civil proceedings. To put the matter crudely at this stage, to make something a crime imports certain protections for the defendant which may not be required if it were merely a civil wrong. The latter seems to have been one reason why the Government chose to place heavy reliance on civil proceedings when tackling 'anti-social behaviour'. All of this explains why the European Court of Human Rights has been fairly active in policing the boundary between criminal and civil proceedings,[49] laying emphasis on the severity of the consequences for the defendant as one of the main elements leading to classification as 'criminal'.

The extra protections granted to defendants in criminal proceedings vary from country to country; indeed, they vary among jurisdictions within the United Kingdom, notably between Scotland and England and Wales. It is hardly controversial to assert that there may be a considerable gap between the rhetoric of safeguards for accused persons and the actual operation of the criminal justice system.[50] The implementation of the Human Rights Act makes it particularly relevant to refer to the European Convention on Human Rights, Article 6.1 of which provides the general right to a fair trial in the determination of all 'civil rights and obligations or of any criminal charge', and Articles 6.2 and 6.3 of which then provide further rights for 'everyone charged with a criminal offence'. Those rights are as follows:

---

[48] Criticisms on this basis are articulated in the writings cited in the previous note. In particular, the only definition of anti-social behaviour is acting in a manner 'likely to cause harassment, alarm or distress' to another (s 1(1)(a)); and, once a court is satisfied of this, it may make an order 'prohibiting the defendant from doing anything described in the order', ie not limited to the kinds of conduct proved (to the civil standard) in court (s 1(4)).

[49] See the decisions cited in nn 22–23, above.

[50] For clear examples, see the *Royal Commission on Criminal Justice: Report* (1993), and the critical commentaries found in S Field and P Thomas (eds), *Justice and Efficiency* (1994); M McConville and L Bridges (eds), *Criminal Justice in Crisis* (1994); A Sanders and R Young, 'The Royal Commission on Criminal Justice: a Confidence Trick' (1994) 14 *OJLS* 435; and A Ashworth and M Redmayne, *The Criminal Process* (2nd edn, 1998), esp Chs 1–4.

'6.2 Everyone charged with a criminal offence shall be presumed innocent until proved guilty according to law.

6.3 Everyone charged with a criminal offence has the following minimum rights:

  a. to be informed promptly, in a language which he understands and in detail, of the nature and cause of the accusation against him;
  b. to have adequate time and facilities for the preparation of his defence;
  c. to defend himself in person or through legal assistance of his own choosing, or, if he has not sufficient means to pay for legal assistance, to be given it free when the interests of justice so require;
  d. to examine or have examined witnesses against him and to obtain the attendance and examination of witnesses on his behalf under the same conditions as witnesses against him;
  e. to have the free assistance of an interpreter if he cannot understand or speak the language used in court'.

There is a considerable and growing ECHR jurisprudence on these provisions, which cannot be discussed here.[51] More pertinent is the international recognition, also found in the International Covenant on Civil and Political Rights,[52] that defendants in criminal proceedings ought to have greater protections because of what is at stake. The protections in Article 6 of the ECHR are expressed to be 'minimum rights', but, even at that, requirements such as free legal aid, the right of confrontation and the burden of proof may make a considerable difference to the balance of power between the parties in criminal cases.

In part 3 of the chapter we discussed the different functions of different branches of the law, noting the tendency to mix civil and criminal, and punitive and compensatory, responses to wrongdoing. However, we had concluded in part 2 that the definition of a criminal offence is likely to emphasise the role of a public authority in bringing proceedings, and the possibility of a (punitive) sentence. The justification for recognising defendants' rights, as embodied in the European Convention, is that significant restrictions on, or deprivation of, liberty may well flow from criminal proceedings, and also that a public authority is bringing the case (with the consequent probability of power and resources far greater than those of an individual defendant). Thus it is contrary to the European Convention on Human Rights for the legislature to label proceedings as civil when the statute provides that, in cases of willful default on the court's order, a person may be committed to prison for up to three months.[53] If the

---

[51]   See Emmerson, Ashworth and Macdonald, n 7 above.

[52]   Notably Article 14: see further DJ Harris and S Joseph (eds), *The International Covenant on Civil and Political Rights and United Kingdom Law* (1995).

[53]   Thus in *Benham v United Kingdom* (1996) 22 EHRR 293, where the English legislation provided for this response to non-payment of the community charge or 'poll tax', the European Court of Human Rights held that the proceedings were in substance criminal, and that therefore the defendant should have been entitled to legal aid and the other safeguards set out in Article 6.

proceedings involve censure and punishment, then the rights of a person 'charged with a criminal offence' should be protected.[54]

This argument is even more compelling where the maximum penalty is as high as five years' imprisonment, as for the offence of breaching an anti-social behaviour order.[55] But it is not merely that the hybrid procedure for anti-social behaviour orders is designed to avoid – at the crucial stage of taking evidence and deciding the terms of the order – the safeguards applicable on criminal charges. It is also that the offence which carries five years' imprisonment has its terms decided by a magistrates' court sitting as a civil court,[56] and that it is one of strict liability. It is committed by a person who 'does anything which he is prohibited from doing by an anti-social behaviour order'. No fault is required, and the only specific defence is 'without reasonable excuse'. It is strongly arguable that persons should not be liable to be deprived of their liberty without proof of fault.[57] Imprisonment is the most severe penalty available in most legal systems, and to condemn an individual to prison without requiring proof of fault – or, at least, without allowing the defendant to establish lack of fault[58] – is a negation of the respect for individual autonomy that ought to be a foundational principle of the criminal law. To provide for up to five years' imprisonment for a strict liability crime is wrong in principle.[59]

1.5 THE SERIOUSNESS OF WRONGDOING

We have already accepted the proposition that neither English law nor the laws of many other countries confine criminal liability to noticeably serious misconduct. Legions of strict liability offences, for example, penalise relatively minor omissions or wrongful acts. But a core element of criminal law, from a normative point of view, is that the criminal sanction should be reserved for substantial wrongdoing. And this prompts questions about how the seriousness of wrongdoing should be assessed.

---

[54] Thus in *Benham v United Kingdom* the Government's argument was that 'the purpose of the detention was to coerce the applicant into paying the tax owed, rather than to punish him for not having paid it'; but the Court emphasised that 'the applicant faced a relatively severe maximum penalty of three months' imprisonment', and that 'where deprivation of liberty is at stake, the interests of justice in principle call for legal representation' and other safeguards: 22 EHRR 293, at paras 55–61.

[55] See nn 47–49 above and text thereat.

[56] By s 1(4) of the Crime and Disorder Act 1998 the court may make an order 'which prohibits the defendant from doing anything described in the order' (not necessarily acts of the kind already alleged), and s 1(6) provides that the prohibitions should be 'necessary for the purpose of protecting [persons] from further anti-social acts by the defendant'.

[57] See Chapter 4 below.

[58] This is the approach taken by the Supreme Court of Canada in *R v City of Sault Ste Marie* [1978] 2 SCR 1299, (1978) 40 CCC (2d) 353, affirmed under the Charter of Rights and Freedoms in *Reference re section 94(2) of the Motor Vehicle Act (BC)* [1985] 2 SCR 486, (1985) 48 CR (3d) 289.

[59] The Privy Council, however, went so far as to approve strict liability for a crime carrying three years' imprisonment in *Gammon v Attorney-General for Hong Kong* [1985] AC 1

The two main dimensions are harm and culpability, and something needs to be said, however briefly, about both of them. The harmfulness of conduct must be judged in terms of its effect on valued interests, which may be individual interests or some form of collective interests.[60] The centrality of the culpability requirement is surely part of the essence of the criminal law: if a person is to be censured publicly by being labelled a criminal and made liable to sentence, then the court should be satisfied not merely that that person caused the consequence but also that he or she did so culpably. Anyone can cause injury, death or damage by misfortune or coincidence, but that should not be enough for criminal liability, however great the harm. The criminal law should require proof of fault as a condition of imposing censure, let alone punishment that involves restriction or deprivation of liberty. I intend to leave this point without further elaboration, in the knowledge that there is room for great debate about the grades of fault that should be required for particular crimes, particularly the debate about the place of negligence.[61] Instead, I would argue for the separate, though not independent, significance of culpability: many of the harms that constitute the conduct elements of different crimes may also give rise to civil liability, but a principal distinction of criminal liability is the requirement that the harm be caused culpably. In particular, the concept of intention (and, to a lesser extent, that of recklessness) would be a requirement of the paradigm crime. Its moral significance was well captured in the *dictum* of Oliver Wendell Holmes that even a dog distinguishes between being kicked and being stumbled over. My reason for stating that culpability is not independently significant is to emphasise its connection with harm, although I do not mean to insist on a connection with actual harm: intended harm towards which a person has taken a substantial step, of the kind typically penalised by the law of attempts, is rightly regarded as within the proper scope of criminal liability.[62] In this paragraph I have given mere sketches of important principles, the justification of which requires fuller argument than I can provide here. For the programmatic purposes of this chapter, however, it is necessary at least to signal these issues and their proper place in the chain of reasoning from the seriousness of wrongdoing to the creation of criminal offences.

It is obvious that both harmfulness and culpability may vary across a wide range of degrees, and this attracts the objection that there is no satisfactory way of distinguishing serious wrongs from non-serious wrongs. Although this is true to some extent, I do not regard it as a significant weakness in my

---

[60] For references, see nn 68–70, below.

[61] On which see AP Simester, 'Can Negligence be Culpable?' in J Horder (ed), *Oxford Essays in Jurisprudence (4th Series)* (2000), and J Horder, 'Gross Negligence' (1997) 47 *University of Toronto Law Journal* 495.

[62] See further A Ashworth, 'Defining Offences without Harm' in PF Smith (ed), *Criminal Law: Essays in Honour of JC Smith* (1987), and J Horder, 'Crimes of Ulterior Intent' in AP Simester and ATH Smith (eds), *Harm and Culpability* (1996).

argument.[63] I accept that there are well-documented differences, over time and between nations at any given point in time, in judgements of whether conduct amounts to a serious wrong or not. I also accept that, even in one country at a particular point in time, there will be no bright line, no categorical difference, that divides serious from non-serious wrongs. I accept further that there will inevitably be some measure of self-reference in whatever criteria are adopted: the wrongs must be serious enough to be condemned and sanctioned by the criminal law.[64] But these are not disabling weaknesses in my approach. For one thing, it is surely possible to identify some clearly substantial and some clearly non-serious wrongs, to which my approach applies without further difficulty. One can then move, assisted by a mixture of human rights principles,[65] applied philosophy and pragmatism,[66] to close the gap between the two extremes. The fact that there is room for argument in the middle-ground is not a fatal flaw – after all, it is a common feature of human affairs and policy-making – so long as the debates to resolve the question are principled, drawing on the kinds of reasons elaborated on here. One can make some headway by demanding internal consistency in the evaluation and treatment of factors relevant to seriousness.

Given the programmatic purpose of this chapter, there will be no detailed analysis of possible approaches to gauging the seriousness of wrongs. In respect of wrongs against individuals, the scheme sketched by von Hirsch and Jareborg may be commended as a starting point for analysis.[67] They develop a method for assessing the effect of the typical case of particular crimes upon the 'living standard' of typical victims, construing 'living standard' as a measure of the means and capabilities that would ordinarily conduce to the achievement of a good life. However, a method must also be developed so as to take account of set-backs to collective interests,[68] and of the public dimension of wrongs inflicted on individuals. The problem of identifying this public dimension has

---

[63] Note the different methodology of M Moore, *Placing Blame: A Theory of the Criminal Law* (1997), Ch 1, for whom the essence of criminal liability is retribution for moral wrongs and who then excludes non-serious wrongs by the application of restraining (mostly, consequentialist) considerations.

[64] In parts 1.7 and 1.8, below, this principle is sharpened through its connection with the grounds of criminal liability and appropriate levels of sentence.

[65] Briefly, (i) the European Convention on Human Rights does not often require the creation of criminal offences, but cf the state's duty to protect citizens from violations of their right to life (Article 2, and *McCann v United Kingdom* (1996) 21 EHRR 97), their right not to be subjected to inhuman and degrading punishment (Article 3, and *A v United Kingdom* (1999) 27 EHRR 611), and their right to respect for their private life, in terms of sexual molestation (Article 8, and *X and Y v Netherlands* (1985) 8 EHRR 235); but (ii) the Convention does generate some strong arguments against criminalising conduct that interferes with the rights of citizens, such as the right not to be discriminated against in sexual offences (Articles 8 and 14, and *Sutherland v United Kingdom* (1997) 24 EHRR CD 22) and the right to freedom of expression and assembly (Articles 10 and 11, and *Steel v United Kingdom* (1999) 28 EHRR 603).

[66] See n 67 below.

[67] A von Hirsch and N Jareborg, 'Gauging Criminal Harm: a Living Standard Analysis' (1991) 11 *OJLS* 1, discussed by A Ashworth, *Sentencing and Criminal Justice* (2nd edn, 1995), Ch 4.3.

[68] See N Lacey, *State Punishment: Political Princiles and Community Values* (1988), Ch 8.

been tackled by Marshall and Duff,[69] who point out that it is not sufficient to say that crimes against individuals (such as homicide, rape and theft) are penalised because they threaten the social order, or some similar phrase, because that diminishes the significance of the victimisation of the individual that is clearly central to the offence. On the other hand, they argue, it is not sufficient to rely merely on the state's duty to ensure protection of these rights of individuals, because that could be achieved by civil law methods or by providing public assistance for private prosecutions. Their argument is that crimes are public wrongs because even those that consist of attacks on the body or property of an individual might be seen as 'wrongs against the community to which the individual belongs', wrongs that are shared by other members of the community with which the victim is identified and by which her or his identity is partly constituted.[70] Now it will be readily apparent that this approach to the public element in crimes draws no bright lines between conduct that should be criminalised and conduct that should not. Nor should it be taken to suggest that wrongs that are merely torts (and not crimes) have no public dimension, or indeed that wrongs which have a substantial community element ought to be treated (for that reason alone) as crimes rather than as aspects of a regulatory scheme. The point is that assessments of the seriousness of wrongs ought to take proper account of this wider community element, even in respect of crimes with individual victims.

Turning to the regulatory sphere,[71] we find differences in wrongs and sanctions that call for re-assessment in the light of broader principles. We have noted that some regulatory bodies are given powers to levy substantial penalties on relevant companies or individuals for breaches of regulations that do not qualify as criminal.[72] On the other hand, some statutes that are chiefly regulatory create criminal offences with substantial criminal penalties – for example, disposing of 'special waste' outside the conditions of a licence has a maximum penalty of five years' imprisonment,[73] and making a misleading statement in relation to investment business has a maximum of seven years' imprisonment.[74] The interests and values protected by these offences need to be assessed in relation to those protected by the 'normal' crimes of theft, making off without payment, and so forth. The creation of offences with such substantial maximum penalties might be taken to suggest that criminal policy-makers are, on occasions, capable of transcending traditional categories and modes of thought so

---

[69] SE Marshall and RA Duff, 'Criminalization and Sharing Wrongs' (1998) XI *Canadian Journal of Law and Jurisprudence* 7.

[70] Marshall and Duff, ibid-,at 21; see also 13, 'to believe that a certain kind of conduct should be criminal is to believe, at least, that it is conduct that should be declared wrong by the community; that it is a matter on which the community should take a shared and public view, and claim normative authority over its members'.

[71] The broad meaning given to the term 'regulatory' (n 12 above) should be recalled.

[72] See, eg the powers of the Occupational Pensions Regulatory Authority, n 25 above.

[73] Environmental Protection Act 1990, s 33.

[74] Financial Services Act 1986, s 47.

as to appreciate the harmful potential of conduct that is often regarded as falling within the 'regulatory' sphere. Some might take the more cynical view that these high maxima were intended as little more than symbolism; but the point to be made here is that all assessments of seriousness ought to be revisited, irrespective of whether a particular type of behaviour has traditionally been thought to belong to the regulatory rather than the criminal sphere, and reassessed in relation to relevant moral values and social interests.

All these observations demonstrate the difficulty of making assessments of seriousness, but there are three overlapping reasons for persevering with the task. First, the decision whether or not to criminalise should be influenced by the seriousness of the wrong. In principle, the criminal law (with all its procedures and consequences) should be used against substantial wrongs and should not be used against non-serious wrongs. There is an element of pragmatism in this: few contemporary societies can afford to grant full procedural safeguards to all those accused of non-serious wrongdoing, and in any event to criminalise the non-serious may be to weaken the significance of the label and the process. Nonetheless, the principle can stand alone, since criminalisation implies a labelling and a liability to punishment that should not lightly be imposed.[75] Secondly, the principle of proportionality in sentencing depends on judgements of seriousness and, even where that principle is not the determining rationale, it ought to be accorded a significant restraining role because it protects individual offenders against excessive demands by society.[76] And thirdly, judgements of seriousness and proportionality are deeply embedded in social intercourse and daily life. They are closely linked to beliefs about fairness, in relation to both wrongdoing and merit. This is not to overlook the genuine and deep disputes over such matters as reward for achievement or for effort, and punishment for harm done or for harm intended. But those disputes are about the indicia of proportionality, and take for granted the importance of the concepts of seriousness and proportionality in these matters.[77]

We have recognised that the task of ranking wrongs according to their relative seriousness is formidably difficult: although there may be some clarity towards the extreme ends of the spectrum, many wrongs that lie between those extremes are of variable and uncertain seriousness. What is needed, to deal with those uncertainties, is an incremental and reflexive approach that builds upon existing relativities and frequently reconsiders them in the light of principled arguments and of practical experience. That should avoid the unthinking adoption of traditional

[75] This is not to overlook or to minimise the problems of line-drawing between substantial and lesser wrongs, which may be acute in spheres such as theft of items of small value. But these are practical issues that do not weaken the principle.

[76] Cf the Council of Europe, *Recommendation R (92) 17 on Consistency in Sentencing*, principle A.4, declaring that, whatever other rationales for sentencing are pursued, it is essential to avoid disproportion between the seriousness of the crime and the severity of the penalty.

[77] Even strong critics of a 'desert' rationale for punishment recognise that there may be sound moral reasons for according a residual role to proportionality: see eg N Lacey, *State Punishment*, 162 and 194.

assumptions, and the frequent reconsideration should stand as an acknowledgement of the permeability of the rankings.

1.6 EQUAL TREATMENT, COUNTERVAILING INTERESTS AND DIFFERENTIAL ENFORCEMENT

Closely connected with the principle of proportionality is the principle of equal treatment – that those who commit wrongs of equivalent seriousness in relevantly similar circumstances should be subjected to censure of a similar magnitude. This is a manifestation of the familiar moral principle that like cases ought to be treated alike: it is a principle of consistency.[78] It begs questions, of course. One question concerns the features that would be regarded as critical for the purpose of judging likeness or similarity: in the context of criminal law, levels of seriousness of wrongs (taking account of actual or potential harmfulness and of culpability) ought to be determinative. Another question concerns the justifications for departing from the principle. Few would maintain that the principle of equal treatment ought to be applied as an absolute rule, especially in the regulation of behaviour in wide ranges of situations. In certain spheres there may be other values and interests that are regarded as so strong as to displace the general principle of equal treatment.

Two possibilities may be considered briefly. Some might wish to argue that criminal law ought to be kept on the outer edges of labour disputes: thus, even though conduct is taking place that would attract the criminal sanction in normal circumstances, there might be a public interest in not penalising that conduct. The argument might be that experience has shown that it is far more effective in the medium and long term to deal with all but the most egregious misbehaviour during these disputes by means of labour relations mechanisms; invoking the criminal law on a 'normal' basis might be counter-productive, possibly leading to an escalation of the conflict. That argument would not be won easily,[79] but it is one example of a possible exception to the principle of equal treatment. Whether it is thought sufficiently strong to draw a distinction between conduct on a picket line and conduct, say, during a demonstration against the breeding of animals for experimentation is a matter for further debate.

Another argument might stem from the policies of family law, based on the rights of family members and the interest in, for example, preserving the family unit so far as possible. It might be argued that the criminal law should be kept on the outer edges of family disputes; that experience has shown that it is far

---

[78] Cf Lacey's 'principle of equal impact', arguing for an 'egalitarian principle' that bears 'not only on the distribution of interest-protection in the substantive law, but also on the potential impact of the law's application' (ibid, 113).

[79] Cf the discussion by PL Davies and MR Freedland, *Labour Legislation and Public Policy* (1993), 495–99.

more effective in the medium and long term to deal with all but the most egregious misbehaviour during these disputes by family law mechanisms; and that such a response shows greater consideration to the other family members involved. Again, this is not an argument that would be won easily: there is rightly an increasing insistence that child abuse and domestic violence should be treated seriously,[80] and that a person's rights should be protected no less in the home than on the street. Thus, whether there are occasions on which family-oriented policies are thought sufficiently strong to draw a distinction between assaults in the street and assaults in the home is a matter for further debate.

The purpose of giving these two examples is to raise the possibility that the principle of equal treatment might be regarded, in certain spheres, as outweighed by the need to protect other values and to assign a more peripheral role to the criminal law. The examples cannot be argued to a conclusion here. However, if the principle of equal treatment is accepted, the burden of justification falls upon the legislature, court or prosecutor to show why offences within a particular sphere should not be dealt with in the normal way. It is, in fact, unusual for there to be specific exceptions or exemptions from the criminal law itself, and we must therefore recognise that we have moved into the realm of law enforcement here. The principle of equal treatment is nothing if not a practical injunction: it should be applied not merely to the enactment of laws, but also to the responses to misconduct in practice. A system of criminal justice that allows the differential enforcement of its laws is not a system that honours the principle of equal treatment.

One source of differential enforcement may be found in the increasing and extensive use of regulatory strategies in the modern state. There is now a wealth of statutes, such as the Trade Descriptions Act 1968, the Consumer Protection Act 1987, the Copyright, Designs and Patents Act 1988, the Financial Services Act 1986 and the Food Safety Act 1990, which are designed chiefly to regulate spheres of commercial activity but which contain criminal offences. Some of these offences carry substantial maximum sentences, and may therefore be thought to be relatively serious – indeed, of roughly equivalent seriousness to other offences carrying the same maximum punishment. There has also been legislation creating new agencies, such as OPRA (the occupational pensions regulator), OFTEL (the telecommunications regulator) and the Environment Agency, with criminal offences at their disposal, as it were. What is clear is that almost all these agencies, and other authorities charged with the enforcement of regulatory schemes, do not regard 'their' criminal offences in the way that the police and Crown Prosecution Service view 'ordinary' crimes. Just as we saw earlier that particular spheres of law (eg labour law, family law) may have their own ethos, focus and techniques, so regulatory agencies tend to have their own order of priority, one that typically involves negotiating for compliance rather

---

[80] See, eg the discussions in J Morgan and L Zedner, *Child Victims* (1992) in C Hoyle, *Negotiating Domestic Violence: Police, Criminal Justice and Victims* (1998), and the Introduction to J Eekelaar and M McLean (eds), *A Reader on Family Law* (1994).

than punishing, particularly where the legislation can be seen as enabling in addition to restricting. In some spheres this preference for negotiating compliance rather than prosecuting breaches may be taken to considerable lengths, so that agencies may believe 'their efforts to attain the wider goals of their legislative mandate to be facilitated by the extensive (formal) nonenforcement of the specific offences' provided in the regulatory legislation.[81]

The contrast in enforcement styles is not absolute, of course.[82] The police caution (rather than prosecute) about one-fifth of all offenders,[83] and the scheme of reprimands and warnings for young offenders under the Crime and Disorder Act 1998 preserves the spirit of avoiding court appearances for the young. Nonetheless, most regulatory agencies use warnings far more frequently, and prosecute far less frequently, than the police. To that extent the contrast in enforcement styles remains a strong one, and it raises the question whether such departures from the principle of equal treatment can be justified. Two kinds of justification can be considered, both of them based on preventive considerations. The first is that a compliance approach (favouring negotiation with offenders and keeping prosecution as a last resort) is more effective than a sanctioning approach (which has prosecution as the favoured response). The claim is that effectiveness should be viewed in terms of conformity to the law and the regulations over a considerable period of time. Thus Ayres and Braithwaite promote a 'pyramid of regulatory strategies', from persuasion as the most-used and least coercive strategy, up to criminal penalties and licence revocation as the most powerful and least-used.[84] The prevailing theory was that compliance is better assured by fostering a relationship between enforcer and (potential) offender which keeps criminal prosecution as a background threat and which allows the enforcer to recognise the pressures on the offender and to steer the latter towards compliance by encouragement and negotiation.[85] Ayres and Braithwaite develop this, in their pyramidal approach, by emphasising the need to adapt enforcement strategies to the context of particular industries and to stiffen the use of deterrent strategies.[86]

---

[81] K Hawkins, *Environment and Enforcement: Regulation and the Social Definiion of Pollution* (1984), 195; see now K Hawkins, *Law as Last Resort* (2003).

[82] Moreover, discretion is exercised at most levels of most enforcement systems. The result may be enforcement practices that are not just selective but 'transformative', in the sense that they alter the impact of the law: see Lacey, 'Contingency and Criminalisation' in Loveland (ed), *The Frontiers of Criminality* (1995), 8.

[83] [The overall cautioning rate was 38 per cent when this chapter was originally written: *Criminal Statistics, England and Wales 1997*, Table 5.4. The rate has declined to 21 per cent in 2011–12: www.justice.gov.uk/statistics/criminal-justice/criminal-justice-statistics Table Q2e; the percentage is higher for females, and also for younger offenders].

[84] I Ayres and J Braithwaite, *Responsive Regulation: Transcending the Deregulation Debate* (1992), Ch 2.

[85] The classic analyses are those of Hawkins, *Environment and Enforcement,* and A. Reiss, 'Selecting Strategies of Social Control over Organisational Life' in K Hawkins and J Thomas (eds), *Enforcing Regulation* (1984).

[86] Ayres and Braithwaite, *Responsive Regulation*, n 84 above, 38–40.

These arguments do not necessarily meet the point behind the principle of equal treatment. If we posit two people who commit two offences of roughly equivalent gravity, one falling within the ambit of traditional policing and the other falling within a regulatory scheme enforced by a specialist agency, the question is whether it is unfair that the former should be prosecuted when the latter receives only a warning and encouragement to comply by a certain date. There may be obvious differences between the two types of case: the former might be a single incident constituting an offence, whereas the latter may be part of a continuing course of conduct which the enforcer wishes to bring into compliance with the law as soon as feasible (but not necessarily right now). Yet it is difficult to see how this weakens the force of the principle of equal treatment: one could just as well reply that the continuing course of conduct constitutes a continuing source of criminality, which ought to be stopped forthwith. The claim must be that the *prima facie* unfairness of departing from the principle of equal treatment can be justified by the extra law-abidance that the compliance approach generates; but it remains to be demonstrated that extra law-abidance is produced, and, if so, that it can only be achieved by means of a compliance approach to enforcement (or, for Ayres and Braithwaite, by a 'responsive' approach). If it transpires that the real argument is that the various inspectorates have insufficient resources to mount more prosecutions, and therefore use the compliance approach partly for cost reasons, then we must accept that the debate has shifted to a rather different terrain.

The second possible justification for departing from the principle of equal treatment is more explicitly economic. It takes us beyond offences typically prosecuted by regulatory agencies, and may also be applied to corporate wrong-doing and even to large-scale fraud by individuals. The claim is that in those spheres the criminal law may be far too blunt a weapon and far too ineffective and costly to employ. In fraud cases the sheer cost of mounting a prosecution is sometimes advanced as a reason for trying to find some other way of dealing with the wrong: if it costs millions of pounds for the Serious Fraud Office to investigate a case and put together the evidence for a prosecution, and then for a court to sit for months as the complex evidence is revealed to a jury, does it not make sense for the state to cut its losses and try to reach some accommodation with the defendant? If the defendant agrees, eg to repay the whole or a substantial proportion of what was taken, and to be subjected to a lesser penalty such as a fine or community sentence, it might be argued that the sacrifice of the appropriate penalty is worthwhile in view of the cost savings. In a similar vein Braithwaite has urged on several occasions that the bringing of criminal prosecutions against companies is likely to be expensive, fraught with legal difficulty, and ineffective in terms of prevention.[87] Braithwaite and Fisse have argued for an entirely different, prevention-oriented approach to corporate wrongdoing

---

[87] See, eg J Braithwaite, *Corporate Crime in the Pharmaceutical Industry* (1983), Ch 9, and *Corporations, Crime and Accountability* (n 88 below).

which, in brief terms, involves imposing requirements on companies to make good the harm they cause and to take remedial measures to prevent a recurrence.[88] The emphasis here would be on the prevention of harm: the authors regard the various attempts of the criminal law to attribute culpability to companies or their officers as futile and even irrelevant, and argue that priority should be given to harm prevention rather than allocating blame for past events.

This perspective opens up possibilities for social policy-making that are well worth exploring. The activities of corporations loom large in contemporary society, and the resources of the criminal justice system are not infinite. My great difficulty with these ideas about serious fraud and about corporate wrongdoing lies in their implications for social justice. Would it not be – is it not – monstrously unfair and intolerable that people who steal from shops are dragged through the criminal courts and subjected to liberty-restricting penalties, when others (whether fraudsters or companies) who culpably inflict far greater harm are dealt with outside the criminal law? In addition, having a criminal record brings various disqualifications from employment and other disadvantages. To put the matter another way, if one person who wrongs another is convicted of a crime whilst another who commits an admittedly more serious wrong is not, this is manifestation of warped priorities and clear injustice. It is not appropriate that the criminal law should be either structured or enforced in such a discriminatory way.

Of course there are ways of contesting this claim. Braithwaite, for example, accepts that most criminal justice systems are excessively punitive in that they use the criminal law and prison sentences too extensively, and he would be unhappy about prosecuting shop thieves and sending them to prison. Both he and I, therefore, might prefer to see a slimmer criminal law. But that does not meet the point. My argument is essentially a comparative one: whatever is the lowliest offence in the criminal justice system, is it fair that a citizen is liable to conviction for that when someone who inflicts an indisputably greater wrong is not? Thus a deep difference between Braithwaite and me concerns the function of the criminal law and the role of prevention. For Braithwaite, the prevention of harm is a primary goal of social policy, and the criminal law is regarded as one among a number of mechanisms for bringing this about. It should therefore be used as and when it is efficient, and replaced by other mechanisms when it is not efficient and/or cost-effective. This view underlies the idea of responsive regulation, as a means of dealing with the varying contexts in which regulatory agencies have to operate. My conception of the criminal law gives primary place to its censuring function, a public function with possibly severe consequences for citizens, which should be exercised in as fair and non-discriminatory a manner as possible. In this context the principle of equal treatment is assigned a high priority. This is not to suggest that the prevention of harm is irrelevant to criminal law: it remains significant as a fundamental justification for having a

---

[88] J Braithwaite and B Fisse, *Corporations, Crime and Accountability* (1993).

criminal law with sanctions attached.[89] But to invoke it as a reason for shaping the criminal law in particular ways would lead to an unacceptably distorted system in which the prospects of effectiveness and prevention, not the seriousness of the wrongdoing, would determine decisions to criminalise, decisions to prosecute and decisions about the appropriate penalty. In principle, the prevention of harm should be pursued through a range of initiatives in social, criminal and environmental policy. In practice, there is no shortage of examples of governments either repeatedly over-estimating the preventive efficacy of the criminal law or deliberately ignoring the poor prospects of prevention in favour of the politically symbolic effect of creating a new crime. The aim should be to produce a set of criminal laws that penalise substantial wrongdoing and only substantial wrongdoing, enforcing those fairly and dealing with them proportionately. There is no justification for differential enforcement systems that detract grossly from the principle of equal treatment and the sense of fairness about proportionate responses to wrongdoing.

This argument should be pressed still further. In principle, the fullest enforcement, with the most frequent use of prosecution and the highest penalties, should be reserved for the most serious forms of criminality. On the same principle, the enforcement agency with the largest powers and the strongest presence should be charged with the investigation of the most serious offences. If this is the police, so be it; but their core tasks should involve the investigation not merely of homicide, rape, robbery and 'normal crimes' but also of transport disasters, major environmental incidents, the making of false representations in investment business (insofar as they belong in this group), and other serious wrongs. At the other end of the scale, there are arguments for re-allocating the enforcement of laws against theft from shops and street nuisances. Of course there are counter-arguments to be discussed, but it is crucial that we re-examine our assumptions about the functions of the police in the maintenance of 'order' and the enforcement of (selected parts of) the criminal law. For too long we have acquiesced in a bifurcated approach whereby the police adopt chiefly a punishment approach and the so-called regulatory agencies, in their unaccountable way,[90] favour forms of negotiated compliance, a division unrelated to the comparative seriousness of the wrongdoing involved. Starting with the principles of proportionality and equal treatment elaborated above, the touchstone of enforcement policy ought to be the seriousness of the offences in question; the choice of investigating and prosecuting agencies may be intrinsically less important, so long as the policies and powers of the agencies are adjusted to the seriousness of the offences.

---

[89] This adopts the rationale advanced by A von Hirsch, *Censure and Sanctions* (1993), Ch 1, in preference to that of M Moore, *Placing Blame: A Theory of the Criminal Law* (1997), 24–29, which finds no place for consequentialist justifications.

[90] The absence of proper accountability mechanisms for the enforcement approaches of regulatory bodies is argued in A Ashworth and Redmayne, *The Criminal Process*, Chs 5 and 6.

Finally, we must recall that there are at least two broader questions of policy that are not concluded by this discussion. The first concerns the style and level of response to crime. Nothing in this essay suggests that there should be increased powers of investigation or higher penalties for offenders: the argument is that, whatever powers and penalties are decided upon (after separate debate), the strongest should be reserved for the most serious forms of crime. Equal treatment should be the principle, with differential enforcement only where it can be justified.[91] Beyond that, it remains important to develop new forms of response to law-breaking and to avoid the fallacy that crime will go down if penalties go up.[92] Secondly, we should not overlook the probability that pursuit of the principles of proportionality and equal treatment will lead to practical conflicts with the pursuit of principles in other areas of social policy, such as health, education and housing. These are not merely resource problems, to be confronted on a political and economic plane. They are conflicts that call for analysis in terms of principle: the contribution of this chapter is to develop the case for a principled approach to criminal justice, prior to debate in the wider forum.

1.7 CRIMINALISATION AND SENTENCING

It has been argued above that judgements of the seriousness of wrongdoing ought to have clear implications for the decision to criminalise, for the procedural protections provided, and for enforcement policy. The two primary sentencing issues – what the maximum penalty for an offence should be, and what sentencing norms should apply in ordinary cases – are so closely bound up with judgements of seriousness that they might be said to be expressive of them. When an offence is created, the maximum penalty set by the legislature ought to place the offence at the appropriate point on the seriousness scale established by other maxima. This may be a contentious decision, particularly when comparisons have to be drawn with the maxima for entirely different forms of wrongdoing. In English law these decisions have often been made in an apparently haphazard and unprincipled manner, as Sir Rupert Cross demonstrated in the *Law Quarterly Review* some 48 years ago.[93] This aspect of English criminal law betrays historical contingency running riot. The one effort to deal with the anomalies ended with an ignominious abdication, supported on the ground that at least the current practice of the courts was not controversial.[94] That

---

[91] This is not to ignore the difficulties of ensuring that policies are translated into practice: see, eg A Ashworth and M Redmayne, *The Criminal Process*, Ch 3, for an overview.

[92] For a careful analysis of the evidence on deterrence, see A von Hirsch, AE Bottoms, E Burney and P-O Wikstrom, *Criminal Deterrence and Sentence Severity: An Analysis of Recent Research* (1999).

[93] In his inaugural lecture as the 12th Vinerian Professor: 'Paradoxes in Prison Sentences' (1965) 81 *LQR* 205 at 211.

[94] Advisory Council on the Penal System, *Sentences of Imprisonment: a Review of Maximum Penalties* (1978), para 164.

assertion was as unconvincing then as it is now. Parliament has continued to raise or lower maximum penalties in an *ad hoc* manner, and there has been no evident enthusiasm for the necessary task of revising maximum penalties so that they have the appropriate degree of principled coherence. In this respect the Government's professed policy of ensuring that a new maximum penalty is 'commensurate with the seriousness of the offence' and that there is 'consistency across the sentencing framework' has a resoundingly hollow ring.[95]

It would be unwise to confine any examination of the coherence of the sentencing framework to maximum penalties, although this would be a desirable and separate first step. Of greater practical relevance are actual sentence levels, for proportionality and equal treatment both require that the degrees of censure embodied in the courts' sentences relate carefully and consistently to the seriousness of the wrongdoing in the particular case. Over the last 30 years the Court of Appeal, under the leadership of successive Lord Chief Justices, has delivered a number of guideline judgments which attempt to provide coherent structures for the sentencing of certain offences.[96] What is needed now is an attempt to review relativities between different offences, to ensure that the sentence ranges for the different offences fit into a sensible pattern informed by the principles of proportionality and equal treatment. This is a task that the Sentencing Council might perform in due course.[97]

Returning to the earlier discussion of the powers of regulatory agencies, there is also the question of what constitutes a 'penalty'. We have seen that the European Court of Human Rights takes the view that one of the three factors relevant to determining whether a person is 'charged with a criminal offence' is whether that person is liable to face 'potentially severe consequences' for doing the act.[98] Since that criterion has been held to apply principally to deprivation of liberty, it is unlikely to form the basis of a challenge to the kind of civil penalties for which the regulatory statutes sometimes provide. The same might be said of the term 'penalty', relevant under Article 7 of the European Convention when it is claimed that a penalty has been applied retrospectively. Although the severity of the measure has been stated to be one of the criteria, the European Court of Human Rights has held that a measure can only be classed as a penalty if it is imposed following conviction for a criminal offence.[99] It therefore seems to follow that, unless a regulator's powers include deprivation of liberty or perhaps the possibility of an enormous financial penalty, no claim for the

---

[95] See the statement of Lord Williams of Mostyn, n 17 above and text thereat. A prime example of this is the maximum sentence of five years' imprisonment provided by s 1 of the Crime and Disorder Act 1998 for the strict liability offence of failing to comply with a (civil) anti-social behaviour order.

[96] For discussion of those judgments, see A Ashworth, *Sentencing and Criminal Justice*, Ch 4.4.

[97] The Sentencing Advisory Panel, constituted under sections 80–81 of the Crime and Disorder Act 1998, began its work in July 1999. As a result of the Coroners and Justice Act 2009, the Panel and also the Sentencing Guidelines Council have been superseded by the Sentencing Council, which issues sentencing guidelines.

[98] See the criteria set out in *Benham v United Kingdom*, nn 22 and 53 above and text thereat.

[99] *Welch v United Kingdom* (1995) 20 EHRR 247, at para 28.

various safeguards provided by Article 6 for defendants in criminal proceedings is likely to succeed.

1.8 THE PRINCIPLED CORE OF CRIMINAL LAW

Although I have tried in this chapter to give some flavour of the proliferation of legal forms and structures for the guidance of conduct, and thereby to demonstrate a blurring of the boundaries between criminal and regulatory and between criminal and civil, the main purpose has been to develop two lines of argument.

The first is that the criminal law is indeed a lost cause, from the point of view of principle. The Government's purported criteria for creating new crimes[100] are not followed in practice, nor have they been in the recent past. *Pace* Lord Williams, new offences have been created to penalise non-serious misbehaviour, sometimes with maximum sentences out of proportion to other maxima. The empirical basis for this claim was illustrated by examples from the 1997 statute book, and particularly the offence in section 1 of the Crime and Disorder Act 1998 of breaching an anti-social behaviour order. The plain fact is that governments often take the view that the creation of a new crime sends out a symbolic message that, in blunt terms, may 'get them off a political hook' – even though the new crime fails to satisfy Lord Williams' criteria on one or more grounds.

The second line of argument is more constructive, in seeking to identify a principled core of criminal law. The core consists, it is submitted, of four interlinked principles:

• *The principle that the criminal law should be used, and only used, to censure persons for substantial wrongdoing.* This principle recognises that the prevention of such misconduct is a reason for criminalising it: if serious wrongdoing can be identified, it is of social importance that its incidence be reduced. However, this should be distinguished from the less acceptable propositions (a) that the prevention of misconduct is a sufficient reason for criminalisation, and (b) that the criminal law is, either on its own or in combination with other social policies, necessarily an effective means of prevention. The tendency to over-estimate the deterrent efficacy of criminal sentencing has already been mentioned.[101] As for crime prevention strategies, these are usually designed to minimise the risk that certain situations or opportunities will come about, or that certain individuals will find it attractive to behave in particular ways. Appropriately targeted social, educational and housing policies may well have a greater preventive effect than the enactment of a criminal offence and the conviction of (what is likely to be) a relatively small proportion of offenders, a point rarely acknowledged in the political and media discussions that lead to

---

[100] See the statement by Lord Williams, n 17 above and text thereat.
[101] Above, n 92; cf N Jareborg, *Essays in Criminal Law* (1988), Ch 5.

the creation of new crimes. However, methods of crime prevention also raise questions of moral and social principle that should be kept in view.[102]

- *The principle that criminal laws should be enforced with respect for equal treatment and proportionality.* The implication is that enforcement authorities and their policies ought to be reorganised so as to reflect the relative seriousness of the wrongdoing with which they are dealing, and should not remain hidebound by traditional divisions of responsibility that fail to reflect proper assessments of the culpable wrongs involved.

- *The principle that persons accused of substantial wrongdoing ought to be afforded the protections appropriate to those charged with criminal offences,* ie at least the minimum protections declared by Articles 6.2 and 6.3 of the European Convention on Human Rights. These minimum protections ought to be regarded as an inherent element of criminal procedure, and this principle as interlinked with the others. Thus, if wrongdoing is regarded as serious enough to warrant the creation of an offence, and if it is thought so serious as to require a substantial maximum sentence, it would be a violation of this principle for a government to avoid or whittle down the protections that a person facing such a charge ought to be accorded. This, it will be recalled, is one objection to the offence of failing to comply with an anti-social behaviour order contrary to section 1 of the Crime and Disorder Act 1998. A maximum penalty of five years' imprisonment has been provided for what is a strict liability offence,[103] all the substantive issues having been determined in earlier civil proceedings without the Article 6 safeguards. Civil-criminal hybrids designed to circumvent Convention rights are wrong in principle.

- *The principle that maximum sentences and effective sentence levels should be proportionate to the seriousness of the wrongdoing.* The implication here, as with the second principle, is that there needs to be a root-and-branch change – a thorough revision of maximum penalties and a re-assessment of sentence levels and of differentials between them.

These are put forward as core principles. It is not claimed that they should be regarded as absolute rules, and indeed at various points above some possible qualifications to them have been discussed. Derogations from them should be argued as derogations, and should be principled in themselves.

The principles also lead in other directions that cannot be examined fully in this context. At the core is the idea that, if a particular wrong is thought serious enough to justify the possibility of a custodial sentence, that wrong should be treated as a crime, with fault required and proper procedural protections for defendants. This has implications for those minor wrongs that are presently made the subject of criminal offences simply because the criminal courts offer

---

[102] A von Hirsch, 'The Ethics of Public Television Surveillance' in A von Hirsch, D Garland and A Wakefield (eds), *Ethical and Social Perspectives on Situational Crime Prevention* (2000).

[103] It was argued above that the use of imprisonment (let alone up to five years' imprisonment) for a strict liability offence is independently contrary to principle: see nn 58–59 above and text thereat.

themselves as a quick and cheap means of dealing with them: many of the 1997 offences fall into this category, as do hundreds of other strict liability offences. A fine solution would be to create a new category of 'civil violation' or 'administrative offence',[104] which would certainly be non-imprisonable and would normally attract a financial penalty; procedures would be simplified but would preserve minimum rights for defendants, such as access to a criminal court.[105] Another implication of the principles should be that any new criminal code for this country ought to declare the most serious offences in English law, rather than simply those traditional offences that have been the focus of textbooks over the years.[106]

What are the prospects for thus re-structuring and restoring integrity to the criminal law? Political reality suggests that they are unpromising: in this sense, the criminal law may be a lost cause. Even governments with large parliamentary majorities, and which profess certain criteria for the creation of new offences, may either give way to the allure of media popularity or simply not care sufficiently to adhere to their own principles. In such political circumstances it is all the more necessary to re-kindle debate about the functions and characteristics that the criminal law ought to have, and to ensure that the close interconnections between criminal law, criminal procedure and sentencing are kept at the forefront of that debate.

---

[104] For discussion, see American Law Institute, *Model Penal Code and Commentaries* (1985), vol 1, 71–73.

[105] The European Court of Human Rights has insisted upon this, whilst recognising that it is not inconsistent with Article 6 of the Convention for minor offences to be dealt with administratively in the first instance: see, eg *Engel v Netherlands* (1979–80) 1 EHRR 647, *Ozturk v Germany* (1984) 6 EHRR 409, at para 56, and *Malige v France* (1999) 28 EHRR 578.

[106] Thus offences such as causing death by dangerous driving, which carries a maximum penalty of 10 years' imprisonment, find no place in the Law Commission's code because that would separate them from the remaining road traffic offences and all the various powers to disqualify drivers that are contained in the Road Traffic Acts, which would be 'inconvenient': Law Com No 177, *A Criminal Code for England and Wales* (1989), para 3A. The convenience of lawyers is thus placed ahead of the importance of restating the most serious offences in the criminal law.

2

Criminalising Omissions

OMISSIONS ARE OFTEN (usually) considered less blameworthy than acts. We tend to react differently to killers and to 'non-savers'. People might form a different moral estimation of P, who pushed a non-swimmer into deep water knowing that he would probably drown and he did, than of Q, who saw a person in a lake calling for help but took no steps to assist (even though she was a strong swimmer) or to call the emergency services, and the person drowned. There is little support for the equivalence or neutrality thesis, whereby there is said to be no general moral difference between acts and omissions in terms of responsibility and culpability.[1] However, one does not have to subscribe to the equivalence thesis in order to appreciate the force of two important points. First, even if omissions are often less culpable than acts, they may still be sufficiently blameworthy to reach the threshold for criminalisation: that is a question for examination below. Secondly, it is possible to conceive of situations in which an omission may be little or no less culpable than an act: if we consider the most straightforward duty-situation, that of parents towards their child, and if we recall a case in which parents gave no food to a particular child and starved the child to death, it is strongly arguable that such an omission is no less culpable than many positive acts of cruelty.[2]

Much depends, for the purposes of the relationship between omissions and the criminal law, on one's conception of an omission. It is surely not coherent to speak of all the things one does not do in the course of a day as omissions. As will be argued below, the things one does not do are best characterised as 'not-doings', and the list may turn out to be tediously long and uninformative. But if one asks the more targeted question of how many omissions someone perpetrated in a day, then the answer should turn on two elements not yet mentioned – whether the person had, in principle, a duty to do x, and whether in the factual circumstances the person had the opportunity and capacity to do x. While the questions of opportunity and capacity will remain in view, the focus here is on the duty element, since it is only proper to speak of something as an omission if it constitutes a failure to carry out a duty. The major questions here are

---

[1] Glover comments that such an approach would 'propose a radical and very demanding morality': J Glover, *Causing Death and Saving Lives* (1977), 109.

[2] See *R v Gibbins and Proctor* (1918) 13 Cr App R 131; T Honoré, 'Are Omissions Less Culpable?' in P Cane and J Stapleton (eds), *Essays for Patrick Atiyah* (1991), 33; and J Rachels, 'Active and Passive Euthanasia' (1975) 292 *New England Journal of Medicine* 78.

twofold: i) in what situations should a person be said to have an affirmative duty to act reinforced by the criminal law; and ii) what is the appropriate intensity[3] of criminalisation?

In its search for criteria for criminalising omissions, this chapter begins (part 1) by reflecting on the place of omissions in the criminal law. This is followed (in part 2) by an outline of the main arguments of principle relevant to the justification of criminal liability for omissions. In part 3 there is a close engagement with the possible justifications for criminalising omissions in four types of social context, considering also the intensity of criminalisation that might be appropriate in each context, and concluding by considering omissions elements in offences of commission. Then there is a discussion (part 4) of what the rule of law requires if omissions offences are to be created. Part 5 turns to the form and intensity of criminalisation that might be most suitable for particular omissions. Part 6 considers some omissions which are elements of broader offence definitions. Part 7 examines what should be required of individuals in these duty-situations. It will be argued that parts 3 through 7 reflect the major issues of principle that need to be settled before a particular offence of omission can be held to be justified. The chapter ends (part 8) with a review of certain major themes in omissions offences.

2.1 THE PLACE OF OMISSIONS IN THE CRIMINAL LAW

The topic of omissions appears towards the beginning of many criminal law courses and books on the criminal law. The standard approach is to state that it is helpful to divide the elements of crimes into *actus reus* and *mens rea*; to argue that one of the basic components of the *actus reus* is the act requirement; and then to confront two types of crime which may appear not to conform to the act requirement – status or state-of-affairs offences and omissions.[4] Focusing on omissions offences, it may be said that they are unusual, and that they depend on recognition of a duty. Omissions can comply with the voluntariness requirement and they can be causes – both of which are obvious if one takes the clear case of a parent failing to feed a child. But normal principles of causation may not apply straightforwardly in all omissions cases: failing to prevent an act from occurring may not amount to a *novus actus interveniens* that breaks the causal chain flowing from a prior positive act,[5] and it may be easier to prove beyond reasonable doubt that an omission was *a* cause rather than *the* cause of an event.[6] Much depends, of course,

---

[3] 'Intensity' refers to the degree of criminal liability, on a scale from an offence of mere failure to report an event (low intensity) to a serious substantive offence such as manslaughter (high intensity).

[4] *Simester and Sullivan's Criminal Law* (4th edn, 2011, by AP Simester, JR Spencer, GR Sullivan and GJ Virgo (eds)), 68–9.

[5] Ibid, 103–7, for analysis; cf I Kugler, 'Two Concepts of Omission', (2004) 14 Criminal Law Forum 421.

[6] Cf G Williams, 'What should the Code do about Omissions?' (1987) 7 *Legal Studies* 92, at 106; W Wilson, 'Murder by Omission: Some Observations on a Mismatch between the General and Special Parts' (2010) 13 *New Criminal Law Review* 1, 8.

on the type and intensity of criminalisation, notably whether causation of a result is required. These and other issues are contested, as is the very distinction between an act and an omission; but most writers conclude that offences of omission can be accommodated within the theoretical structure of the criminal law, even if by way of partial exception.

Having reached this point, usually in a matter of a few pages, it is common for textbooks to turn to the question of duties – what situations should be recognised as giving rise to a duty that can form the basis of an omissions offence? Thus one leading English textbook identifies four categories of duty (parental/family; contractual duties; voluntary undertakings; dangerous situations created) and has a short discussion of them before moving on to the next major topic in criminal law.[7] This way of proceeding glosses over a significant change in the direction of the discussion. Having started off by examining the respects in which omissions offences do or do not differ from the standard (act-related) elements of the *actus reus*, we have now moved to a discussion of the rationales and boundaries of the various categories of duty. These are criminalisation questions, relating to the special part (not the general part) of the criminal law – what should the limits of criminal liability be? Which omissions should the law criminalise?

It therefore follows that these questions ought to be approached by considering principles relevant to criminalisation. We should start with the proposition that criminal law is one of the law's several mechanisms for regulating conduct, along with civil regulatory structures, the law of torts, taxation, planning law, and others. The specific technique of the criminal law is to threaten punishment for non-compliance with its injunctions, to censure offenders publicly, and to impose punishment on them: all these features curtail the normal rights of the individuals who are convicted, and therefore require strong justification. The official censure is made known so as to communicate to the offender, the victims and the wider community that a public wrong was committed. The threat of punishment aims to supply a prudential reason for compliance with the law, by way of deterrence. If the threat fails and an offence is committed, proportionate punishment (involving hard treatment) is, in principle, a deserved supplement to the appeal to the offender as a moral agent that is part of the public censure. Thus 'to criminalise an action is both to declare that the action should not be done and to deploy desert-based sanctions as supplementary reasons not to do it'.[8]

What kinds of conduct ought properly to be criminalised? Are there any defensible criteria for or against criminalisation? This is a deeply contested subject,

---

[7] D Ormerod, *Smith and Hogan's Criminal Law* (13th edn, 2011), 70–76. This has hitherto been my approach too, eg A Ashworth, 'Public Duties and Criminal Omissions: Some Unresolved Questions' [2011] 1 *Journal of Commonwealth Criminal Law* 1. See also M Bohlander, *Principles of German Criminal Law* (2009), 40–45, stating six categories similar in extent to those in English law.

[8] AP Simester and A von Hirsch, *Crimes, Harms and Wrongs: On the Principles of Criminalisation* (2011), 6; note that this quotation confines itself to an 'action'.

which cannot be examined in full here. But we may start with the argument of Andrew Simester and Andreas von Hirsch, to the effect that one necessary pre-requisite of criminalisation is that the conduct amounts to a moral wrong.[9] This does not imply that this is a sufficient condition, merely that it is a prerequisite, since there may be morally wrong conduct (eg forms of lying or sexual infidelity) which, for other reasons, should not be criminalised. Nor does this rule out the criminalisation of what might be termed co-ordination offences, ie those offences necessary to regulate an activity such as driving, where the law must make certain determinations (eg that drivers should drive on the left) which then, through their instrumental value, impart moral force to related requirements.[10] However, before criminalisation is justified, it must be clear that there are not strong countervailing considerations, such as the absence of harm, the creation of unwelcome social consequences, the curtailment of important rights, and so forth.[11] Indeed, given the content and consequences of public censure and punishment – in terms of restrictions on, and even deprivations of, basic liberties – there is a strong case for restricting criminalisation to moral wrongs attaining a certain level of serious-ness. That is straightforward in a system that has a lesser category of 'administra-tive offences' or (as in Germany) *Ordnungswidrigkeiten* with low penalties, which can be used to penalise public wrongs that do not attain the appropriate level of seriousness to be criminalised.

Elements of this brief discussion will be developed further below, but here we must begin to consider how the justifications for criminalisation might apply to omissions. In liberal theory the characteristic form of the criminal law is that it prohibits people from inflicting serious wrongs on others and provides for the conviction and punishment of those who do so. It is not generally thought that the core prohibitions in English law amount to such a restriction on people's liberty of action as to prevent them from pursuing their conception of a good life, according to their own goals and values. This is not to ignore or to mini-mise the potentially chilling effects on liberty of the controversial extensions of the criminal law which penalise pre-inchoate and preparatory offences.[12] But the central point is that being prohibited from killing, wounding, sexually violat-ing, stealing from or defrauding others cannot be regarded as an unfair or excessive narrowing of people's options; indeed, such prohibitions rule out sev-eral means of pursuing one's own ends that in themselves deny respect for oth-ers, and liberty to pursue one's own conception of a good life must always be subject to recognition of a similar liberty of others to pursue their own concep-tion of a good life. This may be termed the 'equal freedom' principle, developed

---

[9] Ibid, 22 and Ch 2 *passim*.

[10] Ibid, 27.

[11] For a fuller exploration, see ibid, Ch 11, and D Husak, *Overcriminalization: The Limits of the Criminal Law* (2008), Chs 2 and 3.

[12] See, eg, V Tadros, 'Justice and Terrorism' (2007) 11 *New Criminal Law Review* 658; A Ashworth and L Zedner, 'Prevention and Criminalization: Justifications and Limits' (2012) 15 *New Criminal Law Review* 542.

most fully in those strands of Kantian philosophy which insist on the absolute worth of each rational being and on the principle of acting 'so that you treat humanity, whether in your own person or that of another, always as an end and never as a means only'.[13] A similar prescription is found in Rawls' 'first principle', that 'each person is to have an equal right to the most extensive total system of equal basic liberties compatible with a similar system of liberty for all'.[14] Thus, even in a political system that ascribed supreme value to individual autonomy, there would have to be some limitations on freedom of action, although the general thrust of liberalism is that they should be kept to the minimum. When it comes to prohibitions embodying the censure and sanctions of the criminal law, minimalism is even more in order.

It may be argued that this strand of liberal theory, with its insistence on individual autonomy, tells against liability for omissions. The contention would be that, whereas the criminalisation of wrongful acts narrows people's options only in a general and residual manner, leaving a large area of freedom of action, the criminalisation of omissions may reduce a person's options to one – a requirement to perform a certain act now – and is thus 'far more intrusive upon individuals' autonomy and freedom than is the prohibition of acts'.[15] Andrew Simester has argued that it would be 'a denial of respect for the idea that one's practical choices should be determined by one's own goals and values' if one were saddled with 'untrammelled responsibility for harms the occurrence of which one is *prima facie* unconnected with'.[16] This proposition seems to be founded on a somewhat constricted conception of autonomy: a broader conception, such as that espoused by Joseph Raz, might allow governments to compel people to take actions in order to improve other people's options and opportunities.[17] Whichever view of autonomy is adopted, any responsibility for the safety of others imposed by omissions offences is hardly 'untrammelled', since in a well-drafted law it would be dependent (at the very least) on our capacities and costs in discharging any responsibilities, as well as on the nature of our relationship to the other(s). Much more will be said below about the positive obligations that might appropriately be placed on individuals in a liberal democracy.

However, even if one were to accept the thrust of Simester's 'extra intrusiveness' argument, it would have to be subject to two major qualifications. First, the degree of intrusiveness has a temporary duration which the argument neglects.[18] The criminal law's prohibitions (negative duties) curtail one's freedom of action at all times, whereas omissions offences (positive duties) only

---

[13] I Kant, *Foundations of the Metaphysics of Morals* ([1785]; trans L Beck, 1959), 429.

[14] J Rawls, *A Theory of Justice* (1972), 302.

[15] *Simester and Sullivan's Criminal Law* (above, n 4) 69; also M Moore, *Placing Blame: A Theory of the Criminal Law* (1997), 278.

[16] AP Simester, 'Why Omissions are Special' (1995) 1 *Legal Theory* 311, at 333.

[17] J Raz, *The Morality of Freedom* (1986), 416.

[18] See also V Tadros, *Criminal Responsibility* (2006), 196–200.

impinge at particular times. An omissions offence arising from the duty to avert a dangerous situation one has created or the duty to assist in law enforcement (both examined in part 3 below) does indeed reduce one's options to one, preventing all other activity, but only for a short space of time. Moreover, it is unlikely that those kinds of circumstance, or a rescue situation, would occur with any frequency; so to refer to us as citizens being forced 'constantly to interrupt our own actions and plans in order to prevent outcomes that are brought about by others' is surely an exaggeration.[19] However, the more offences of omission are created, the greater the incursion into individual autonomy, an incursion that is further increased if the ambit of the duties on which those offences are founded rests on vague concepts such as 'reasonable'.[20] Yet many omissions offences differ from prohibitions in that the duty-situation is essentially conditional: if a certain situation arises, then an obligation to do x is imposed and the failure to do x is an offence. This conditionality, combined with the temporary duration, renders it doubtful whether omissions offences are more intrusive than prohibitions, all things considered. To argue that prohibitions have a different impact on liberty than laws that require actions is correct but, as Waldron argues, it is doubtful if this can be translated 'into a broader theorem about quantum of liberty'.[21] Secondly, only a small number of omissions offences require action at a particular time. The thrust of the 'extra intrusiveness' argument is that an omission offence requires an individual to 'drop everything' and attend to a particular circumstance at a particular time (often, immediately). This is definitely the case in legal systems that have an 'easy rescue' offence, and it applies equally to duties such as those mentioned above (arising from the creation of a dangerous situation and the duty to assist in law enforcement). There are, however, other duties that are more constant and yet can be fulfilled without any enormous time-pressure, such as the duties to provide the necessaries for one's children and to protect others from the effects of hazardous materials. Details of the various duties will be discussed fully in part 3 below, but it is important to signal at this stage that the 'extra intrusiveness' argument, insofar as it applies, is much stronger in relation to those omissions offences that call for immediate action.

Finally in this section, we should return briefly to the question whether acts and omissions are equally blameworthy – to whether the law should recognise a distinction between P, who pushes a non-swimmer into deep water knowing that there is a real risk that he will drown, and Q, who is walking beside a lake

---

[19] *Simester and Sullivan's Criminal Law* (above, n 4) 70. Cf P Smith, 'Omission and Responsibility in Legal Theory' (2003) 9 *Legal Theory* 221, 232. Jeremy Waldron draws attention to the anxious nature of the choices in 'easy rescue' situations, there being 'a restriction upon a "choice" that is already torn and conflicted between the impulse the help and the aversion to getting involved, a choice whose cheerful autonomy is most likely already drained or polluted by bad conscience': 'On the Road: Good Samaritans and Compelling Duties' (2000) 40 *Santa Clara Law Review* 1053, 1082.

[20] See part 2.4 below for elaboration.

[21] Waldron (above, n 19), 1083–85, taking aim particularly at Moore (above, n 15), 278.

and sees someone in the water calling for help and decides to quicken his step away from the incident, despite realising there is a real risk that the person will drown. If we think a distinction should be drawn between P and Q, then it cannot be a distinction in terms of the mental element, because they both appreciate that there is a real risk that the person will drown. We might suggest two significant differences arising from this example. First, one reason for drawing a moral distinction between P and Q would be in terms of the degree of responsibility for initiating the incident, a distinction that finds itself reflected in ordinary language (in English, at least), since one would say that P killed the non-swimmer or caused her death, whereas probably neither description would be used in relation to Q. Put differently, P has clearly broken a prohibition by pushing the non-swimmer into deep water; but whether Q has a duty to mount a rescue is much more debatable, especially if (as we may assume) Q is not the parent of the drowning person. The question, in other words, is whether Q's conduct amounts to an omission, or simply to a not-doing. In terms of the criminalisation principles discussed briefly above, one question is whether Q's conduct in this situation was morally wrong; and if we decide that it was, there is the further question whether or not it is appropriate to criminalise it – or whether there are strong arguments against this.[22] Secondly, even if we do distinguish between P and Q in terms of their respective degrees of responsibility, that does not mean that Q should not be liable to criminal conviction. That is a separate issue for debate. Thus, although this article does not set out to argue in favour of introducing an 'easy rescue' offence,[23] it is important to recognise that such an offence is perfectly compatible with the intuition that people are generally less responsible for omissions than for acts. The appropriate intensity of criminal liability requires discussion too: 'easy rescue' offences are typically middle-range crimes with a moderate maximum penalty, and the reasoning does not (necessarily) render Q liable for murder or manslaughter, let alone to the same degree as P. It is important to establish this difference at the outset: one can reject the equivalence thesis in general,[24] and embrace the idea of recognising a moral distinction between P (action) and Q (omission), but that has no bearing on the acceptance or rejection of the case for criminalising a failure to effect an easy rescue. As Jeremy Waldron puts it, 'points about failures of equivalence between an omission to rescue and the active infliction of harm are therefore simply irrelevant'.[25] Thus the question of criminalisation, on which we focus below, is not simply a threshold issue; there is also, and in all instances, a question of the appropriate intensity of criminalisation.

---

[22] See text at nn 27–30 below.

[23] See my earlier argument in A Ashworth, 'The Scope of Criminal Liability for Omissions' (1989) 105 *LQR* 424. I still adhere to this view, but the current chapter is not concerned to advocate such a change in the law.

[24] Subject to the possibility of a few cases of equivalence: see n 2 above and accompanying text.

[25] Waldron (above, n 19), 1082.

2.2 THE FOUNDATIONS OF LEGAL DUTIES

In part 1 above it was accepted that there is a general (but not absolute) distinction in blameworthiness between acts and omissions, but it was argued that some omissions offences may nevertheless satisfy the principles of criminalisation – depending on the nature of the duty, and the intensity of the offence. We now move to an examination of the moral, political and social foundations for imposing positive obligations on individuals and organisations. While the question whether to criminalise certain not-doings cannot be answered by deduction from any fundamental propositions, there are some general principles that may be helpful.

It is uncontroversial to declare that one of the state's primary duties is to prevent harm to its citizens, or, more narrowly and specifically, 'to seek to reduce the incidence of the kinds of conduct that are properly criminalised, since it is a proper part of the state's responsibility to seek to protect its citizens from suffering such wrongs'.[26] In order to examine the proper role of omissions offences, we need to know more about the foundations of that state duty, and of the reciprocal duties of citizens. Unfortunately these issues of political obligation have always been controversial. Three lines of argument may be considered briefly.[27] First, it may be argued that voters consent, actually or tacitly, to the authority of the state by virtue of their involvement in the political process. Either by voting, or at least by accepting the legitimacy and outcome of the election, citizens may be taken to grant to the state various powers, such as the monopoly of force, and with them various duties, such as the duty to put in place mechanisms and laws for the reduction of harm. It is moot how many citizens can be said to have consented, in this way or any other. Secondly, it may be argued that we may fairly posit a hypothetical contract as the basis of political obligation, inasmuch as citizens can be taken to have agreed to the authority of the state in exchange for the state's promise to assure various benefits to citizens, including security from harm. But this approach, whether based on Hobbes or Locke or a more modern theory, raises the question whether a hypothetical contract can do the work required. Somewhat similarly, a third argument is that citizens' obligations to the state stem from the acceptance or positive seeking of benefits provided by the state, including education, health, transport and so forth. Whether based on a form of gratitude or fair play, this argument does not enable us to say how much taking of benefit requires how much shouldering of burdens.

None of these grand theories of political obligation is precise about the nature and degree of the obligations of the citizen to the state or the state to the

---

[26] RA Duff, *Answering for Crime: Responsibility and Liability in the Criminal Law* (2007), 87.

[27] For elaboration, see R Dagger, 'Political Obligation' and, more fully, D Knowles, *Political Obligation: A Critical Introduction* (2010), Chs 7, 8 and 9.

citizen. One might begin by arguing that the state has a duty to provide security and that it should, at a minimum, provide emergency services trained and equipped to protect citizens from harm and to deal with dangerous situations. One could go further and argue that the state has a duty of justice as well as a duty of security. Thus, not only should it provide a reasonable measure of security by taking steps to prevent harms of certain kinds, in the last resort by criminalising those who culpably cause or attempt to cause harms, but it should do so in a way that respects the autonomy of all citizens. Thus it should ensure that its use of the criminal sanction is contingent on the operation of fair procedures, for example. None of this, however, is specific about the lengths to which the state may properly go in taking measures for the prevention of harm. Even if one inserts the principle of the least restrictive appropriate alternative – arguing that, in recognition of the autonomy of citizens, the criminal law should be kept as a last resort – the ambit of the state's obligations remains vague.[28]

The same may be said of citizens' duties. It is one thing to accept that citizens should adhere to prohibitions on physical violence, sexual assault, theft, fraud and so on. It is quite another to determine whether those negative duties should be supplemented by positive duties to prevent physical or sexual abuse by others behind closed doors, to assist fellow citizens in peril, to inform the authorities about suspicions of wrongdoing, and so forth. One might construct an argument to the effect that the state should make a priority of the preservation of human life, or (more broadly) human wellbeing, but that proposition may be open to contradiction on the basis of the principle of the least restrictive appropriate alternative. Thus a prominent view in nineteenth-century England was that, in general, 'the penal law must content itself with keeping men from doing positive harm, and must leave to public opinion, and to the teachers of morality and religion, the office of furnishing men with motives for doing positive good'.[29]

This view did not deny the justifications for some offences of omission, notably those which reinforce the duties of parents to provide properly for their children. But such offences were to be confined to clear and strong cases, and the major difference between English and continental approaches was apparent from Stephen's famous statement:

> 'A number of people who stand around a shallow pond in which a child is drowning, and let it drown without taking the trouble to ascertain the depth of the pond, are no doubt shameful cowards, but they can hardly be said to have killed the child'.[30]

As it stands, the argument of this passage is unpersuasive, resting as it does on ordinary language (the limits of the word 'killed') as a justification for reaching

---

[28] For other sceptical comments, see D Husak, 'The Criminal Law as Last Resort' (2004) 24 *OJLS* 207.

[29] Lord Macaulay, *Speeches and Poems, with the Report and Notes on the Indian Penal Code* (1867), vol 2, 408.

[30] JF Stephen, *A History of the Criminal Law of England* (1885), vol 3, 10.

a momentous legal conclusion.[31] But it embodies the then spirit of the common law, which was reinforced in contemporary debate by worries about the insecurity that would be created for citizens if a duty of easy rescue were criminalised, since it was thought that it would be virtually impossible for the law to define what was expected of a citizen who, for example, came across a beggar lying hungry and destitute in the street.[32] The question of definitional uncertainty will be examined in part 4 below, but for the moment it can be said it appears not to have caused problems in the several continental European jurisdictions which have a 'duty of easy rescue' in their criminal law.

Four possible limiting considerations – the principle of the least restrictive appropriate alternative, the proper scope of moral and social reprobation, the problem of definitional uncertainty, and the possibility of producing greater evils[33] – will be kept in mind as we move through the potential duty-situations. But they must be placed in the context of the state's duty to prevent harm, to protect its citizens, and to provide them with an adequate level of security. Even if we leave aside the security questions raised by terrorism in the modern age, there may still be a strong case for the state to impose positive obligations on citizens when there is a threat to life – to start with the clearest case. Thus three decades ago the Law Reform Commission of Canada examined the case for a general 'duty of easy rescue' offence and, recommending its introduction into Canadian law, stated that 'where one person's life can only be preserved at the cost of another's small inconvenience, the community conscience would be shocked at a refusal to shoulder the inconvenience'.[34] The Commission noted that such an offence is not a homicide offence, and is committed irrespective of whether the person in peril suffers death or serious injury. What such an offence does is to signal the social importance of citizens offering some basic assistance to persons *in extremis*, insofar as it lies within their power to do so without endangering themselves.

While it is not the purpose of this chapter to argue in favour of an offence of 'easy rescue', this Canadian approach suggests an answer to what Lord Hoffmann once described as the 'why pick on me?' argument.[35] We can identify three points of general principle that have a particular relevance to questions of criminal liability for omissions:

---

[31] The fact that many common verbs (eg kill, drown, even 'cause the death of') assume a positive act and sound wrong when applied to omissions does not mean that omissions cannot be causes. Much depends on the presence or absence of a duty, or at least an expectation. If the child's parent had been standing beside the shallow pond, we would surely not hesitate to say that the parent was responsible for allowing the child to die without making an effort to save it. We would ascribe causation to the parent, but would not use the active verb 'kill'. See further J Feinberg, *Harm to Others (The Moral Limits of the Criminal Law vol 1)* (1984), Ch 4.

[32] Macaulay (above, n 29), 407.

[33] On which see JS Mill, *On Liberty* ([1859], Penguin, 1985), 70.

[34] Law Reform Commission of Canada, *Omissions, Negligence and Endangering* (1985), 19.

[35] In *Stovin v Wise* [1996] AC 923, at 943–44, arguing against omissions liability in tort.

(a) *The Principle of Urgency:* the case for recognising a positive duty to act is at its strongest when there are circumstances of urgency or emergency. On the rare occasions when action needs to be taken immediately, in order to preserve something of fundamental value, there is a clear argument for departing from the normal legal ordering, in favour of individual autonomy, and imposing a duty on persons present.

(b) *The Priority of Life:* the survival of each individual is a supreme value, as recognised, for example, by Article 6 of the International Covenant on Civil and Political Rights. Thus, combining (b) with (a), where urgent action is needed in order to preserve life, there is a strong argument for recognising a duty to act. That duty should probably be allocated to the state in the first place, but (i) the emergency services will be unable to help unless alerted, and (ii) there may be situations in which it is reasonable to expect an individual to do more than simply alert the emergency services. The same argument could perhaps be applied to the preservation of other human rights, such as the right not to be subjected to inhuman or degrading treatment or the right to liberty and security of person, but the strongest case is surely the survival of the rights-bearing subject – the right to life.

(c) *The Principles of Opportunity and Capacity:* where principles (a) and (b) already apply, the duty to act should fall on the person who has the opportunity and the capacity (physical and psychological) to render some assistance.[36] Thus no duty could properly be cast on a person who is not physically present, except in cases (i) where that person was already subject to a duty to safeguard another (eg a parent who ought to have been present, caring for his or her young child) or (ii) where a person is or ought to have been undertaking surveillance (eg a lifeguard). The effect of physical presence or live surveillance is to connect the person who has the opportunity and capacity to render assistance with the predicament of the other person whose life is in danger and who urgently needs that assistance.[37]

It will soon become clear that these points of principle do not apply equally to all the many duty-situations that might fairly give rise to criminal liability, and so the discussion below will range more widely. The submission – differing from Lord Macaulay's prescription for the Indian Penal Code in the mid-nineteenth century[38] – is that the case for omissions liability is strong where life or another fundamental interest is at stake; where someone has the opportunity and capacity to protect those interests; where protecting those interests is urgent; and where taking action will not sacrifice more important interests. There may also, it will be argued, be a strong case for omissions liability flowing from a person's

---

[36] Cf the 'best position' argument developed by G Mead, 'Contracting into Crime: a Theory of Criminal Omissions' (1991) 11 *OJLS* 147, at 168.

[37] Simester (above, n 16) would deny that this is a sufficient connection, but cf the doubts discussed by Smith (above, n 19).

[38] See above, nn 29 and 32, and accompanying text.

role-responsibility (eg professional, familial), and in some other well-defined situations. To those we now turn.

2.3 A RE-APPRAISAL OF DUTY-SITUATIONS

We turn now to consider the foundations of criminal-law duties. Contemporary legal systems contain a wide range of omissions offences. All contain an offence of failing to pay required taxes. There are many further offences of failure to report, or failure to comply with other requirements, which form part of a regulatory structure. One example would be the UK offence of failing to give the required information to an authorised officer under the Eggs and Chicks Regulations;[39] a more serious offence, carrying possible imprisonment, is that of a parent who fails without reasonable justification to cause to attend school a child whom the parent knew was not attending school regularly, contrary to section 444(1A) of the Education Act 1996 (UK).[40]

Our main interest here, however, is in the more general duties and their rationales. For the purpose of analysis, these duties are divided into four broad groups. Those groups, and their constituent duties, are as follows:

(i) Family Obligations:

A. Duty of parents to provide the necessaries of life for their children.
B. Duty of members of a household to protect children and vulnerable adults in the household from serious violence from other members of the household.

(ii) Voluntarily Incurred Obligations:

C. Duty of persons in possession of hazardous materials (such as explosives, ammunition or inflammable substances) to protect people from the dangerous effects of those materials.
D. Duty of persons working in the financial sector to disclose certain information to the government (as when dealing with large amounts of money that may have been laundered), or of a contracting party to disclose information to the other party to the transaction (as when entering insurance contracts).
E. Duty of persons having a contractual duty or voluntary undertaking of care for one or more others, or having the lawful custody of one or more others, to ensure the health and welfare of those individuals.
F. Duties of those involved in a chosen and regulated activity (in relation to owning a car, driving, or participating in a business and financial undertaking) to bear certain positive obligations.

---

[39] Law Commission Consultation Paper No 195, *Criminal Liability in Regulatory Contexts* (2010), 82, referring to regulation 15(1)(b) of the Eggs and Chicks Regulations 2008.
[40] Law Commission, ibid, 41, for contextual discussion.

(iii)   Obligations Arising from Personal Responsibility:

G.   Duty of a person deriving from a chosen situation, or from a non-chosen situation for which one is causally responsible (as by unintentionally causing a dangerous situation), to take steps to deal with the danger.
H.   Duty of the owner of property to use one's power and authority in order to prevent crime (as by forbidding criminal activity on or with one's property).

(iv)   Civic Obligations:

I.   Duties to assist in law enforcement, of a police officer to intervene to prevent a crime (from continuing) or of a citizen to assist in law enforcement when called upon by a constable to do so.
J.   Duty of all persons to notify police about suspected terrorist offences being committed by another.
K.   Duty of professionals to notify the authorities about suspected child abuse or elder abuse.
L.   Duty of all persons to make reasonable efforts to ascertain the criminal law.

This list is certainly not comprehensive, but is intended to include those duties recognised most widely across legal systems as a basis for criminal conviction. Some of the listed duties may appear strange, but in the re-appraisal that follows it is hoped to deal with unusual listings such as the duty in L. The 'duty of easy rescue' is not listed above, on the ground that such an offence is rarely found in common law jurisdictions, but there are many countries in which a person is liable to conviction for failing to take steps to render assistance to a person in peril.[41] The possibility of recognising such a duty is kept in view, even though it is not central to the discussion. The purpose of examining the four groups of duties here is to assess the strength of the grounds for imposing criminal conviction on those who fail to carry them out.

(i)   Family and Household Obligations

The first source of obligations may be found in the family. The core obligation is the duty of a parent towards his or her child. That is a general duty to ensure the welfare of one's child,[42] which in English law translates into an offence of child cruelty that penalises neglect, abandonment, and exposure to 'unnecessary suffering or injury to health', and failure to provide 'adequate food, clothing, medical aid or lodging'.[43] That particular statutory duty lasts only until the child is

---

[41]   For discussion, see A Cadoppi, 'Duties to Rescue' in M Menlowe and RA McCall-Smith (eds), *The Duty to Rescue* (1993); cf s 93 Merchant Shipping Act 1995 (UK), duty of ship's master to assist persons in distress.

[42]   A common law duty: see PR Glazebrook, 'Criminal Omissions: the Duty Requirement in Offences against the Person' (1960) 76 *LQR* 386, and *R v Lunt* [2004] 1 NZLR 498, on which see J Tolmie, 'The "Duty to Protect" in New Zealand Criminal Law' [2010] *New Zealand Law Review* 725.

[43]   Children and Young Persons Act 1933, s 1; see also s 152 of the Crimes Act 1961 (NZ) for a parent's duty to provide the necessaries of life for her or his children.

16, and it overlaps with a parent's common law duty to ensure the safety of the child (the duty broken by a parent who fails to take the opportunity to rescue her or his child from a shallow pool).[44] The justifications for these duties lie in the appropriateness of placing primary responsibility on the person who brought the child into the world (or who adopted the child),[45] to provide care until the child reaches majority. This responsibility should arise irrespective of marriage. Some parents may demonstrate from the outset that they have no wish to care for the child, and the state should have services for adoption and support in such circumstances. Thus we may say that parents should have the primary duty, stemming from the act of giving birth to (or adopting) the child, the priority of life and the principles of opportunity and capacity;[46] but that, insofar as the modern state values and relies on family units, it is reasonable to expect the state to support them in various ways (eg healthcare, day nursery provision, social services support, education). This is not the place to attempt a full account of the respective duties of parents and of the state towards children, not least because (beyond the important minima established by the UN Convention on the Rights of the Child) different political compromises may be appropriate in different political and cultural settings. Our focus here is on the avoidance of life-threatening circumstances (although there are lesser forms of neglect), and we can surely affirm that there is good reason to place the primary responsibility with the parents, while insisting that they should also be able to look to the state for appropriate support, particularly in their wider responsibilities.

Accepting the parent's or carer's primary duty as the core,[47] how much further (if at all) should family obligations be taken? It could be argued that parents should assume responsibility for children who are under the age of majority (18) and still dependent on them, since children under 18 are not yet full citizens. On the one hand, the law allows 16-year-olds to leave their parents' home and to apply for state benefits as a single person, which may be thought to contradict any continuing responsibility of parents for their welfare; on the other hand, if a child of 17 is still living at home, the parent(s) ought surely to have an obligation to summon medical assistance in case of illness – in other words, to bear responsibility (at a minimum) for the avoidance of life-threatening circumstances. A child of that age is not a full member of the political community, and children aged 16 and 17 receive special protection from the law (eg against sexual activities with persons in a position of trust),[48] which suggests a certain vulnerability.

---

[44] As in Stephen's famous example, above, n 30 and accompanying text.

[45] Appropriate adjustments must be made for step-parents and for others, such as foster-carers, who voluntarily assume the role of parent within a certain framework. This qualification should be borne in mind throughout this chapter.

[46] T Honoré, 'Necessite Oblige' in his *Making Law Bind: Essays Legal and Philosophical* (1987), 128–29; Mead (above, n 36), 163 and 170.

[47] To avoid repeating 'parent or carer' (see above, n 45), I will use 'parent' henceforth to include both.

[48] See the offences in the Sexual Offences Act 2003, ss 16–24.

There is inconsistency in the English case-law about the extent of a parent's duty to safeguard a child's life after the child has reached the age of majority, and also about the duty towards an adult child who has some mental or physical incapacity.[49] There is even greater doubt about whether the duty would extend to other relatives, such as cousins or aunts or adult brothers or sisters. In one case it was held that there was no duty towards a younger half-sister, without any implication that the position would have been different if the younger girl had been a full sister.[50] Thus Lord Lane's assertion that the deceased woman 'was a blood relation of the appellant Stone', as a reason for finding that Stone had a duty towards his sister, is unconvincingly wide insofar as it suggests that any blood relation should be (potentially) within the duty category.[51] All the above cases are weaker than that of parent and child under 16. Whilst there are degrees of moral responsibility towards older children and other relatives, few of them approach the clarity and strength of the rationale for parents to assume responsibility for their under-age children.

What about an adult's responsibility to care for his or her parents? Since the parents are adults, their primary obligation is to care for themselves. Beyond that, much depends on culture and the prevailing political morality. In the United Kingdom it would seem that, even in respect of the duty to safeguard life, the obligation of the state is placed ahead of any obligations of the elders' children.[52] The state is assumed to bear the responsibility to provide a decent minimum for older people unable to care for themselves, partly because these older people will have contributed by paying taxes throughout their working life. On the other hand, while it can be said that children do not choose to have parents (whereas parents choose to have children), it is usually true that parents make sacrifices in bringing up their children and that this might give grounds for some reciprocal obligation. Similar arguments cannot usually be relied upon in relation to brothers, sisters and more distant relatives:[53] whatever the family ties that might be identified, there is no political argument (or, is no longer a political argument) and a weaker moral argument in favour of recognising an obligation so strong that its breach should lead to criminal conviction. This would seem to support the current dividing line between legal obligation and social/moral obligation.

A different rationale is called for when we turn to consider a husband or wife's duty to a spouse, recognised in many systems of law.[54] Any such obligation is based on the loyalty required of partners in a marriage, fortified by the

---

[49] For discussion, see Glazebrook (above, n 42), and Williams (above, n 6), 99–100.

[50] *R v Evans* [2009] 1 WLR 1999.

[51] *R v Stone and Dobinson* [1977] QB 354, at 361; this reason was one of three given by Lord Lane for finding a duty, and it is possible that the reasons were intended to be cumulative. Cf *R v Barrass* [2012] 1 Cr App R (S) 452.

[52] See generally J Herring, *Older People in Law and Society* (2009).

[53] There may be a separate argument for a voluntarily incurred obligation, as in *Stone and Dobinson* (above, n 51); see part 3(ii) below.

[54] See, eg GP Fletcher, *Rethinking Criminal Law* (1978), 612, on US and German laws.

marriage vows,[55] rather than by the kind of relationship of dependence evident between infant child and parent. However, there are also many relationships between people who are not married but who share an ongoing partnership: in these cases the degree of commitment may be no less than that in marriages (although without the formality). George Fletcher suggests that 'the facts of communal living and prolonged interdependence' are sufficient to ground mutual obligations in such cases.[56] This would blur the clear line drawn by marriage, but rightly so if account is to be taken of real-life situations. It would be for the court to determine whether there was a settled relationship of interdependence between the parties such as to give rise to mutual duties to safeguard life, a judgement that would be difficult to make in the early or late stages of co-habitation, where ambiguity abounds. Such judgements would be necessary for unmarried couples living together, for adult sisters or brothers who have shared living arrangements for years, and for long-term flat-mates, among others. The key question is whether joining or forming a 'household' may fairly be said to give rise to a set of reciprocal duties;[57] and, in cases where the priority of life arises, whether the duty is justifiably reinforced by criminal liability for a substantive offence (murder or manslaughter) or merely for a lesser offence of failure to report. At least two English authorities favour the existence of such a duty, with manslaughter liability for failure.[58]

There remains the question of short-term guests who become ill or otherwise indisposed – a 'friend' or distant relative who comes for the weekend, for example. In these instances there is the same priority of life and basic physical integrity and the same principle of physical presence and capacity. What is missing is any continuing relationship sufficient to amount to 'communal living and prolonged interdependence' – in some cases, any interdependence at all. Unless it is argued that the act of inviting someone to stay or agreeing to someone's request to stay implies an undertaking to summon medical aid if they fall ill – not an outrageous proposition, but one that might be thought to raise questions about

---

[55] However, any duty may be overridden if the spouse refuses to have a doctor called: compare *R v Bonnyman* (1942) 28 Cr App R 131 (wife very weak, husband qualified doctor, wife refused intervention initially, wife became helpless and lost weight dramatically; husband convicted of manslaughter on ground of failing to supply necessaries when having 'care and custody of someone who is helpless') with *R v Smith* [1979] *Crim LR* 251 (husband failed to call doctor for several days to ill wife, because she refused to have a doctor; wife died, husband acquitted of manslaughter); cf *Hood* [2004] 1 Cr App R (S) 431, where a husband was convicted of manslaughter on the basis that he had a duty to call an ambulance for his injured wife (even though she did not want him to call assistance, and did not do so herself).

[56] Fletcher (above, n 54), 613.

[57] In their report to the English Law Commission, the Criminal Code Team took it to be established common law that a duty rests on 'a member of the same household' to ensure that another member of the household is not subjected to death, serious injury or detention: *Codification of the Common Law: a report to the Law Commission* (Law Com No 143, 1985), cl 20(2) and paras 7.11–7.12.

[58] *R v Sinclair* (1998) 148 *NLJ* 1353 (close friend and flat-mate supplied heroin and stayed with V), approved by the full Court of Appeal in *Evans* [2009] 1 WLR 1999, at [28] (half-sister supplied heroin and stayed with V).

the boundary between legal and merely moral obligation[59] – then these cases must stand or fall with the decision whether or not to create an offence of 'failure of easy rescue', which requires all citizens to take reasonable steps when they come across someone in peril.

In recent years, many jurisdictions (including England and Wales) have introduced a 'failure to protect' offence which imposes a positive duty on members of a household (which includes frequent visitors) who have frequent contact with either a child or a vulnerable adult living in that household. The duty is one of safeguarding the child or vulnerable adult from a significant risk of physical harm, and it arises only if the member of the household ought to have been aware of that risk and could reasonably have been expected to take steps to protect the child or vulnerable person. In South Australia, for example, the offence is committed if death or serious harm is caused to the child or vulnerable adult,[60] and the same now applies in England and Wales,[61] whereas the New Zealand provision extends to death, serious injury or serious sexual assault.[62] The essence of these new offences is that any such household member should have the duty to raise the alarm, even if he or she cannot be expected to try to stop the abuse personally. This partly reflects the priority of life and basic physical integrity (awareness of a significant risk of serious harm), and partly the principle of physical presence and capacity (opportunity to report); but it also draws from two relationships implicit in the statutory definition, the interdependence of household members as compared with the dependence (vulnerability) of the child or vulnerable adult.[63] This duty would not extend to an obligation to protect, say, an adult woman cohabitant from repeated violence from her partner, unless the very fact of being subjected to domestic violence qualifies her as 'vulnerable'.[64] But if there is indeed a general common law duty towards members of the same household,[65] that might be mobilised in such a situation.

The introduction of statutory 'failure to protect' offences may be seen as a significant step towards the protection of children, in the very situations (behind closed doors) where their physical security is most at risk. The offences give

[59] Cf the famous case of *People v Beardsley* (1907) 150 Mich 206, 113 NW 1128 (woman stayed with D for weekend of sex, alcohol and drugs; eventually became unconscious, whereupon D and others moved her to a neighbouring apartment and left her; she died; manslaughter conviction reversed because no sufficient relationship or responsibility established), discussed by Fletcher (above, n 54) at 613–14, with *R v Ruffell* [2003] 2 Cr App R (S) 330 (friend staying overnight, attempt to revive friend when he became unconscious, 'sufficient nexus' for a duty of care, manslaughter with sentence of 2 years' imprisonment) and *Lewin v CPS* [2002] EWHC 1049 (friend left asleep and drunk in car on a hot day and died, no duty of care found).

[60] The amended s 14 of the Criminal Law Consolidation Act 1935 (SA).

[61] Domestic Violence, Crime and Victims Act 2004 (UK), s 5, as amended by the Domestic Violence, Crime and Victims (Amendment) Act 2012.

[62] Section 195A(1) Crimes Act 1960 (NZ) as amended.

[63] Compare the extensive definition of 'same household' in s 195A(4) of the New Zealand provision.

[64] See further *R v Khan* [2009] 1 WLR 2036.

[65] See n 56 above.

some extra protection to the basic rights of children, although some aspects of the legislation (a requirement of negligence, not gross negligence, combined with a maximum sentence of 14 years for a non-perpetrator) may be thought disproportionate.[66] The protection comes from casting a serious duty on 'members of the household', going beyond those with responsibility as a parent or carer to include frequent visitors; but, so long as that duty is publicised, the three principles of urgency, the value of life and physical presence/capacity may be triangulated so as to justify the imposition of the obligation. However, Jonathan Herring urges caution in relation to 'failure to protect' offences, for three main reasons.[67] First, he argues that the offence may be used to switch the focus from the perpetrator of the violence to the household member who fails to intervene: we must not overlook the primary responsibility of the attacker, in relation to which the non-intervener's role is distinctly secondary. This accords with the above suggestion that the English offence bears down unduly severely on non-perpetrators. Secondly, the reason why the other party (often the mother) fails to intervene may be fear: Herring demonstrates how women subjected to 'domestic violence' may be or feel threatened, and how they may try to distract the bully rather than alerting the authorities, thereby incurring liability for this offence.[68] Thirdly, he argues that the offence distorts the proper relationship between family obligations and the duties of the state: the state has international obligations to safeguard the lives and physical well-being of children,[69] and this means putting in place mechanisms for family support that show awareness of, and are responsive to, problems of domestic abuse. The many fatal cases of child abuse in recent years, involving failures of the authorities to respond adequately and swiftly, remain a blot on English family policy. Herring's points are well taken, but the appropriate reaction may be to focus on improving family services and to review the statutory provisions (notably, the need for a broader defence to the 'failure to protect' offence for those in genuine fear), rather than to abandon the offence altogether. We will return to this debate in part 3(iv) below.

This discussion of family obligations raises several points about omissions liability. The family is a basic social unit, in which reciprocal duties are inherent. If we accept the principle of urgency, the priority of life and the principles of opportunity and capacity, and assuming a legal system without a general duty of easy rescue, there seems to be a strong argument for reinforcing family duties

---

[66] On this, and on the evolution of the English offence, see M Hayes, 'Criminal Trials where a Child is the Victim: Extra Protection for Children or a Missed Opportunity?' [2005] *Child and Family Law Quarterly* 307.

[67] J Herring, 'Familial Homicide, Failure to Protect and Domestic Violence: Who's the Victim?' [2007] *Crim LR* 923.

[68] For discussion of the prevalence of domestic violence, see C Hoyle, 'Victims, the Criminal Process and Restorative Justice' in M Maguire, R Morgan and R Reiner (eds), *Oxford Handbook of Criminology* (5th edn, 2012), 401–4.

[69] Eg under the UN Convention on the Rights of the Child, and Arts 2 and 3 of the European Convention on Human Rights.

with criminal liability where there is a clear risk of death or serious injury. That argument becomes even stronger where the victim is a child or vulnerable family member. The next question is whether the basis for such obligations can fairly be broadened from the family to the household: in many cases there may be no real difference, but in others there will be members of the household who do not count as 'family' (a concept pregnant with uncertainties, as we have noted). Beyond that we have noted several borderline cases in which, if there is no common household membership, there is much room for debate: for example, a parent's duty towards an adult child, an adult child's duty to parents, and a person's duty to a guest or friend with whom there is no relationship of interdependence. These are questions to which the general theories of political obligation supply no ready answers. We should recall that the state has a duty to maintain emergency services and family support services, as reinforced by instruments such as the UN Convention on the Rights of the Child. But the individual also has duties, and the question is whether it is in any way unreasonable to impose a criminal law duty on the individual to summon emergency services or to report abuse, particularly in view of the principle of urgency, the priority of life, and the principles of opportunity and capacity. One approach would be to leave the relationship of parents to non-adult child to be regulated by an obligation to care and a substantive offence in the event of failure to care; to re-draft the 'failure to protect' offence, retaining its reach to members of a household in respect of children or vulnerable members of that household; and to deal with all other cases by means of a lesser 'duty of easy rescue' offence, which would apply to all people in respect of all people, distant relatives and weekend guests included. These suggestions are taken further in parts 4 and 5 below.

(ii) Voluntarily Incurred Obligations

This category includes a range of activities and relationships into which a person chooses to enter. It highlights the way in which the relevant duties take the form of conditional positive obligations – if you choose to engage in *x*, then you must bear certain positive obligations. Among the examples to be considered below are certain business and financial activities, the ownership and driving of a motor vehicle, contractual duties, and voluntary care undertakings.

First, many financial and business activities are regulated by official agencies, and anyone who engages in that kind of activity is rightly expected to become acquainted with the various obligations that go with involvement in that activity. A prominent example, discussed in detail in part 3(iv) below, is those businesses which involve the movement of money (banks, accountants, solicitors, financial advisers etc), and which give rise to a duty to report to the authorities anyone whom they suspect of money-laundering. Some positive obligations attach to ordinary people who engage in certain types of transaction, notably the various duties of disclosure of information imposed on persons entering into contracts and other legal arrangements, most typically insurance contracts. The criminal law sometimes founds an offence on the breach of such a duty, an example being section 3 of the Fraud Act 2006, which penalises the dishonest failure to disclose information 'which he is under a legal duty to disclose', with intent thereby to make a gain or to cause a loss. The criminal offence therefore reinforces and depends on the civil law, where the range of duties has been explained as follows:

> 'Such a duty may derive from statute (such as the provisions governing company prospectuses), from the fact that the transaction in question is one of utmost good faith (such as a contract of insurance), from the express or implied terms of a contract, from the custom of the particular trade or market, or from the existence of a fiduciary relationship between the parties (such as that of agent and principal)'.[70]

Most of these duties arise from voluntary involvement in a particular type of transaction. However, the duties are not confined to people in a certain line of business, and so it is possible that ordinary members of the public may be unaware of the particular duty (eg in insurance contracts). The issue of fair warning is crucial to the criminalisation of omissions (see part 4 below).

Secondly, both the ownership and the driving of a motor vehicle give rise to a range of positive and negative obligations related to those activities. Thus the driver of a car has a duty to stop after an accident; and the owner of a vehicle has a duty to state who was driving it at a given time and place, if an official request is made.[71] These and other positive obligations may be justified as elements of the fair regulation of an activity that (i) is so complex as to require firm co-ordination and (ii) has the potential to cause danger to people's physical safety. To this end the drivers of motor vehicles have to pass a test, which requires familiarity with the obligations that go with engagement in the activity. Thus there is a similarity with category C in relation to handling or storing hazardous materials: that activity can be said to have been chosen or voluntary – no person is required to engage in it – and it should be well known that, if one does decide to engage in it, certain positive obligations follow. The role of the criminal law is as reinforcer, mostly as an ultimate sanction in a regulatory system for businesses, but also for road traffic laws.

A third type of voluntarily incurred obligation is the direct contractual duty to care for another person or to carry out a protective role. It appears not to matter whether the contract is directly between defendant and eventual victim, as suggested in *R v Instan*,[72] or between the defendant and his employer, as in

---

[70] Law Com No 276, *Fraud* (July 2002), para 7.28; see further D Ormerod and DH Williams, *Smith's Law of Theft* (9th edn, 2007), 166–69, and SP Green, 'Theft by Omission' in J Chalmers, F Leverick and L Farmer, *Essays in Criminal Law in Honour of Sir Gerald Gordon* (2010).

[71] Road Traffic Act 1988 (UK), ss 170 and 172. Such duties exist in many legal systems; see *Weh v Austria* (2005) 40 EHRR 890.

[72] [1893] 1 QB 450, where D lived with her aunt, who paid for the food, and the Court held that she impliedly undertook the reciprocal duty of caring for her aunt. Whether this was a contractual obligation is unclear; but D neglected to buy food for her aunt, who died, and D was convicted of manslaughter.

R v Pittwood;[73] the fact of a contractual obligation is thought to be sufficient to form the basis for, and constitute a fair warning of, the criminal law duty-situation. This argument needs to be scrutinised carefully:[74] indeed, Glanville Williams went so far as to condemn the inference from breach of a contractual duty to breach of duty in criminal law as 'impermissible reasoning'.[75] Why should it be assumed that a mere civil wrong is sufficient to ground liability for a serious offence such as manslaughter? It is one thing to suggest that failure to discharge a voluntarily incurred obligation can properly give rise to a free-standing offence of omission with a moderate penalty, as in the first two examples above (duty of regulated sector to report suspected money-laundering, duty of driver to stop and report accident). It is quite another thing to suggest that failure to discharge a civil obligation is enough to support conviction for the second most serious criminal offence, ie manslaughter. Indeed, the 'failure to protect' offence has a maximum sentence of 14 years,[76] and it is debatable whether the culpability there is usually greater or less than in the contractual duty cases. These differentials cannot turn on the priority of life, since that is common to all these cases. The contractual duty cases are clear that the nature of the assumed obligation concerns life and death,[77] but then it may be questioned whether gross negligence is an appropriate standard of culpability, and manslaughter an appropriate label, in relation to the culpability of the non-fulfilment of the duty.

A fourth example is the voluntary undertaking to care for a person by welcoming him or her into the household. Thus one of the three reasons given for imposing a duty in *Stone and Dobinson*[78] was that Stone's sister had been accepted into his home and allowed to occupy a room there, the implication being that voluntarily receiving someone into the household creates an obligation (whereas turning someone away would not do so, unless, perhaps, weather conditions were atrocious at the time). This takes us back to the discussion in part 3(i) about the interdependence and reciprocity involved in communal living. Dobinson's kindness in washing the sister and changing her bedclothes was also held to create a duty,[79] founded presumably on an expectation of continuance, which was then neglected. Insofar as a single act of kindness is held to provide the foundation for a continuing obligation, this may seem not only unduly burdensome but also unfair on someone whose motivation was

[73] (1902) 19 TLR 37, where D was employed to open and shut the gate on a railway crossing; he was convicted of manslaughter after forgetting to close the gate, causing several deaths.

[74] See Mead (above, n 36).

[75] Williams (above, n 6), 94.

[76] See part 3(i) above.

[77] The judgment in *Instan* (above, n 72) may be unduly severe in this respect.

[78] Above, n 51 and accompanying text.

[79] Lane LJ stated erroneously that Dobinson 'undertook the duty of washing her', but it was not a duty when she did it, it was an act of kindness only. Interestingly, the judgment in *R v Ruffell* [2003] 2 Cr App R (S) 330 (at 333) contains the same erroneous locution, stating that D 'had taken upon himself the duty of trying to revive' the deceased, when actually D had simply tried to effect a revival.

altruistic. However, an alternative line of reasoning is suggested by the Australian decision in *R v Taktak*,[80] where T had been asked to collect a friend from a party and found her in an unconscious state through drug-taking. He took her to his home and made various attempts to bring her back to consciousness. He then left her to sleep, resolving to call a doctor if she was no better in the morning. She died in the night. On appeal from his manslaughter conviction, the Court held that a duty arose in this situation because, in assuming the care of a helpless person, he had 'secluded' her and had thereby removed the possibility of others rendering assistance.[81] The concept of 'seclusion' offers a more convincing rationale for these cases of voluntary undertaking: it is not so much that one person who takes another into her or his home enters into an unbounded obligation of caring, as that this action prevents others from rendering assistance.[82] As the principles of opportunity and capacity would indicate, this strongly favours placing an obligation on the person who 'holds out the hand', and the priority of life and principle of urgency are also applicable. This obligation must, however, remain consistent with the proper sphere of the state's duties. As argued earlier, the state should provide emergency services to deal with situations of this kind, but their operation often depends on an individual to alert them. Thus in cases such as *Stone and Dobinson* and *Taktak* the reasoning should be that, by taking a sick person into his home, the defendant had effectively secluded that person from state help (ie from the probability that others would call for help), and so the duty to call the emergency services must fall on the person who (albeit out of kindness) took the person in.[83]

The potential duty-situations in this category may, again, be seen as conditional positive obligations: if D voluntarily enters into an undertaking, that carries with it certain obligations. This reasoning applies strongly to cases of contract, where D has already agreed to be bound to do certain acts.[84] Its application to activities such as carrying on a particular profession or business, or driving a car, may sometimes stretch the element of voluntariness. But it remains fair to say that a person engaging in certain activities is rightly presumed to know that it is regulated, and that the criminal law reinforces the regulations.

---

[80] (1988) 34 A Crim R 334 (New South Wales, Court of Appeal); cf Honoré (above, n 2), 45–46, deploying a somewhat similar concept of 'dependency'.

[81] The conviction was quashed, on the ground that D had made reasonable efforts to discharge the duty.

[82] A similar rationale was mentioned in *R v Evans* [2009] 1 WLR 1999, Lord Judge CJ holding that a duty might arise 'where, for example, a voluntary assumption of [responsibility] by the defendant had led the victim, or others, to become dependent on him to act' at [36]. See also Green (above, n 70), 167, applying similar reasoning (in the context of theft) to a person who finds property and takes it elsewhere.

[83] It is not suggested that this justifies the finding of a duty on the facts of *Stone and Dobinson*, inasmuch as the defendants were unaware of her condition when they initially allowed her to occupy a room in their house. Nor is it suggested that the defendants in *Stone and Dobinson* had the requisite capacity, given their low intelligence and unfamiliarity with the telephone. That question of fact would need resolution. Cf also the awkward facts of *Ruffell* (above, n 79).

[84] For elaboration, see Mead (above, n 36).

The state bears a duty to make it known that these obligations attach to certain activities, particularly those in which it may not be obvious. Lastly, some undertakings may be said to be constructive – as where a person decides to show kindness towards an incapacitated person and thereby 'secludes' them from other sources of assistance, yielding good reasons for imposing a duty on the person who showed kindness.

However, recognition of such duty-situations leaves the related questions of the appropriate fault element and the appropriate level of criminalisation. The duties arising from certain businesses or activities may or may not involve the priority of life; where they do, as in some road traffic cases, the argument for serious offences with significant penalties grows stronger, but for lesser omissions such as failure to stop after an accident or failure to inform the police who was driving the car at a particular time, the appropriate intensity of the criminal offence should be much lower. Whether failure to fulfil a contractual obligation should lead directly to a conviction for manslaughter by gross negligence has been doubted above: even assuming that the risk of death was known, what is it in a contractual duty that points to conviction for so serious an offence as manslaughter if the duty is breached? Part of the answer must be the priority of life: not just any contractual obligation would be relevant in such cases, there must be a contractual duty relating to safety or to subsistence. As for the 'seclusion' cases, there is an argument that these lie closer to the duty of easy rescue than they do to other cases of voluntarily incurred obligations. We will return to these issues in part 5 below.

(iii) Obligations arising from Causal Responsibility

We now turn to a type of situation that is explicitly non-chosen – where a person accidentally creates a danger. This might occur when D falls asleep while smoking and unintentionally sets fire to a bed or sofa,[85] or when D accidentally bumps into P beside a lake and pushes P into the water, for example. As the author of the accident D is causally responsible for it, and so ought to bear the duty to take action to minimise further harm, as by summoning help or trying to do something to alleviate the situation (within capacity, and without incurring personal danger). If the author of the initial damage was at least negligent, he or she may be liable for damages in tort. Should the criminal law become involved? In cases where the principles of urgency, priority of life and opportunity and capacity are all applicable, there is a clear and strong case for criminal liability – so long as it can be shown that D, the author of the damage, realised what he or she had done. If despite that awareness D takes no remedial action, is it not right to treat D on the basis that he or she intended, or at least knowingly risked, the harm that resulted? If, as in the leading case

---

[85] *R v Miller* [1983] 2 AC 161 cf s 92 Merchant Shipping Act 1995, duty on ship's master after collision at see.

of *R v Miller*,[86] two of the three principles are present (urgency, opportunity and capacity), the extra connection provided by D's causal responsibility should form a sufficient basis for liability for a property crime or other offence, eg for criminal damage by fire, if D is aware that he has accidentally set fire to a mattress. This is therefore a stronger obligation than that which could be said to arise in cases of failing to take steps to rescue a person in peril (in jurisdictions where a duty of easy rescue applies), where the person on whom the duty falls may not be responsible for causing the situation. Both persons have the opportunity to make efforts to remove the danger; the distinguishing factor in the present category is D's causal responsibility for creating the situation of danger. Even if the causation is the purest of accidents, it suffices to create a degree of responsibility that explains why D, more than anyone else, should bear the primary duty of taking steps to remove or remedy the danger.

The discussion so far has been premised on the causation of danger being accidental. If D did the dangerous act knowing of the danger or, worse, intending to create danger, then clearly D would have the duty to prevent the danger from materialising or to minimise its effects. Those are much stronger cases. By way of contrast, a much weaker case would be *R v Evans*,[87] where E had provided her half-sister with heroin, which the half-sister administered to herself, and then became very ill. The Court of Appeal held that E's initial act of providing the heroin created a dangerous situation, which E then had the responsibility to remedy. However, this analysis fails to attribute significance to the half-sister's voluntary intervening act of administering the heroin to herself, an action that distinguishes the case from others in this group and may render the *Miller* principle inapplicable.[88]

Perhaps closer to the 'accidental' cases are those in which D, the owner of a car or house, allows P to have possession of the car or house, and P then commits an offence of which D is aware. The owner of a car has the power and authority to instruct someone whom he or she has allowed to drive the car on what not to do;[89] the owner of a house has the power and authority to insist that

---

[86] Ibid; the same principle may be found in German law: M Bohlander, *Principles of German Criminal Law* (2009), 44, 'a duty to act arising out of prior conduct which created a source of risk or danger'. The duty appears to apply if the creation of the dangerous situation was accidental.

[87] [2009] 1 WLR 1999.

[88] See G Williams, 'Gross Negligence Manslaughter and Duty of Care in 'Drugs' Cases' [2009] *Crim LR* 631, discussing interpretations of the causal principles in *R v Kennedy (No 2)* [2007] UKHL 38.

[89] See *Du Cros v Lambourne* [1907] 1 KB 40, where the owner sat next to the permitted driver while she drove at excessive speed through an urban area. The decision in *Rubie v Faulkner* [1940] 1 KB 571 is *a fortiori*, since it involved a driving instructor who failed to intervene when his pupil embarked on a dangerous manoeuvre. The Law Commission originally supported these decisions on 'passive encouragement' (Law Com No 177, *A Criminal Code for England and Wales* (1989), vol 1, cl 27(3)), but subsequently came to regard them as an 'over-extension' of the criminal law: Law Com No 300, *Inchoate Liability for Assisting and Encouraging Crime* (2006), para 5.68.

visitors refrain from certain activities; and so on.[90] These are situations where ownership carries with it various rights. The question is whether the law should require those rights to be exercised for certain public ends, notably for the purpose of preventing crimes from being committed. This is a challenge for the 'equal freedom' perspective, since the basis of criminal liability here would simply be that the owner has given them permission to use something that belongs to him or her. The law-breaking in which the permitted driver (or permitted house guest) is indulging is, for the owner, a non-chosen activity but the owner bears causal responsibility for it since his permission made it possible and the withdrawal of that permission could put a stop to the law-breaking. That would trade on an analogy with the decision in *Miller*,[91] an analogy that is not perfect because the owner of the car or house does not cause the offence so much as provide an opportunity for someone else to commit it.

However, the fundamental question is why an owner or employer should have a duty to take steps to prevent crime being committed by another autonomous actor: the question is whether the owner's 'but-for' causal responsibility, in terms of providing the opportunity for the eventual crime, ought to be sufficient to impose a positive obligation even though there is an intervening voluntary act. Is the situation really any different analytically from that in *Evans*?[92] We may accept that a third party (another passenger in the car or guest in the house) should have no obligation to take steps to prevent the offence, so the issue is the significance of the owner's legal power to control the offender. Is the combination of the power of ownership, with the causal element in permitting the wrongdoer to stay or to drive, and the principles of opportunity and capacity, sufficient to justify the criminal law in co-opting the owner as a law-enforcement officer or convicting the owner for failing to exercise the power? This question is revisited in part 5 below. Connected with it is the question of the intensity of criminal liability: conviction as an accomplice to the principal offender is the chosen approach for dealing with property owners,[93] and convicting of the relevant substantive offence the person who originally created the danger is the approach in the *Miller* situation. These approaches underline the closeness of the causal connection, but they go too far in treating the owner or originator as falling into the same legal category as a perpetrator.

---

[90] A further example would be the managing director of a company, who knows that employees are falsifying official tachograph records and fails to prevent this: *R v JF Alford Transport Ltd* [1997] 2 Cr App R 326.

[91] Above, n 85 and accompanying text.

[92] Above, n 87 and accompanying text.

[93] Or an offence of assisting or encouraging the crime, contrary to the Serious Crime Act 2007, ss 44–46 and 47(8)(a); cf s 65(2)(b).

(iv) Civic Obligations

This is perhaps the most contestable of the four categories of obligation, since it is founded on the ill-defined concept of the civic duty of individuals. In (iii) above we have just raised the question whether a person with the legal power to control others (car owner; house owner; employer) should be co-opted into law enforcement, effectively, by being liable to conviction for failing to exercise that power to prevent the commission or continuation of an offence. Now we move to wider questions about the justifications for imposing on certain persons the duty to report a known or suspected offence. None of the political theories sketched at the beginning of part 2 above offers a clear answer to the question of the proper extent of a citizen's duties. It is generally assumed that the state and its law enforcement officers will take charge of trying to prevent crimes from occurring and investigating crimes that have occurred, with a view to bringing the offenders to justice, and that citizens ought to concede limited powers to the police (eg stop and search, surveillance, arrest) in order to make this work. However, just as the state's duty to provide emergency and support services will only achieve its objective if people alert them to dangerous situations, so the responsibility of state officials to investigate and prevent crimes will only achieve its objective if members of the public are co-operative. But that leaves unresolved the question whether an active crime-preventive role should be assigned to the citizen and reinforced by the criminal sanction.

What duties (if any) should a person have to assist in law enforcement? There is long-established common law authority for a duty to go to the assistance of a police constable if such assistance is necessary and is requested. The authority is that of the Court for Crown Cases Reserved in *R v Brown*,[94] where the duty was said to apply if assistance was necessary and could be given 'without any physical impossibility or lawful excuse'. While those exceptions are significant, there is no reference to the risk that the citizen might be harmed in the encounter. If an officer is outnumbered by an angry crowd – as was the situation in *Brown*, where two illegal prize fights were taking place – requesting one citizen to assist means, almost certainly, requesting that citizen to place herself or himself in physical danger. Whatever the position was in the early days of policing, one might doubt the acceptability today of requiring a citizen to run the risk of physical injury; yet, in their brief endorsement of the rule, two members of the House of Lords made no reference to this implication of the duty.[95] There would be a much stronger argument for requiring the citizen to summon assistance, not least since the advent of mobile telephones. That should place the citizen in no danger, particularly if it were subject to a 'reasonable excuse' exception. Thus, while it may

---

[94] (1841) Car & M 314, on which see D Nicolson, 'The Citizen's Duty to Assist the Police' [1992] *Crim LR* 611.
[95] In *R (Laporte) v Chief Constable of Gloucestershire* [2007] 2 AC 105, at [83] per Lord Rodger and at [123] per Lord Brown; cf, however, s 65(3) of the Serious Crime Act 2007.

be appropriate that a police officer should be required to take action to prevent a serious crime from being committed, perhaps intervening physically,[96] at least unless the prospects appear hopeless without support from other officers, the citizen should have an obligation only to summon assistance and not to give physical support. It is suggested that the *Brown* rule requires more than should fairly be expected of a citizen, and that the decision to give physical support to a constable should be left to morality and conscience.[97]

At the other end of the spectrum of potential civic duties is that of making reasonable efforts to ascertain the criminal law. This is not a duty like the others considered so far, in the sense that failure to ascertain the criminal law is not an offence, but simply a non-defence. However, it is considered here because it can lead to criminal liability in some jurisdictions, notably England and Wales, where the prevailing doctrine is that ignorance of the criminal law is no excuse. That approach can be criticised as imposing too great an obligation on citizens and also on foreign visitors, given the frequency of new criminal legislation, not least because the state does not make great efforts to spread knowledge about developments in the criminal law. Is it not unfair and disrespectful of autonomy to impose this peremptory duty, and would it not show proper respect for autonomy to place people under a duty to make reasonable efforts to ascertain the criminal law? This is the rule in several countries, yielding a defence of rea-sonable ignorance or mistake of law;[98] but English law excludes that defence and thus incriminates people – although, as already stated, there is no crime of failing to know the law. Correspondingly, the state should bear a duty to publi-cise widely any new offences that are applicable to people in general, rather than to a particular business or financial sector, for which targeted publicity is more appropriate. Such reciprocal duties, of citizens and of the state, ought to have beneficial results in terms of reducing ignorance of the criminal law and even reducing offending,[99] while remaining grounded in realistic expectations of ordinary people. Once again, therefore, it can be argued that the common law doctrine (that ignorance of the criminal law is no excuse) is not consistent with the proper political relationship between the state and individuals, particularly in its application to omissions offences.

If the duty to make reasonable efforts to ascertain the criminal law is politically acceptable and a duty to give physical assistance to a police officer seems unduly demanding, both on the grounds of what can fairly be expected of citizens, what about the credentials of possible intermediate duties? Brief consideration must

---

[96] Eg *Dytham* [1979] QB 722, where a police officer saw a man being severely beaten outside a club but turned away rather than intervening, and was convicted of the common law offence of misconduct in a public office.

[97] The duty remains in other legal systems, however: see s 176 of the Indian Penal Code 1860, creating an offence of failure to assist a public servant when called upon to do so, and (among oth-ers) s 129(b) of the Canadian Criminal Code.

[98] For discussion, see A Ashworth, 'Ignorance of the Criminal Law, and Duties to Avoid it' (2011) 74 *MLR* 1, reprinted as Chapter 3 below.

[99] Ibid, 19–23.

now be given to four omissions offences in English law which consist of a failure to report a crime:[100]

(a) *Failure to Report Suspected Money-Laundering (Regulated Sector):* sections 330 and 331 of the Proceeds of Crime Act 2002 create two offences of failure to disclose money-laundering activities, applicable only to persons working in the regulated sector who have reasonable grounds for knowing or suspecting that another person is engaged in money-laundering.[101] Some 240,582 SARs (suspicious activity reports) were made in the year ending September 2010, slightly more than in the previous year: over three-quarters came from banks, with money service providers, lawyers, accountants, casinos and others making up the remainder.[102] It is not clear how many of these reports led to a prosecution, a statistic of some importance for the justification of this duty. It is easy to claim that such duties to report are indispensable to law enforcement, and to claim that organised criminals, particularly those involved in the drugs trade or in terrorism, rely on the laundering of money in order to thrive;[103] but we are entitled to require objective evidence before accepting the argument for imposing criminal law duties with substantial maximum penalties.

(b) *Failure to Report Suspected Financial Offences related to Terrorism (Regulated Sector):* section 21A of the Terrorism Act 2000 creates a similarly-structured offence for persons working in the 'regulated sector' who fail to disclose suspicions of an offence under sections 15 to 18 of the Terrorism Act – offences of fund-raising for the purposes of terrorism, the use or possession of money or other property for the purposes of terrorism, being concerned in an arrangement to fund terrorism, and 'laundering' terrorist property.[104] The range of defences is similar, and the maximum sentence is also five years' imprisonment. The number of suspicious activity reports made in respect of terrorist finance was 599 in the last full year, or some 0.25 per cent of all SARs made, with three-quarters coming from the banks;[105] it is not known how many led to prosecutions.

(c) *Failure to Report Suspected Financial Offences related to Terrorism (General Employment):* wider than the above offences is the offence in section 19 of the Terrorism Act 2000, which now applies to information that comes to any person

---

[100] See also S Wallerstein, 'On the Legitimacy of Imposing Direct and Indirect Obligations to Disclose Information on Non-Suspects' in GR Sullivan and I Dennis (eds), *Seeking Security* (2012).

[101] For discussion in the financial services context, see EP Ellinger, E Lomnicka and CVM Hare, *Ellinger's Modern Banking Law* (5th edn, 2011), 101–5.

[102] Serious Organised Crime Agency, *Suspicious Activity Reports Regime Annual Report 2010* (2011), 13.

[103] Cf the similar provisions in the United States, requiring financial institutions to make SARs when they suspect money-laundering or another criminal transaction. The provisions of the US Patriot Act extended the reporting requirements to sellers of high-value goods (eg jewellery, luxury cars, boats and planes). See SG Thompson, 'The White-Collar Police Force: "Duty to Report" Statutes in Criminal Law Theory' (2002) 11 *William and Mary Bill of Rights Journal* 3, at 25–31.

[104] For analysis, see CP Walker, *Blackstone's Guide to the Anti-Terrorism Legislation* (2nd edn, 2009), 97–100.

[105] Serious Organised Crime Agency (above, n 102), 58; on SARs more generally, see L Campbell, *Organised Crime and the Law* (2013), 70–74.

in the course of employment (whether or not in the course of a trade, profession or business). The original section 19 was aimed at professional people who handled financial matters, but in 2008 it was broadened so as to include information coming to all persons in the course of their employment, and by section 22A (inserted into the 2000 Act) 'employment' includes work experience, voluntary work and work under a contract for services.[106] This considerably extends the reach of the offence, but on the other hand the fault element is somewhat narrower than the 'regulated sector' offences since it does not include the objective 'reasonable grounds' condition. Thus the prosecution must prove that D knew or suspected that one of the four terrorist offences was being committed by another person, and that D failed to report that. The defences are broadly similar to the 'regulated sector' offences, and the maximum penalty is five years' imprisonment.

(d) *Failure to Report Information about Acts of Terrorism:* moving away from financial offences, section 38B of the Terrorism Act 2000 makes it an offence to fail to disclose information which D 'knows or believes might be of material assistance (a) in preventing the commission by another person of an act of terrorism, or (b) in securing the apprehension, prosecution or conviction of another person, in the United Kingdom, for an offence involving the commission, preparation or instigation of an act of terrorism'.[107] Section 38B thus creates two offences, one relating to the prevention of future acts of terrorism and one relating to terrorist acts that have already occurred (albeit that this may include acts of preparation, encouragement or assistance). The fault element of these offences is knowledge or belief, and suspicion is not enough. However, the referential point of that knowledge or belief is different from the financial offences above, since the knowledge or belief need only be as to a *possibility* of material assistance ('might be'), which lowers the threshold considerably. The prosecution is required to prove that the offence involved is an 'act of terrorism', rather than an 'ordinary' crime.[108] The conduct element is a failure to disclose the relevant information to a constable as soon as is practicable. The maximum sentence is five years' imprisonment. Section 38B(4) provides that it is a defence for P to prove that there was a reasonable excuse for not making the disclosure, but the cases make it clear that family ties, however close, cannot amount to a reasonable excuse.[109]

It is not known how frequently disclosures are made in response to the obligation imposed by section 38B. Prosecutions are certainly infrequent: 15 in Great Britain between 1984 and 2001 (many more in Northern Ireland), and 27 in Great Britain between 2002 and 2007.[110] There is little evidence that the existence of the

---

[106] See Walker, above, n 104, 97–98.
[107] For analysis, see C Walker, 'Conscripting the Public in Terrorism Policing: Towards Safer Communities or a Police State?' [2010] *Crim LR* 441, and Walker (above, n 104), 124–31.
[108] *Attorney-General's Reference (No 3 of 1993)* [1993] NI 50, applying *R v Rock*, 29 June 1990 (Northern Ireland, unreported).
[109] *R v Abdul Sherif* [2009] 2 Cr App R (S) 33, particularly at [45]; *R v Esayas Girma* [2010] 1 Cr App R (S) 172.
[110] Walker (above, n 104), 129–30.

section 38B offence has helped to combat terrorism by increasing the flow of information to the police and security services. For that effect to occur the existence of the offence would need to be widely known, and that cannot simply be assumed. Recent cases suggest that the offence is used chiefly after the event to penalise family members who either do not know that the duty exists, or prefer not to contact the police, or resolve their conflicting loyalties by not 'betraying' family members or close friends. Should such conduct be criminalised?

(e) *Failure to Report: Crime or mere Civic Duty?* The offences of failure to report suspected money-laundering and other financial offences, discussed in (a) and (b) above, apply only to the regulated sector. Would it be convincing to rely on 'voluntary obligation' reasoning to justify these offences, arguing that by deciding to work in the regulated financial sector a person assumes some responsibility for ensuring the lawfulness of transactions of which he or she becomes aware? The force of this cannot derive simply from the argument that if one voluntarily takes on a position one must accept all the duties that go with it, because that is to assume the answer to the question. Nor is it persuasive to maintain that a person who reaps the benefits of working in that sector should submit to certain burdens (including that of reporting) – there might be no great 'benefit' for a lowly employee, and the burden is that of acting as an unpaid law enforcement officer, which may be quite demanding. Why should that burden be imposed on workers in the financial sector and not (on the basis that they accept the benefits of the security provided by the state) on all citizens? Insofar as part of the reasoning for co-opting the regulated sector into law enforcement stems from the limitations of conventional policing, should we not review those limits in order to see what other groups of workers ought to be co-opted as required reporters? If the argument is that the police have no access to bank accounts and other details in the financial sector, can it not also be said that they have insufficient access to accounts within companies and other organisations? This reasoning would embrace (c), the duty imposed on persons who do not work in the regulated sector but who simply have some form of employment (even unpaid) which brings them within range of financial dealings that may be related to terrorism. Given the broad definition of 'employment', that falls little short of a general duty on citizens, of the kind in (d) that relates to past or future acts of terrorism.

However, the duty in (d) may be thought to be considerably more powerful, since it concerns not mere financial dealings but the priority of life, the principle of opportunity and capacity, and (in some cases) urgency. Money-laundering is wrong, but, even if the claimed links with organised crime and gang culture are substantiated,[111] it is a crime that should not be ranked as high as significant physical or sexual abuse. Thus in the United States all jurisdictions have an offence of failure to report child abuse, applicable to those who may come into

---

[111] For sceptical views, see M Levi, 'The Organisation of Serious Crimes for Gain' in M Maguire, R Morgan and R Reiner (eds), *Oxford Handbook of Criminology* (5th edn, 2012), 609–12, and Campbell, above n 105, Chs 2 and 9.

professional contact with children, whether as doctors, nurses, educators, child-care workers etc.[112] All States also impose a similar duty on relevant professionals to report elder abuse.[113] In at least 17 States these offences of failure to report have been extended to all citizens who come to know of an incident of child abuse or elder abuse. This may lead to a heavily gendered enforcement policy, predominantly against women who know that their partner is committing child abuse, and it is important that this be tackled by adequate support services and sensitive prosecution policies.[114] Some States go even wider, and have laws penalising failure to report any serious offence of which a person becomes aware (with a relatively low maximum penalty, usually a fine, for failing to report or summon help).[115] These American developments raise two questions: should there be a general duty on citizens to report serious offences? Is there a strong argument for a special duty to report abuse of the vulnerable?

The first question depends on the principles of criminalisation and, in particular, on conceptions of the appropriate relationship between the state and its citizens. Most theories of political obligation accept some kind of arrangement whereby citizens pay taxes and the state undertakes to provide a level of security, through emergency services such as ambulances, fire-fighters and police. The question here is: what may the state properly demand of citizens in relation to criminal law enforcement? It is normal to have a constitutional 'principle of compulsory process', which ensures that a witness can be compelled to attend and to give evidence at a person's trial, subject to being found in contempt of court for refusal.[116] This is currently one of several duties of citizenship, alongside the duty to serve on a jury (unless excused), and the duty to submit to arrest if a constable reasonably suspects a person of an arrestable offence, and so forth. But there is ambivalence about the proper extent of the principle of compulsory process. Thus in the famous case of *Rice v Connolly* [117] the Divisional Court held that at common law a citizen is entitled to refuse to answer a question put by a police officer (unless there is a statutory power involved), even though that makes the officer's task of law enforcement more difficult. Similarly, a person is not required to accompany a police officer to the police station, unless the officer has arrested him or her. Plainly the limits of the state's legitimate demands on citizens are contestable, so it may help to consider a specific question.

---

[112] Thompson (above, n 103), 13–19; see also L Remick, 'Failing to Report and False Reporting of Elder Abuse' (2009) 31 *Bifocal* 1–13.

[113] Remick, ibid.

[114] Ibid; Thompson (above, n 103, 15–16) states that prosecutions are rare in most States, and that the duty is used to ground civil actions against health professionals and educators who fail to report.

[115] DB Yeager, 'A Radical Community of Aid: a Rejoinder to Opponents of Affirmative Duties to Help' (1993) 71 *Washington University Law Quarterly* 1, 23; SJ Heyman, 'Foundations of the Duty to Rescue', (1994) 47 *Vanderbilt Law Review* 673, 689.

[116] P Roberts and A Zuckerman, *Criminal Evidence* (2nd edn, 2010), 307.

[117] [1966] 2 QB 414; see also *Sekfali v DPP* [2006] EWHC (Admin) 894 and, for empirical research, A Sanders, R Young and M Burton, *Criminal Justice* (4th edn, 2010), 94–96.

Should it be an offence to fail to report any serious crime? The justifications for such an offence must rest on the purpose of criminalisation, which may be either to ensure that offenders are brought to justice or to protect victims from violation of their rights. If it is to ensure that those who commit offences are brought to justice, then that comes close to the old common law offence of misprision of felony, which existed for many centuries and was abolished in 1967 following a recommendation of the Criminal Law Revision Committee.[118] Is there, as that committee implied, a fundamental social objection to offences such as misprision of felony, which (even if limited to *knowing* failures to report *serious* offences) would compel citizens to align themselves with the police and to betray their fellow-citizens? A general duty to report serious crime does not 'align' citizens with the police: it requires citizens to assist the police in the discharge of one of the state's primary obligations, which is to investigate crimes. Nor can such a duty to report be said to require the 'betrayal' of fellow-citizens, since loyalty can rarely be more important than bringing a serious offender to justice. There may be cases of intimidation or threats, and this raises questions about the proper scope of the defence of duress.

However, the main thrust of the argument in this chapter is that the purpose of an offence of failure to report is to improve the protection of victims. The chief argument here is for an offence of failure to report ongoing offences, with a view to ensuring that the emergency services (and child protection services) are informed about the commission of the offences. The obvious application of this is to offences of child abuse, elder abuse and abuse of vulnerable adults, not least because they tend to take place over a period of time and so the reporting should lead to the prevention of future victimisation. The broader question is whether this should be a general duty applicable to all serious crimes, or a specific duty in relation to crimes against vulnerable people such as children and the mentally disadvantaged. For example, is English law right to hold that going to watch a crime in progress does not incur criminal conviction? There is no duty to intervene (unless the victim is someone in respect of whom D stands *in loco parentis*), and so long as the witness does not encourage or in any way assist the offender, there can be no liability, even if the witness went to the place knowing that a crime was occurring.[119] It is noteworthy that the way in which this question is framed is whether the onlooker is liable as an accomplice to the ongoing offence,[120] in which case the witness would be liable to be convicted and sentenced as a principal. Surely there should be a significant distinction made between the actual perpetrator of the offence and the onlooker. If the onlooker or witness is to be guilty of an offence of failure to report, the proper level of

[118] Criminal Law Revision Committee, *Seventh Report – Felonies and Misdemeanours* (Cmnd 2659, 1965), [39-42].

[119] *R v Clarkson and Carroll* [1971] 1 WLR 1402; see also *R v Francom* [2001] 1 Cr App R 237 and *Robinson v The Queen* [2011] UKPC 3, at [15].

[120] Cf s 65(3) of the Serious Crime Act 2007, which provides that a person who fails to respond positively to a constable's call for assistance cannot be held liable for encouraging or assisting the principal offence.

criminalisation should be a civic duty to report the offence, reinforced by a crime of failure to report with a moderate maximum penalty.

If we have put forward a *prima facie* case for criminalisation, based on the better protection of victims, what countervailing considerations should be weighed in the decision whether or not to create an offence of this kind? There is an obvious conflict with the values placed on the institution of marriage. Thus, returning to the 'principle of compulsory process', English law excuses a spouse or civil partner from being a compellable witness in order not to jeopardise the 'special status of marriage' by forcing one party to testify against the other.[121] However, the legislation creates an exception to that exception, where the trial involves an assault on the spouse or civil partner or on a person under 16, or a violent or sexual offence against a person under 16.[122] These exceptions leave the law in a somewhat incoherent state: the immunity applies to a spouse but not to a long-time partner, sister, brother, parent or child; and the immunity does not apply to a spouse alleged to have kissed a 15-year-old but does apply to one alleged to have committed murder or rape on anyone over 16.[123] But, anomalies apart, the statutory hierarchy suggests that marriage and civil partnership are valued so highly that only trials for domestic violence and physical or sexual abuse of children are of sufficient public importance to displace the marital immunity. It is questionable whether the importance of the marital bond should be allowed to outweigh the desirability of bringing other serious offenders to justice. The 'failure to protect' offence in English law is explicit about this, since the offence is aimed at criminalising family and household members including spouses, in order to protect the young and vulnerable.[124] The offences of failure to report information about acts of terrorism have also been interpreted, as we have seen, so as to rule out the possibility that loyalty to family and friends (even to a spouse) can amount to a 'reasonable excuse' for not reporting.[125] Similarly a new offence of failure to report a crime against the person should, in principle, apply equally between family members.

However, in relation to 'failure to protect' offences, some doubts were raised earlier about the opportunity and capacity of those (usually women) who, as wives or partners of abusers, may be subject to abuse themselves and therefore unable through fear to discharge their duty to protect; it was suggested that this undoubted problem is better approached through a broader defence and sensitive prosecution policy than by abolishing the 'failure to protect' offence. The duty to protect can often be fulfilled by raising the alarm and reporting the abuse. In those situations, the offence is similar to the American 'failure to

---

[121] Per Lord Salmon in *Hoskyn v Commissioner of Police for the Metropolis* [1979] AC 474, at 495; see also Criminal Law Act 1977, s 2(1)(a), D cannot be liable for criminal conspiracy with spouse or civil partner. There is not space here to discuss what the relevant marital value is, and the extent to which it is undermined by a duty to give evidence or a duty to report.

[122] Police and Criminal Evidence Act 1984, s 80(3).

[123] See the comments by Roberts and Zuckerman (above, n 116), 314–17.

[124] See above, nn 60–69 and accompanying text.

[125] Above, part 3(iv)(d).

report' offences in cases of child abuse and elder abuse. It is because children and elders are at risk through usually being violated in a private sphere (removed from the public gaze, and where they should be able to feel secure) that they have a particular claim to protection from abuse – reporting is likely to be the most appropriate course for professionals and for members of the household.[126] A duty to report that was inapplicable within the family would leave vulnerable people without protection. Yet a duty to report that applies to family members requires sensitive handling, because they too may be 'vulnerable' given the real risk of violence in some households. Imposing a general duty to report should not be taken as a suggestion that public services of support for families and for the vulnerable should in any way be diminished; indeed, in many situations it will be more realistic to look to professionals to raise the alarm.

Other countervailing arguments against such an offence should also be considered. One is whether the police might take more power than the offence was intended to give them, abusing it by routinely accusing the partners of suspects of this offence, as a means of pressuring the true suspects to confess. The offence might then become a controlling or bargaining tool in the hands of the police, rather than performing the civic function intended. This makes the case for close monitoring of the use of the offence, and guidelines for the police and prosecutors that explain the way in which the offence should and should not be used.

Perhaps the most intractable issue is the problem of definition. The argument so far has been that there is a strong case for an offence of failure to report serious crimes; but there is no simple way of defining serious crimes, at least so as not to include simple thefts, and certainty is of particular importance when defining offences of omission (see part 4 below). A preferable approach may therefore be to argue in favour of an offence of failure report a crime against the person, including offences of violence and sexual offences. This also has the merit of coming close to implementing the priority of life, by targeting crimes that involve the most serious kinds of wrong against individuals. One remaining counter-argument is that the police might abuse such an offence by using it to exert pressure on the families and associates of suspects: this is a less convincing argument now than it was in 1964,[127] since there are now greater safeguards for people being questioned by the police (right to legal representation, tape-recording of interviews), but it is an argument that should be taken seriously and tackled through close monitoring of the police and sensible prosecution policy.

---

[126] Failure to report, by a parent or other person standing *in loco parentis*, may be sufficient to amount to wilful neglect of a child in English law: *R v Emma W* [2006] EWCA Crim 2723. See further Herring (above, n 52), 195, supporting a duty to report elder abuse but pointing out the reluctance of many nurses to make reports, for fear of reprisals or of having misunderstood the situation.

[127] This was one of four arguments against the common law offence of misprision of felony listed by the Criminal Law Revision Committee, above n 118.

Assuming that these counter-arguments can be overcome in the manner suggested, the argument in favour of an offence of failure to report offences against the person remains strong. Can the argument be taken further, so as to demand some form of physical intervention to stop an ongoing crime? That question was discussed earlier in relation to the offence of failing to assist a constable when called upon to do so, and it was argued that such a duty asks too much of citizens – that, even if it was appropriate in the early days of professional policing, it is unjustifiable now to expect a citizen to place himself or herself in the line of physical danger.[128] A duty to report and to call for immediate assistance should be sufficient, and any further involvement should be left to conscience. The same should apply to any general duty to report crimes against the person: it is too much to require a person who observes a crime not only to report it but also to make some intervention, since that may place the person in danger.[129] However, it will be recalled that the failure to protect offence (discussed in part 3(i) above) imposes a further-reaching criminal law duty in relation to children and vulnerable adults. This is the duty to take such steps as could reasonably be expected to protect such persons from death or serious bodily harm, a duty borne of proximity to the abuse (the principles of opportunity and capacity) rather than the professional responsibility of a person whose employment brings them into contact with children or vulnerable people. What kind and degree of intervention can be reasonably expected in familial abuse situations is not clear, but in principle the duty should extend to at least an attempt at physical intervention to save a child or vulnerable person from violence. We have already noted the practical difficulties and gendered unfairness to which this may give rise, insofar as it imposes the duty (often) on women who are themselves at risk of attack. As well as sensitive prosecution policy and better support services, there may be a case for a defence broader than duress to be introduced. In general, even where there is urgency and a form of opportunity and capacity, the law should not require physical intervention in a situation involving aggression, at least unless it involves a parent and child or police officer and a crime victim. If a duty of easy rescue were introduced into the law, with the usual capacity defence, that would be one thing. But it is a significant step further to require a citizen to step into a situation of aggression, even if there were opportunity and capacity conditions attached.

---

[128] Above, nn 94–97 and accompanying text. Cf Heyman (above, n 115), 685–89, summarising the authorities from Bracton onwards on the citizen's earlier duty to raise the 'hue and cry'. Cf also the sources discussed in Lord Denning's speech in *Sykes v DPP* [1962] AC 528 with the analysis by PR Glazebrook, 'Misprision of Felony – Shadow or Phantom?' (1964) 8 *American Journal of Legal History* 189, 283.

[129] An alternative approach would be to add to the 'failure to report' offence the kind of requirement found in 'failure of easy rescue' statutes, which typically require a person to become involved to the extent that they can do so without danger to themselves. The application of this clause would be contentious in situations such as *Clarkson and Carroll* (above, n 119): could the two soldiers have overpowered the soldiers who were engaged in the rape, without danger to themselves?

2.4 OMISSIONS OFFENCES AND THE RULE OF LAW

According to the principle of legality and the 'rule of law', legal norms, and especially those of the criminal law, must be clear, stable, and not retrospective in their operation. The law's primary function is to guide people's conduct, and in this context Lon Fuller, in his catalogue of 'eight ways to fail to make a law',[130] emphasised the fundamental importance of publicising laws and making them available to citizens. In similar vein, John Gardner has argued that 'those of us about to commit a criminal wrong should be put on stark notice that that is what we are about to do'.[131] This principle should apply to offences of commission and *a fortiori* to offences of omission, where a person might be unaware of the duty to act. Thus:

> 'According to the ideal of the rule of law, the law must be such that those subject to it can reliably be guided by it, either to avoid violating it or to build the legal consequences of having violated it into their thinking about what future actions may be open to them. People must be able to find out what the law is and to factor it into their practical deliberations. The law must avoid taking people by surprise, ambushing them, putting them into conflict with its requirements in such a way as to defeat their expectations and frustrate their plans'.[132]

These rule-of-law standards give rise to four major issues in omissions liability – the creation of duty-situations; the issue of knowledge of the law; the role of *mens rea*; and the problem of vagueness.

First, the list of duty-situations in English law remains open for judicial development, so that individuals often cannot know whether their failure to intervene in a given situation will lead to liability for the serious offence of manslaughter. Surely if we accept the fundamental principle that the criminal law should not be retroactive, and that fair warning should be given, the judicial recognition of new duty-situations in these serious cases would seem to violate this.[133] The Law Commission of New Zealand recommended that 'in the interests of certainty and transparency' duties that are not set out in legislation should not be recognised:

> 'It is a cornerstone of the rule of law that people should only be held criminally liable for conduct that was criminal at the time that it occurred, so that, if they were inclined to do so, they would be able to ascertain whether it is prohibited. This is not possible in relation to the common law duties discerned by the courts from time to time;

---

[130] LL Fuller, *The Morality of Law* (rev edn, 1969), Ch II; see also J Waldron, 'The Concept and the Rule of Law' (2008) 43 *Georgia Law Review* 1, at 7.

[131] J Gardner, 'Wrongs and Faults' in AP Simester (ed), *Appraising Strict Liability* (2005), 69–70.

[132] J Gardner, 'Introduction' in HLA Hart, *Punishment and Responsibility: Essays in the Philosophy of Law* (2008), xxxvi.

[133] Recognition of new duty-situations in cases such as *R v Wacker* [2003] QB 1203 and *R v Willoughby* [2004] EWCA Crim 3365 is far more problematic than the English Court of Appeal admitted.

bluntly put, it invites the courts to "make it up as they go along" according to the circumstances of the individual case'.[134]

Although this may seem a counsel of perfection, it is a necessary implication of taking the rule of law and its values seriously. A degree of judicial interpretation of legislative categories is to be expected, but courts should avoid taking individuals by surprise.[135] Thus in principle the New Zealand Law Commission's recommendation is to be preferred to the 'hands-off' approach of the English Law Commission,[136] particularly if combined with an explicit restraint on the judicial creation of new categories or extensions of existing categories.

The second major problem is that there may be nothing to put the individual on notice of the duty-situation, not least because there may be a widespread belief that there are few legal duties to care for one's fellow human beings.[137] The parable of the good Samaritan is an indication of what it may be morally right to do, but, we are told, not of the common law. This is quite a well-known difference of orientation between the common law and continental European criminal law. Thus the problem for the individual is that the existence of duty-situations is exceptional, since English criminal law's general stance is not to impose positive duties to act. As already noted, the English Law Commission decided that the relevant law was too uncertain to re-state in codified form,[138] a position that Glanville Williams had earlier criticised pithily:

> 'If the top lawyers in a Government committee find the law hard to state clearly, what hope have the Stones and Dobinsons of this world of ascertaining their legal position, in advance of prosecution, when they find themselves landed with a hunger-striking relative?'[139]

In part 3(i) we noted the uncertainty about the ambit of duties to assist relatives, household members and friends who fall ill. To conform to the rule of law, these issues should be resolved rather than left open for judicial development; and governments must then make a concerted effort to communicate

---

[134] Law Commission of New Zealand, *Review of Part 8 of the Crimes Act 1961: Crimes against the Person*, Report 111 (2009), para 4.17. It has also been argued in the Canadian context that the creation of new duty-situations by the courts would 'come precariously close to creating common law crimes contrary to section 9 of the *Criminal Code*': K Roach, *Criminal Law* (4th edn, 2009), 109.

[135] See the powerful arguments of Glanville Williams, 'What should the Code do about omissions?' (1987) 7 *Legal Studies* 92, at 94–95.

[136] In Law Com No 177 (1989), the Law Commission stated that it felt unable to make a list of duty-situations in English law, and that therefore liability for omissions 'must remain a matter of construction and, so far as duties to act are concerned, of common law': vol 2, 187.

[137] Surveys suggest that the position is more nuanced: eg PH Robinson and JM Darley, *Justice, Liability and Blame: Community Views and the Criminal Law* (1995), 42–50, and B Mitchell, 'Public Perceptions of Homicide and Criminal Justice' (1998) 48 *British Journal of Criminal Law* 453.

[138] Law Com No 177, para 5.43.

[139] G Williams, *Textbook of Criminal Law* (2nd edn, 1983), 266.

duty-situations to citizens. Without such steps, it is doubtful whether much of the criminal law on omissions would conform to the principle of legality.[140]

A third and related problem concerns the fault element required for liability. Even if the list of duty-situations were not to remain open for judicial development, it would be important to confine liability to those who knowingly fail in their duty, so as to ensure an appropriate level of fairness. It may be acceptable to impose a duty of care on persons in a particular field (eg the regulated sector in financial services; car drivers), with a negligence basis for liability. But in the absence of some such special grounds for putting people on notice, the case for liability based on negligence, or even on gross negligence, is precarious.

Fourthly, one aspect of the rule of law is that people are entitled to know what is expected of them. Omissions law creates difficulties in this respect insofar as it relies on concepts such as 'reasonable steps' and 'such steps as could reasonably be expected'. As John Rawls has argued:

> 'If the precept of no crime without law is violated, say by statutes being vague and imprecise, what we are at liberty to do is likewise vague and imprecise . . . And to the extent that this is so, liberty is restricted by a reasonable fear of its exercise'.[141]

As will appear from part 6 below, this is a particular problem for the law on criminal omissions, since what it requires is often (not invariably, of course) phrased in terms of making reasonable efforts. To the household member who asks whether she must call the police or must try to intervene herself, we cannot give a confident answer. In continental European law 'duty of easy rescue' legislation usually includes a phrase such as 'without danger to oneself' and refers to one's capacity too,[142] and these must surely be implicit. Can it not be said that, in practice, a person who makes a genuine effort to do something is unlikely to incur liability (or even prosecution)? That is not a proposition of law, of course. True it is that the concept of reasonableness is much less objectionable as an element in a defence than as an element in an offence,[143] but it could satisfy most of the objections if it were supported by indications of relevant factors and explicit provision for limiting factors such as capacity and avoiding personal danger.

2.5 THE CONTOURS OF OMISSIONS LIABILITY

The justifications for basing criminal liability on failures to act were examined in part 3. We considered family and household obligations, voluntarily incurred

---

[140]   This was conceded by the Law Commission in Law Com No 177 (1989), para 3.16. For the common law application of this standard, see Lord Bingham in *R v Rimmington and Goldstein* [2005] UKHL 63. In the UK the European Convention on Human Rights reinforces this requirement: see B Emmerson, A Ashworth and A Macdonald (eds), *Human Rights and Criminal Justice* (3rd edn, 2012), Ch 16.

[141]   J Rawls, *A Theory of Justice* (1972), 239.

[142]   The requirement of capacity is discussed further in part 2.7 of this chapter.

[143]   L Alexander, 'Criminal Liability for Omissions: an Inventory of Issues' in AP Simester and S Shute (eds), *Criminal Law Theory: Doctrines of the General Part* (2001), 130.

obligations, obligations arising from personal responsibility, and civic obligations. Some of those obligations arise where another person is the principal offender: in such instances, the duty is one of reporting, or of taking steps to protect the victim or to stop the offending. Some of the obligations arise where the omitter bears the primary duty, such as a duty to secure the wellbeing of another or a duty to prevent further harm after accidentally creating a dangerous situation.

It is evident from part 3 that the grounds for criminalising the breach of certain duties are contestable. But those arguments cannot be pursued to a conclusion without determining the *form* and *intensity* of criminalisation, since it might be easier to justify creating a simple 'failure to report' offence with a low maximum penalty than treating a breach of duty as the basis for conviction of a substantive offence. Without purporting to be exhaustive, five different levels of the intensity of criminalisation (LC) can be distinguished:

LC1 – offence of failure to report;

LC2 – offence of failure to call for assistance and, where possible without danger, to intervene physically;

LC3 – offence of failure to care for a dependent or to take necessary precautions;

LC4 – complicity in principal offence, through failure to intervene;

LC5 – conviction of substantive offence (eg murder, manslaughter) for failure to perform a particular act.

Examples of these different offence structures have already been given at various points in part 3 above. The important point is that any decision to criminalise an omission is not simply a yes/no issue: there are further questions about the nature and the level of intensity of criminalisation, and the appropriate maximum sentence. There are also questions about whether the offence should be formulated so as to penalise the omission itself (irrespective of consequences), or so as to criminalise the causing of a result by failure to fulfil a duty. Thus what is here referred to as the *intensity* of criminalisation covers both the question of the relative seriousness of the offence and the question whether the offence is conduct-based or result-based in its formulation.

The most basic form of omissions offence is that of 'failing to do *x*' (LC1). Examples of such formulations would be the road traffic offences of failing to stop and report an accident (see part 3(ii) above), and the various failure to report offences (see part 3(iv) above). One common feature of these offences is that they do not specify a result or consequence: the omission itself is what is criminalised. However, the seriousness of the offence – whether it is triable on indictment, whether its maximum sentence involves imprisonment and, if so, at what level – must be assessed on the basis of the seriousness of the omission and its possible consequences. Thus, to work through the three examples just mentioned, the rationale for the two road traffic offences is more concerned with identification of the driver than of preventing harm, and therefore a summary offence with a moderate non-custodial penalty is in order. The failure to report offences that relate to terrorist activities ought to be pitched at a higher level and, while the current maximum of five years' imprisonment for failure to report terrorist activities pays appropriate regard to the fact that the non-reporter is not the primary offender, the similar maximum for failure to report money-laundering seems not to pay appropriate regard to that element and to be disproportionately high compared to the wrong involved.

Into the second category (LC2) fall offences of 'failure to effect an easy rescue', which are essentially offences of failure to call the emergency services and, if this can be done without personal danger, intervening physically to prevent death or serious injury. Such offences are rare in common law jurisdictions but frequently found in continental European systems. It was argued in part 3(i) above that the introduction of such an offence would be more appropriate than persisting with the current English distinction between duties towards family members which, if violated with fatal consequences, may lead to conviction for the serious offence of manslaughter (LC5) and situations where there is no duty at all towards a family member or house guest. It would be both fairer and proportionate to put in place a general offence of failure to report and to take steps towards an easy rescue.

The third category includes some serious offences, such as wilful neglect of a child by failing to provide food, medical care etc (see part 3(i) above). The current maximum sentence is 10 years' imprisonment, a maximum designed to cover a range of forms of child abuse including assaults and ill-treatment. In most cases this offence will have involved actual abuse of the child, ie not just a failure to feed or provide medical aid but a consequence flowing from that failure. However, the offence is formulated so as not to require proof of such a consequence.[144] In cases of intentional failure to fulfil the duty, with fatal results, English law provides for the offence to come within LC5, with conviction of either murder or manslaughter, depending on the degree of fault proved. Also falling within LC3 are offences of failure to take the necessary precautions when storing or using explosives and failure to obtain a licence for a firearm. These may be regarded as regulatory offences but, given the potential harm of unauthorised use of firearms or explosives, the 'regulatory' tag should not be taken to suggest that such offences are at the level of LC1 when it comes to maximum penalties.

Category four has been used in English law to hold liable as an accomplice the owner/employer who fails to countermand the offending behaviour of someone over whom he has the power of control. This is a strongly contested duty-situation, as we saw in part 3(iii) above; but, if one accepts the duty, then it is the very presence and opportunity of the owner/employer that indicates

---

[144] For cogent proposals for reforming this offence, see R Taylor and L Hoyano, 'Criminal Child Maltreatment: the Case for Reform' [2012] *Crim LR* 871. See also the offence of wilful neglect of a person lacking capacity: Mental Capacity Act 2005, s 44.

criminal liability. This is a high intensity imposition, since it renders the owner/accomplice liable to conviction and sentence as if she or he were the principal. As argued in part 3(iii) above, this may be regarded as an excessive reaction to the owner or employer's failure to try to exert control over another voluntary actor. Liability for a form of secondary crime such as encouraging or assisting an offence might be more appropriate; but, even then, the penalty should not be high. Accepting that the principal actor is behaving voluntarily, the culpability of failing to attempt to dissuade the principal should be at a modest level, on a similar level to failure to report.

In the fifth category we find probably the most controversial forms of omissions offences – those in which a failure to fulfil a duty may serve as the *actus reus* of a substantive offence. Thus parents who intentionally refrain from feeding their child are liable to be convicted of murder if the child dies and it can be proved that they intended to cause death or serious bodily harm by their behaviour;[145] and this is surely justifiable, since starving a child to death seems hardly less heinous than assaulting the child physically. Any distinction in terms of culpability between acts and omissions vanishes at this point. It re-emerges, however, when we consider a failure to summon medical assistance, by parents who believe that God will save their child. Such parents would surely be aware of the possibility of death, and so a conviction for the very serious offence of manslaughter may be appropriate. William Wilson argues that the law of manslaughter gives the court a greater opportunity to consider the context and motives of the defendant than does that of murder; but, referring to *Senior*,[146] where parents followed their religious beliefs in not calling a doctor to their sick child, he speculates:

> 'that the absence of bad motive may yet have stifled consideration of whether murder was the more appropriate charge. That this was at least plausible can be demonstrated by the little remarked upon fact that this was the seventh time one of his children had died under such circumstances'.[147]

That point is well taken. There are clearly cases in which an omission may rightly serve as the *actus reus* of a serious offence, where matters of life and death are unmistakeably involved and the path of duty is clear. But should that reasoning be extended to all family and household obligations, and to all contractual duties? In the family and household cases there is a difference between cases where another person is the principal offender (where the duty is to report and/or intervene) and cases where the defendant owes a duty directly to the victim. We have dealt with the latter eventuality when discussing a parent's liability towards children. In cases where the defendant is not the principal offender, English law now adopts a middle way – the 'failure to protect' offence, which imposes a duty to take steps to prevent the death or injury of the child or vulnerable adult, and which has a

---

[145] *R v Gibbins and Proctor*, above n 2, a rare example of the equivalence principle.
[146] [1899] 1 QB 293.
[147] Wilson, 'Murder by Omission' (above, n 6), 16.

maximum sentence of 14 years' imprisonment.[148] This approach does not convert the defendant who fails to protect another into an accomplice (as, for example, with cases of the owner of property or employer, discussed in the previous paragraph), largely because of the problem of identifying a principal in many of these 'failure to protect' cases. An uncomfortable social reality – the difficulty of identifying the perpetrator of child abuse in the home – has led to an unusual criminal law solution.

As for contractual duties, even if we confine ourselves to contracts for the provision of necessaries or for the avoidance of accidents, there is still a serious question whether the breach of contract ought to be sufficient to form the basis for conviction of manslaughter. The historical explanation for this appears to reside in the significance attached to the causing of death. A breach of contract with no bad consequences[149] may amount to a breach of laws on health and safety but is unlikely to be prosecuted; the self-same breach with fatal consequences amounts to manslaughter. Some would argue that the defendant's fault is the same in the two cases, and that a conviction for manslaughter attributes too much significance to what is truly a matter of chance – although that is a general criticism of the offence of constructive manslaughter. An intermediate offence, such as that which penalises breaches of the law on health and safety, would be the proportionate response. Others would contend that the causing of death is part of what the defendant did, and his conduct cannot properly be described without it; or that the risk of death was just what the contract was drafted to guard against, and so a manslaughter conviction is justified on a 'scope of risk' principle.[150] This approach may not lead to a severe sentence, however, even if it does lead to the imposition of a strongly condemnatory label (manslaughter) on the result of the defendant's omission.

Finally, also in LC5 are those who accidentally cause danger and then have a duty to prevent further harm. The presence and opportunity of the causer of the accident not only points to him or her as the person who should take action, but suggests that failure to do so (with the required culpability) should amount to commission of the substantive offence. That person is the principal, and the duty arises from his or her causal responsibility. The appropriate substantive offence depends on the circumstances, but may be criminal damage by fire (as in *Miller*)[151] or may even be manslaughter or murder (in the hypothetical example

---

[148] For present purposes we leave out of account the history of this offence, which shows that it was intended also to cover cases where it was impossible to prove which of two parents or carers inflicted the abuse. These are more serious cases than simply a failure to protect, since the defendant would then be the principal actor (although this could not be proved). See further Hayes (above, n 66) and Herring (above, n 67).

[149] Eg if the keeper of the railway crossing had left the gates open while taking his lunch and no accident had occurred: *R v Pittwood*, above, n 73.

[150] For references to the debate, see A Ashworth, 'The Criminal Law's Ambivalence about Outcomes' in R Cruft, M Kramer and M Reiff (eds), *Crime, Punishment and Responsibility* (2011).

[151] Above, n 85 and accompanying text.

of D who accidentally bumps into V on a lakeside path, and then takes no steps to prevent V from drowning).

2.6 OMISSIONS AS OFFENCE-ELEMENTS

Thus far we have been considering situations in which the breach of a duty is the most significant aspect, and is the main reason for criminalisation. But reference should also be made to a further type of case in which the breach of a duty is a significant element of an offence: these are offences that would not generally be referred to as offences of omission, but where the breach of a duty is or may be one element in the reason for criminalisation. Two examples are (i) failure to ascertain whether the other participant in sexual activity is consenting; and (ii) failure to ascertain the age of a young participant in sexual activity, or the mental capacity of a vulnerable participant in sexual activity. Like many of the other duties discussed above, these are in the nature of conditional positive obligations. If a person embarks on a given course of conduct, he or she has a duty to make certain enquiries.

Since the enactment of the Sexual Offences Act 2003, the four major offences – rape, sexual penetration, sexual assault and causing sexual activity – all require an absence of consent by the other party, and require that the defendant 'does not reasonably believe' that the other party was consenting. The effect of the word 'reasonably' is that a person can be convicted of this offence on the basis of a failure to do what was reasonable in order to make himself or herself aware of the other party's view of the conduct. As subsection (2) of each offence-creating provision puts it:

> 'whether a belief is reasonable is to be determined having regard to all the circumstances, including any steps A has taken to ascertain whether B consents'.[152]

Thus, in practical terms, a person who wants to engage in sexual conduct with another has a positive obligation to take some steps to find out whether the other party is consenting, ie whether that person 'agrees by choice, and has the freedom and capacity to make that choice'.[153] The situation in which this duty arises is one of his or her own choosing, and the failure or omission to make enquiries constitutes a significant element in the distinction between a voluntary encounter and a serious sexual assault. The doctrine of 'equal freedom' enjoins respect for the other person as a choosing being, and condemns the imposition of the defendant's will in such a way as to use the other person 'as a means only'. It is therefore right that if the defendant is proved not to have taken reasonable steps to ascertain that the other person is truly consenting, and the other was not consenting, he (or, rarely, she) is liable to conviction for one of those four major offences on the basis of the omission.

---

[152] Sexual Offences Act 2003 (UK), ss 1(2), 2(2), 3(2), and 4(2).
[153] Ibid, s 74.

Moving from (i) to (ii), we must consider whether adults have wider duties towards children and the vulnerable. All adults are subject to various prohibitions against sexual activities with the young, and combined with those prohibitions are some positive obligations, of which the most prominent is the duty to take reasonable steps to ascertain the age of the young person. In England and Wales the age of consent is 16, and so the offences against children aged under 16 include the requirement that 'B is under 16 and A does not reasonably believe that B is 16 or over'.[154] This means that A (the defendant) may be convicted of a child sex offence on the basis of a failure to take sufficient steps to ascertain the other party's age, or a general failure to have a good reason for making an assumption. So the duty arises as a concomitant of a situation into which A enters voluntarily: if A wishes to have sexual activity with a person who appears to be young, A must ensure that he or she has reasonable grounds for believing that the other party is at least 16 years old. Similar duties arise when a person wishes to engage in sexual activity with a person who appears to be and is mentally disordered. For example, one requirement is:

> 'A knows or could reasonably be expected to know that B has a mental disorder and that because of it or for a reason related to it B is likely to be unable to refuse'.[155]

Thus a significant element in the offences relating to sexual activities with people who may be too young or mentally disordered is that the actor fails to take reasonable steps to make himself or herself aware of the lack of capacity, a duty that in practice requires the actor to know the law and to realise that the intended sexual partner may fall into one of the prohibited groups. These duties to take reasonable steps form a significant element in these offences, and can be supported as demonstrating proper respect for the rights and limited capacity of the young or mentally disordered.

How far should this argument be taken? English law imposes a peremptory duty where a person engages in sexual activity with a child under 13. There is no requirement of reasonable grounds: if the child is under 13, the other party is liable to conviction for a most serious offence (rape of a child under 13) irrespective of lack of knowledge or mistaken belief. There are strong arguments both for and against imposing this absolute duty, which cannot be pursued to a conclusion here.[156] Two points will be made, however. First, the effect of imposing this strict liability as to age is to impose on adults a duty to make full (and successful) enquiries as to the age of a child who may be under 13. If the adult gets it wrong, by (for example) taking on trust what he or she is told, or even because he or she was tricked by someone, this is no excuse in English law. Clearly the policy behind this approach is to ensure the maximum protection of very young children from sexual molestation and premature sexual experiences,

---

[154] See, eg Sexual Offences Act 2003 (UK), s 10(1)(c), s 11(1)(d), s 15(1)(d), and others.

[155] Sexual Offences Act 2003 (UK), s 30(1)(d); cf, slightly differently, s 34(1)(e) and s 38(1)(d).

[156] For discussion, see A Ashworth, 'Should Strict Criminal Liability be Removed from all Imprisonable Offences?' (2010) 45 *Irish Jurist* 1, reprinted as Chapter 4 below.

and this policy must be seen in the context of the fact that, even if the child was 13, 14 or 15, the sexual interaction would still be unlawful. Should a person be able to say that he or she was prepared to have sex with a child of 14 or 15 (maximum sentence 10 years) but not with one of 12 or younger (maximum sentence life imprisonment)? English law makes no concession to this argument, but if we assume that the defendant has taken reasonable steps to check the child's age and has formed the conclusion that the child is 14, then that ought to be grounds at least for some mitigation of sentence. But it remains to be decided whether it is fair to convict of such a serious offence those who have made reasonable efforts to ascertain the child's age. Secondly, English law makes no concession for young defendants either. So if a boy aged 15 has consensual sex with a girl who tells him that she is also 15 (when in fact she is 12), the strict liability rule applies no less, and the boy is liable to be convicted of the most serious offence.[157] This is inconsistent and oppressive: whether in sexual offences or more broadly, defendants who are children themselves ought not to bear the obligations of adults and full citizens, but should rather benefit from some of the protection normally accorded to children as victims.[158] If a child under 16 is deemed incapable of consenting to sexual activity, is it not inconsistent to hold him or her liable to the same standards as someone who is regarded as fully capable of consenting? To impose strict liability as to age on children who are themselves under age is plainly out of order.

2.7 WHAT DUTY-SITUATIONS SHOULD REQUIRE

The prohibitions of the criminal law take different forms, as is well known. Some prohibit the culpable causing of a result (as in the law of homicide and of offences against the person); some prohibit conduct irrespective of whether it produces a result (such as dangerous driving, or possession of an unregistered firearm), and so on. There are also various forms of omissions offence, as explained in part 5 above. What they require of the individual differs significantly, and this raises points of principle.

The basic model of an omissions offence is a failure to do *x*. Usually this takes the form of non-compliance with a duty, such as the duty to report a road accident or to report suspicions of money-laundering. No result is specified in this type of offence. So far as the general part of the criminal law is concerned, two requirements stand out. First, the duty-bearing person must know that the circumstances giving rise to the duty have arisen: it would be unfair to hold a person liable for failing to report a matter of which he or she was unaware,[159]

---

[157] See *R v G* [2008] UKHL 37 and *G v United Kingdom* [2012] *Crim LR* 46.
[158] For discussion, see A Ashworth, 'Child Defendants and the Doctrines of the Criminal Law' in J Chalmers, F Leverick and L Farmer (eds), *Essays in Criminal Law in Honour of Sir Gerald Gordon* (2010), reprinted as Chapter 7 below.
[159] As Lord Goddard CJ held in *Harding v Price* [1948] 1 KB 695.

unless the individual is subject to a positive duty of care in respect of looking out for such events, as in the offences of failure to report suspected money-laundering which relate to persons working in the regulated sector.[160] Secondly, compliance with the duty must not have been impossible for the individual concerned. This is the cutting edge of the principle of capacity, which has been mentioned several times above. In effect, here as elsewhere in omissions offences, a defence of impossibility must be recognised. If it was physically impossible for the defendant to carry out the duty, he or she should not be liable to conviction for failing to do so. This is unlikely to arise in the context of reporting suspected money-laundering, but it might arise in connexion with the duty to report an accident. A good reason for not prosecuting someone seriously injured in such an accident is that they might have been unable to report it because of their physical state (eg unconsciousness); and, in the unlikely event that they are prosecuted for this offence, they should have a defence of impossibility. The importance of such a defence was also recognised in *R v Brown*,[161] where the Court upheld a citizen's duty to go to the assistance of a police officer when requested, where assistance could be given 'without any physical impossibility or lawful excuse'.

A defence of impossibility would certainly be relevant to the second (ii) group of omissions offences, where the omission serves as the *actus reus* for a substantive offence such as murder or manslaughter. What is required in these duty-situations is a failure to fulfil the duty, together with a fault element of gross negligence (manslaughter) or an intention to kill or cause serious harm (murder). However, our primary interest here lies in what the offence requires of the individual, and it ought to require the fulfilment of a duty which is, in most instances, a duty to take reasonable steps or, perhaps, a duty to do one's utmost. Thus the draft English code of 1985 provided that the act must be 'one which, in all the circumstances, including his age and other relevant personal characteristics, he could reasonably be expected to do'.[162] Somewhat similarly, section 1(2)(a) of the Children and Young Persons Act 1933 states that a parent is deemed to neglect a child by failing to provide adequate food, clothing or medical aid; but it also states that if the parent is 'unable otherwise to provide such food, clothing' etc, the parent will be liable only if he or she has 'failed to take steps to procure it to be provided . . .'. Although the word 'reasonable' is not used in this formulation, that seems to be its gist. Where the duty arises from a family obligation or from a relationship of interdependence within a household, as in the much-criticised decision in *R v Stone and Dobinson*,[163] the failure to fulfil the duty must be culpable in the sense that fulfilment of the duty must have been within the defendant's power. That decision is put in doubt by the defendants'

---

[160]   See part 2.3(iv)(a) above.

[161]   Above, n 94 and accompanying text.

[162]   Law Com No 143, *Codification of the Criminal Law: A Report to the Law Commission* (1985), cl 20(2)(a). This provision did not survive into the Law Commission's draft criminal code: Law Com No 177 (1989), cl 16.

[163]   Above, nn 51 and 78 and accompanying text.

borderline mental handicap and their lack of basic social skills (eg being unable to use a telephone). This is a case where the principle of capacity should have been invoked to support a defence to liability.

On these facts, as in many other omissions situations, all that the law can properly require of someone is that they take reasonable steps to fulfil their duty. To require that an individual succeed in averting death or injury, for example, would be most unfair. English law is much clearer about this where another person is the principal actor and the defendant's duty is to report or to protect. Two duty-situations may serve as illustrations here. First, the 'failure to protect' offence is committed where the defendant 'failed to take such steps as he could reasonably have been expected to take to protect V from the risk'.[164] In such situations it would usually be reasonable to expect the defendant household member to notify the police or child protection services about what is going on. The wording of the statute suggests that in some situations it may be reasonable to expect the household member to intervene physically, by interposing herself or himself in order to give protection to the child or vulnerable person. But this would be to ask a great deal if the principal perpetrator is violent and powerful or armed, or if there is a history of violence in the household;[165] it is difficult to accept a criminal law requirement that one should put oneself in physical danger, although preventing the violent abuse of a child might be one of the strongest conceivable situations for this, unless the witness is also vulnerable. A second illustration might be where the owner of a car is sitting in the car while someone whom the owner has allowed to drive is driving dangerously. The car owner may not be able to stop the dangerous driving, but is surely able to order the driver to stop the vehicle, and so that is what the law should reasonably require.

Similar principles should apply where the primary duty lies on the defendant. For example, in cases where the defendant has accidentally created a dangerous situation and has a duty to do something about it, that duty can only be to do what is reasonable.[166] The law could not fairly demand that the defendant should act to remove the danger created; it can only properly require the person to take reasonable steps to remove the danger, as by alerting the emergency services and taking any positive action that can be taken without personal danger. The same approach should be taken to knowledge of the criminal law, as was submitted in part 5 above: it is not reasonable for complete knowledge to be expected, only that every person should take reasonable steps to acquire an understanding of relevant laws and equally that the state should take steps to publicise new or misunderstood laws.

However, almost all these formulations place reliance on the concept of reasonableness. As argued in part 4 above, this term alone does not give adequate warning of what the law requires of the individual. It is fair to say that the law should not generally require more than the taking of reasonable steps or taking

[164] Domestic Violence, Crime and Victims Act 2004, s 5(1)(d)(ii); see above, part 3(i).
[165] Cf the arguments of Herring (above, n 67) and the evidence of domestic abuse (above, n 68).
[166] Above, part 3(iv).

such actions as can reasonably be expected of the defendant, especially calling the emergency services. But the fairness of that statement relates to the quantitative element of individual responsibility – what it is reasonable to expect of a person in such situations – and does not necessarily satisfy the communicative element – how to give people fair warning of what they are actually required to do. The duty to report is clear, but the problems begin when there is an argument in favour of requiring more, even some kind of physical action in cases where the defendant's duty might be said to be strongest (perhaps where the defendant is the parent of a child in peril, or is the creator of the dangerous situation that threatens another).[167] Certainly the principle of capacity should be given prominence, to the extent that a defence of impossibility should be recognised in appropriate circumstances.[168] In *Brown*, as noted above,[169] the Court referred 'any physical impossibility or lawful excuse'; if that could be stretched to 'reasonable excuse', then this could take account of fear, shock and other emotions that may prevent a person from reacting appropriately in a known duty-situation. Moreover, English law rightly draws the line at family loyalty, and neither in 'failure to protect' cases nor in suspected terrorism cases are close family ties permitted as mitigation, let alone as grounds for a defence.[170] Rule-of-law principles require greater specificity than that, however, and the law must clarify the nature of the obligations imposed by 'failure to protect' offences, by duties to family and friends, and by voluntarily incurred obligations which do not arise from contracts or other agreements. As argued in part 2.4 above, because of the relative rarity of affirmative duties imposed on individuals by the criminal law, it is especially important that rule-of-law values are respected.

2.8 CONCLUSIONS

Omissions are 'special' in some senses: our psychological and social reactions to those who allow things to happen are different (and usually less condemnatory) from our reactions to those who make things happen. The equivalence or neutrality thesis – that omissions should always be treated in the same way as acts – is untenable: omissions are generally less culpable, although we have identified a few cases where the equivalence thesis holds.[171] The main task above has been to focus on the arguments in favour of recognising a criminal-law duty in various sets of circumstances. What has become clear, however, is that it is

---

[167] Alexander (above, n 143), 129.
[168] For elaboration, see A Smart, 'Responsibility for Failing to do the Impossible' (1987) 103 *LQR* 532; see also s 2.01(1) of the American Law Institute's *Model Penal Code* (1962), referring to 'the omission to perform an act of which he is physically capable'; and s 4.2(4) of the Commonwealth Criminal Code Act 1995 (Australia), which provides that 'an omission to perform an act is only voluntary if the act omitted is one which the person is capable of performing'.
[169] Above, n 161.
[170] See above, n 125 and accompanying text.
[171] See n 2 above and accompanying text.

necessary to grapple with some fundamental issues of what the state may properly require of individuals if progress is to be made on the criminalisation of omissions, within a rule-of-law framework.

The context must be set by a conception of the appropriate political relationship between the state and its citizens. This is a vast issue, but two elements stand out here. First, the state has an obligation to make provision for security and the prevention of harm, and for the prevention and investigation of crimes; this should entail duties to provide police and emergency services, services for the protection of children, for the support of families, and so forth. Secondly, the state also has an obligation of justice, which includes respect for individual rights. Thus rights such as the presumption of innocence and the privilege against self-incrimination should be respected by any procedural or substantive criminal laws. The state's obligation of justice means also that it has a general duty to publicise its criminal laws and, given their unusual or exceptional nature, particularly its omissions offences. As for the individual, she or he must accept certain strong limits on behaviour (the prohibitions of the criminal law), and also certain obligations such as those flowing from the 'principle of compulsory process' (eg the duty to give evidence, to serve on a jury if required, etc).

There may be good reasons for the criminal law to place further obligations on individuals. A precondition is that failing to do *x* in the given situation is morally wrong. The strongest sense of moral wrongness arises when three principles can be triangulated – the principle of urgency, the priority of life, and the principle of opportunity and capacity. The priority of life suggests that situations involving possible death should give rise to duties to act, particularly in terms of reporting an event (or, if conditions are favourable, making some physical intervention).[172] The arguments are therefore much stronger for life-threatening situations than for 'terrorism' (as a general proposition, ie not confined to life-threatening situations), or for money-laundering. There are also strong arguments for the recognition of duties in 'closed' situations such as the home or household, where vulnerable people (such as children or the physically or mentally challenged) might be particularly at risk of physical or sexual harm. We also noted that many duty-situations may be characterised as conditional positive obligations: if a person undertakes a certain activity or enters a certain business, he or she should expect to take on certain duties. Conditional affirmative obligations are also to be found in sexual offences law: there is a duty to take reasonable steps to ascertain whether the other party consents to sexual activity, and also a duty to ascertain the age of young people involved in sexual activity, and to that extent the relevant offences involve an omission.

---

[172] Cf the protestations of Fletcher (above, n 54), 633: 'As a category of "criminals", people who fail to avert harm are hardly dangerous to society. Bank robbers, rapists, hired assassins, muggers – they are dangerous because they take the initiative in causing harm'. What little purchase this statement has is derived from the choice of the term 'dangerous' and its implication of positive action. Conceding that omissions may be less reprehensible than acts, but insisting on the priority of life, would indicate a different conclusion.

Finally, the justifications for each duty must be scrutinised in relation to the level and intensity of liability and to the clarity and demands of the duty. It is unacceptable to leave to the courts the question whether a duty arises in a given type of situation, and absolutely unacceptable if conviction for so serious an offence as manslaughter may follow. Further, any criminalisation of omissions should require of the citizen only what can be reasonably expected in the situation. Imposing a duty on professionals to report ill-treatment is straightforward. Imposing a general duty on individuals to report serious offences (or, further, their suspicions about serious offences likely to occur) is a much more sensitive issue. At present legal systems tend to have a mixture of *ad hoc* reporting requirements, reflecting the priority of life, the importance of protecting children, fear of terrorist activity and other concerns. A general reporting requirement for serious crimes would therefore be a major step; moreover, any such requirement raises issues such as conflicting loyalties (the priority of life should outweigh private loyalties), police use of the offence as a controlling or bargaining tool, and uncertainty about what qualifies as a 'serious offence'. Beyond a duty to report, some physical intervention might appropriately be required in clear and urgent situations such as police officer–victim, parent–child, or perhaps household member–vulnerable person, but generally should not be expected of ordinary citizens.

3

Ignorance of the Criminal Law, and Duties to Avoid It

'IGNORANCE OF THE law is no defence', so we are told from an early stage in our legal studies. Or, to be more accurate, 'ignorance of the criminal law is no defence to a criminal charge'. That appears to be the rule in this country, apart from a couple of well-established exceptions and another possible one. I will argue that it is a preposterous doctrine, resting on insecure foundations within the criminal law and on questionable propositions about the political obligations of individuals and of the state. In developing these arguments, I will draw attention to the differing problems of ignorance of the criminal law in three broad areas – regulatory offences, serious crime, and offences of omission – with a view to suggesting that there is a great deal more that the state needs to do if the issue of ignorance of the criminal law is to be dealt with adequately and fairly.

I begin by scrutinising the relevant rule of English criminal law and the justifications offered for it. I then go on to situate the 'ignorance-of-law' doctrine in the context of the principle of legality and the rule of law, those bastions of liberal criminal law theory. Part 3 then explores the three broad areas of the criminal law, and parts 4 and 5 carry the debate into the political obligations of individuals and of the state in these matters.

3.1 IS IGNORANCE OF THE CRIMINAL LAW NO DEFENCE?

Although there is no codified or definitive statement of English criminal law, there is agreement among judges and scholars that at common law the general principle is that ignorance of the criminal law is no defence. Thus Blackstone stated that mistake or ignorance of the law 'is in criminal cases no sort of defence'.[1] Likewise the current edition of Smith and Hogan contains the proposition that ignorance of the criminal law 'is no defence even where the crime is not one commonly known to be criminal', adding that 'ignorance of any of the

---

[1] 4 Bl Comm 24. For fuller exploration of the history, see ER Keedy, 'Ignorance and Mistake in the Criminal Law' (1908) 22 *Harvard Law Review* 75.

thousands of regulatory offences is no defence'.[2] Similarly, in leading cases such as *Johnson v Youden* (1951)[3] and *Churchill v Walton* (1967),[4] the proposition that ignorance of the criminal law is no defence was treated as fundamental to the court's reasoning; and in *Grant v Borg* (1982)[5] Lord Bridge delivered the strong statement that:

> 'The principle that ignorance of the law is no defence in crime is so fundamental that to construe the word "knowingly" in a criminal statute as requiring not merely knowledge of the facts material to the offender's guilt but also knowledge of the relevant law, would be revolutionary and to my mind wholly unacceptable'.

Although there is no legislative re-statement of the principle, certain statutory provisions assume it to be the general position.[6] When the English Law Commission reviewed the subject in the context of the draft criminal code, no change was proposed.[7]

There are some recognised exceptions, which will not be examined in detail here. They include cases where a statutory instrument has not been appropriately publicised,[8] where the making of an expulsion order has not been drawn to the attention of its subject,[9] and where mistake or ignorance of the (civil) law negatives the definition of particular crimes.[10] It is also possible that reasonable reliance on an official statement of the law may provide either a defence or a procedural bar to conviction.[11]

More significant for our purposes are the foundations of the doctrine that ignorance of the criminal law should be no defence. Blackstone followed many of his predecessors in asserting that 'every person of discretion . . . is bound and presumed to know' the law;[12] but, as Austin pointed out, that is merely an assertion without normative force, and as a statement of fact it is plainly an

---

[2] Smith and Hogan, *Criminal Law* (12th edn, 2008, by D Ormerod), 319; see also AP Simester and GR Sullivan, *Criminal Law: Theory and Doctrine* (4th edn, 2010), 680; A Ashworth, *Principles of Criminal Law* (6th edn, 2009), 220–24.

[3] [1950] 1 KB 544, at 546 per Lord Goddard CJ.

[4] [1967] 2 AC 224, at 236 per Viscount Dilhorne, followed eg by Lord Taylor CJ in *Attorney-General's Reference (No 1 of 1995)* [1996] 2 Cr App R 320, at 333.

[5] [1982] 1 WLR 638, at 646B.

[6] For a recent example, relating to the offences of encouraging or assisting a crime, see the Serious Crime Act 2007, s 47(2), (3) and (4).

[7] Law Com No 177, *A Criminal Code for England and Wales* (1989), vol 1, cl 21; vol 2, paras 8.29–8.32.

[8] Statutory Instruments Act 1946, s 3(2).

[9] *Lim Chin Aik v R* [1963] AC 160. For similar exceptions to the principle in the Model Penal Code, see s. 2.04 of the Code and the comments by MD Dubber, *Criminal Law: Model Penal Code* (2002), 103–4; in Australia, see Criminal Code Act 1995 (Commonwealth), s 9.4(1) for the rule and (2) for the exceptions; in Canada, see s 19 of the Criminal Code ('ignorance of the law by a person who commits an offence is not an excuse for committing that offence').

[10] Eg *R v Smith (DR)* [1974] QB 354 (knowledge that property 'belonged to another'), *Secretary of State for Trade and Industry v Hart* [1982] 1 WLR 481 (knowledge that disqualified from auditing company's accounts because of positions previously held).

[11] Model Penal Code s 2.04 (USA); the English authorities are reviewed by A Ashworth, 'Testing Fidelity to Legal Values: Official Involvement and Criminal Justice' (2000) 63 *MLR* 633, at 635–42.

[12] See n 1 above.

exaggeration.[13] Austin relied on a consequentialist rationale: that allowing a defence of ignorance of the law would create insuperable difficulties for prosecutors in proving that defendants knew the law, resulting in acquittals of guilty people.[14] Others have preferred the consequentialist argument that to allow the defence would be to create a perverse incentive, since it would inevitably have the effect of encouraging ignorance of the law.[15] These two consequentialist reasons seem to have been regarded as sufficient to sustain the English rule, subject only to the exceptions mentioned in the previous paragraph. The only argument of principle that is sometimes invoked is that, since serious offences are *mala in se*, individuals should know that they are wrong and therefore criminal.[16] More will be said about this argument in due course.

3.2 THE IGNORANCE-OF-LAW DOCTRINE AND THE PRINCIPLE OF LEGALITY

We must begin by challenging the two consequentialist arguments for the strict doctrine, since they are unpersuasive and inadequate. The first one – Austin on the difficulty of proof for the prosecution – seems no more powerful in this context than in relation, for example, to the doctrine of *mens rea*.[17] Jurisdictions that allow ignorance of the criminal law as a defence appear not to experience significant practical difficulties.[18] As for the second consequentialist argument, the 'false incentive' reasoning, this is inapplicable to any legal system that allows the defence only where there are 'reasonable grounds', since a form of reasonableness requirement would remove any perverse incentive to remain in ignorance.[19]

As for the argument of principle based on a distinction between '*mala in se*' and '*mala prohibita*', the best we can do at this stage is to place a huge question-mark over it. The two terms are highly contested, and do not represent agreed categories of offence. It is extremely doubtful whether there is a sufficiently robust distinction between *mala in se* and *mala prohibita* to provide reassurance that people who are ignorant of the criminal law will be convicted only if they are blameworthy. The ignorance-of-law doctrine crystallised at a time when perhaps the contours of the criminal law were reasonably knowable and widely

---

[13] J Austin, *Lectures on Jurisprudence* (5th edn by R Campbell, 1885), I, 482.

[14] Ibid 482–83.

[15] See generally G Williams, *Textbook of Criminal Law* (2nd edn, 1983), 452; DM Kahan, 'Ignorance of Law *is* an Excuse – but only for the Virtuous' (1997) 96 *Michigan Law Review* 127; F McAuley and JP McCutcheon, *Criminal Liability* (2000), 570–75; J Chalmers and F Leverick, *Criminal Defences and Pleas in Bar of Trial* (2006), Ch 13, 261–65.

[16] See the discussions of this in the case of the Pitcairn Islanders, *Christian v R* [2007] 2 AC 400.

[17] Indeed, this counter-argument was made as long ago as 1881 by OW Holmes in *The Common Law* (M DeWolfe Howe (ed) (1963) [1881]), 48. See further ATH Smith, 'Error and Mistake of Law in Anglo-American Criminal Law' (1985) 14 *Anglo-American Law Review* 3, 17.

[18] See the discussion of South Africa, n 26 below and accompanying text.

[19] For further discussion, see nn 29–31 below and accompanying text.

known;[20] in the pages that follow, I will raise doubts about whether this is true now, even if it was then. The use of terms such as *mala in se* assumes a moral consensus that is unlikely to exist, except in relation to a small core of egregious crimes. Questions about the justice or injustice of the ignorance-of-law doctrine are therefore unlikely to be resolved by applying these Latin labels.

At least, however, that argument has brought our discussion to the question of fairness and justice. Leaving aside the (in any event unsustainable) consequentialist reasons, is it not unjust and morally wrong to convict people of crimes the existence of which they were not aware? Douglas Husak and Andrew von Hirsch argue in favour of courts being allowed to assess the moral legitimacy of the defendant's belief or ignorance, except in cases where the defendant knows that his conduct is injurious.[21] Two of the issues they discuss will be taken further here – the relevance of ignorance of the criminal law to the concepts of *mens rea* and guilt, and to culpability and excuse.

First, can it be argued that knowledge of the criminal law is so fundamental to the idea of criminal guilt that it should be recognised as part of the doctrine of *mens rea* or, at least, as a precondition of criminal liability? Two lines of argument are relevant here. First, criminal conviction involves public censure, and that should be limited to cases of culpable wrongdoing. Insofar as ignorance of the law negatives culpability, it should be relevant either to *mens rea* or as a defence. Secondly, there is a link with the principle of legality or rule of law, which in this context requires legal norms, and especially those of the criminal law, to be clear, stable, and not retrospective in their operation. The principle of legality is usually said to require fair warning of clear and certain criminal laws that do not operate retrospectively. An individual living under the European Convention on Human Rights can expect to be protected from retrospective criminal laws (Article 7), from laws that are not sufficiently certain and from powers that do not contain sufficient safeguards against arbitrariness (the 'quality of law' test derived from Article 7).[22] All of these points of principle relate to the law's function of guiding people's conduct, and it was Lon Fuller, in his catalogue of 'eight ways to fail to make a law',[23] who emphasised the fundamental importance of publicising laws and making them available to citizens.

The next question, then, is whether the element of notice and fair warning is properly seen as crucial to criminal liability. For example, John Gardner has argued that 'those of us about to commit a criminal wrong should be put on

---

[20] Compare the confidence with which Thomas Hobbes, *Leviathan* (1651), II. xvii. 4, proclaimed that 'ignorance of the law of nature excuseth no man', since everyone is supposed to have a developed sense of reason, with Keedy's denunciation of the presumption that everyone knows the law as 'absurd': Keedy, n 1 above, at 91.

[21] D Husak and A von Hirsch, 'Culpability and Mistake of Law' in S Shute, J Gardner and J Horder (eds), *Action and Value in Criminal Law* (1993).

[22] See further B Emmerson, A Ashworth and A Macdonald (eds), *Human Rights and Criminal Justice* (3rd edn, 2012), Ch 16; B Juratowitch, *Retroactivity and the Common Law* (2008), Ch 3; and ATH Smith, 'Judicial Lawmaking in the Criminal Law' (1984) 100 *LQR* 46, at 69–73.

[23] LL Fuller, *The Morality of Law* (rev edn, 1969), Ch II; and see also the discussion by J Waldron, 'The Concept and the Rule of Law' (2008) 43 *Georgia Law Review* 1, at 7.

stark notice that that is what we are about to do'.[24] He goes on to argue, developing Hart, that it is through the ideal of the rule of law that 'the mental element in crime is connected with individual freedom:

> 'According to the ideal of the rule of law, the law must be such that those subject to it can reliably be guided by it, either to avoid violating it or to build the legal consequences of having violated it into their thinking about what future actions may be open to them. People must be able to find out what the law is and to factor it into their practical deliberations. The law must avoid taking people by surprise, ambushing them, putting them into conflict with its requirements in such a way as to defeat their expectations and frustrate their plans'.[25]

In so far as this points in the direction of recognising knowledge of the criminal law as part of *mens rea*, or at least as standing on a par with it, this would be a radical departure from the common law tradition. It is a step that has been taken in South Africa: in *S v De Blom*[26] the Appellate Division held that the defendant's ignorance of the law prohibiting her from taking jewellery out of the country negated the *mens rea* required for the offence. This law has been applied for over 30 years without causing great problems of proof. Thus criminal liability 'invariably depends upon intention in respect of the unlawfulness element, as well as the other elements, of the crime in question'.[27] It appears that, for offences of negligence, ignorance of the law may only lead to acquittal if it was not reasonable to expect the defendant to know about the law.

Should English law adopt this approach, and reject the traditional doctrine entirely? The importance of individuals not being taken by surprise by the criminal law is, as Gardner argues, fundamental to the rule of law. The South African approach is one way of ensuring that the individual has fair warning that he or she is about to violate the law, and thereby that the rule of law is complied with. The problem, however, is that this approach does indeed offer a perverse incentive to people to remain ignorant, or, more realistically, it fails to require people to make an effort to understand the criminal law. Thus part of my argument is that it is fair and right to expect people to make a reasonable effort to find out what the law is; the other part of my argument, to be developed more fully below, is that the state should also have an obligation to provide more information about the criminal law and about changes made to it, thus making the citizen's task easier. To impose this moderate duty on people is not inconsistent with the rule of law, so long as the state discharges its duty to make the criminal law sufficiently accessible.

[24] J Gardner, 'Wrongs and Faults' in AP Simester (ed), *Appraising Strict Liability* (2005), 69–70; although there may be situations, as Husak and von Hirsch have argued (n 21 above), where it would not be reasonable to excuse someone who knew that he was injuring another.

[25] J Gardner, 'Introduction' in HLA Hart, *Punishment and Responsibility: Essays in the Philosophy of Law* (2008), xxxvi; and see also the use of Hart's arguments by ATH Smith, n 17 above, 23.

[26] 1977 (3) SA 513; for discussion see J Burchell, *Principles of Criminal Law* (3rd edn, 2005), 494–507.

[27] Burchell, ibid, 503.

My provisional conclusion, then, is that there is a fundamental problem of principle with the English ignorance-of-law doctrine. It subjects people to the censure of conviction when they may not have been culpable. It is not suited to protecting individuals from conviction in situations in which it would not be reasonable to expect them to have discovered the criminal prohibition, a failure that contravenes the rule of law and which cannot be justified by reference to any broader 'public interest'.[28] Three ways of responding may be considered. *First*, ignorance of the criminal law could be allowed to negative liability, as part of or on a par with *mens rea*. That was rejected above, on the ground that it is fair and right to expect citizens to acquaint themselves with the criminal law and wrong to give them an incentive to remain ignorant. *Secondly*, ignorance of the law could be treated as a bar to trial, resulting in a stay of proceedings.[29] This would recognise the state's role in the matter, and would of course avoid subjecting the defendant to trial. The Crown Prosecution Service would have guidance to the effect that a person who was reasonably ignorant of or mistaken about the law should not be prosecuted; to prosecute in spite of that guidance would be an abuse of process. However, the state's role would typically not have been so great as in cases of entrapment and of acting on official advice as to the law,[30] and it is questionable whether reasonable ignorance of the law is not more appropriately dealt with by a lay tribunal (magistrates, jury) in the same way as duress and other excusing conditions.

My preference is therefore for a *third* approach: that of introducing a general but circumscribed defence of excusable ignorance of the law. This implies that citizens rightly have duties to try to find out about the criminal law, and these should be linked to the kind of duties of the state advocated by Fuller – notably the duty to give adequate publicity to laws, and particularly to criminal laws. Thus where a new piece of legislation introduces a whole raft of offences, the details of which receive little publicity (as a possible example, the Sexual Offences Act 2003), it may be understandable that an individual remains ignorant of some of the legislative changes, in the sense that there has been nothing to put her or him on notice. In those circumstances the law should recognise excusable ignorance of criminal law as a defence, supporting it by reference to (for example)

---

[28] *Pace* Holmes, who wrote that 'It is no doubt true that there are many cases in which the criminal could not have known that he was breaking the law, but to admit the excuse at all would be to encourage ignorance where the law-maker has determined to make men know and obey, and justice to the individual is rightly outweighed by the larger interests on the other side of the scales'. *The Common Law*, n 17 above, 46.

[29] I am grateful to Jeremy Horder for pressing this form of response. Its claims would be strongest in sexual offences cases where a prosecution has been brought contrary to the Crown Prosecution Service guidance, although (as he pointed out) such guidance is not law.

[30] See, eg, *R v Looseley* [2002] 1 Cr App R 29 (entrapment), *Postermobile plc v Brent LBC*, *The Times*, 8 December 1997 (acting on official advice as to the law). Abuse of process would be relevant if the law had not been adequately published, as was argued (unsuccessfully) in relation to Pitcairn Island in *Christian v R* [2007] 2 AC 400, on which see H Power, 'Pitcairn Island: Sexual Offending, Cultural Differences and Ignorance of the Law' [2007] *Crim LR* 609, at 619–25, and D Oliver (ed), *Justice, Legality and the Rule of Law: Lessons from the Pitcairn Prosecutions* (2009).

Gardner's argument that the individual must have 'lived up to expectations in a normative sense'.[31] Thus the defence should be based on an appropriate objective standard – what could reasonably be expected of an individual in the defendant's position – perhaps a little broader than the defence in Germany and Sweden.[32] The grounds of excuse would be negligence-based, what could 'reasonably be expected', and it would be proper for this to be subject to capacity-based exceptions for those unable to perform this citizen's duty.[33]

On this model the rule of law cuts both ways, being part of the framework that constrains those in positions of public authority by imposing on them duties relating to the way in which they should carry out their legislative functions.[34] There is room for debate about the degree of certainty that is required to fulfil the ideal of the rule of law: that ideal is sometimes expressed as if absolute certainty of definition is achievable and desirable, whereas in practice it is not and the law can be used to guide behaviour even if it does not achieve maximum certainty.[35] Insofar as the criminal law employs both rules and standards, it should strive to ensure that terms such as 'reasonable' or 'dishonest' are supplemented by illustrations or sub-principles that enhance people's ability to use them as a guide.[36]

3.3 THREE DIFFERENT CONTEXTS FOR IGNORANCE OF THE CRIMINAL LAW

In this section I consider the different problems created by three different strains of criminal law – first, regulatory offences; secondly, serious crime; and thirdly, offences of omission. Given the frequent references in the press to the large numbers of new criminal laws created in recent years, it is important to assess the nature of the problem. I have directed surveys of the new criminal laws created by primary legislation in 1995 and in 2005. The overall numbers of criminal offences catalogued – 188 for 1995 and 165 for 2005 – are somewhat lower than those commonly cited, but the surveys were confined to primary

---

[31] J Gardner, *Offences and Defences* (2007), 124; Gardner does not refer specifically to ignorance of the criminal law, so this is my application of his doctrine.

[32] Some support for this approach was expressed by Glanville Williams, *Criminal Law: The General Part* (2nd edn, 1961), 291–293]. For the German position, providing a defence of 'unavoidable mistake of law', see M Bohlander, *Principles of German Criminal Law* (2009), 119–21, and Husak and von Hirsch, n 21 above, 169–70; for the Swedish approach, providing a defence of 'manifestly excusable' or 'clearly excusable' mistake of law, see S Wennberg, 'Criminal Law' in M Bogdan (ed), *Swedish Law in the New Millenium* (2000), 172.

[33] See the discussion in Ashworth, n 2 above, 185–89; and, in German, by U Neumann, 'Die Schuldlehre des Bundesgerichtshofs – Grundlagen, Schuldfähigkeit, Verbotsirrtum' in C Roxin and G Widmaier (eds), *50 Jahre Bundesgerichtshof, Festgabe aus der Wissenschaft* (vol IV, 2000), 83–109.

[34] See Waldron, n 23 above, 11: 'the Rule of Law aims to correct abuses of power by insisting on a particular mode of the exercise of political power: governance through law'.

[35] Eg Gardner, n 24 above, 52, Fuller, n 23 above, 41–44 on the 'morality of aspiration' and, more fully, TAO Endicott, 'The Impossibility of the Rule of Law' (1999) 19 *OJLS* 1.

[36] See L Alexander and K Ferzan, *Crime and Culpability* (2009), 291–92.

legislation, whereas considerable numbers of new offences (almost entirely 'regulatory') are created by subordinate legislation.[37] In terms of culpability requirements, some two-thirds of the offences in both years imposed strict liability, mostly without providing for a defence of reasonable excuse. There was otherwise considerable diversity in the culpability requirements,[38] but it is not necessary to explore them here. It may, however, be worth adding that there was express provision for placing a burden of proof on the defendant in 15 (8 per cent) of new offences in 1995 and 19 (12 per cent) in 2005.

(A) 'Regulatory' Offences

In order to elucidate the context of the new laws, let us focus on 2005 – a year in which there was no 'traditional law reform', in the sense of changes to the kinds of criminal law that are commonly taught in universities and contained in textbooks on the subject. It appears that the predominant purpose of 2005's new offences was to reinforce the regulatory state, by creating offences that support or underpin regulatory mechanisms. The concept of the regulatory state refers to the state's withdrawal from providing services directly and the creation of regulatory and licensing authorities to govern other organisations that provide the services.[39] In this context, the role of the criminal law is increasingly that of handmaiden to the regulatory state, a reinforcement mechanism that is seen as an essential part of the package. However, the title 'regulatory offences' for this section is a loose one, and should not be taken to suggest that all these offences are minor or non-imprisonable, for example.

The research suggests that, typically, a regulatory structure is supported by offences of three kinds – offences of failure to comply, offences of giving false information, and offences of obstruction. Five examples of offences of failure to comply are:

- failing without reasonable excuse to notify the regulatory authority of a change of position in relation to a gambling licence (section 101(6) Gambling Act 2005);
- failing without reasonable excuse to notify the regulator of a relevant conviction (section 138(3) Gambling Act 2005);
- failing without reasonable excuse to comply with a litter clearing notice (section 20 Clean Neighbourhoods and Environment Act 2005);

[37] A point well made in Law Commission Consultation Paper No 195, *Criminal Liability in Regulatory Contexts* (2010), paras 1.17–1.20.

[38] For example, some offences had strict liability as to one element and intent or full knowledge as to another. Some offences used terms such as 'permitting', 'connivance', 'invites' and other operative words that do not fit into a simplified scheme. I am grateful to Dr Rhonda Powell for research assistance on this project.

[39] Cf D Osborne and T Gaebler, *Reinventing Government* (1992) with M Moran, *The British Regulatory State – High Modernism and Hyper-Innovation* (2003).

– failing without reasonable excuse to furnish name and address to an officer who believes that controlled waste is being transported (section 37 Clean Neighbourhoods and Environment Act 2005);
– failing without reasonable excuse to comply with requirements in a disclosure notice (section 67 Serious Organised Crime and Police Act 2005).

It is readily apparent that the obligations imposed on individuals by these various offences are different. In particular, the first two examples, from the Gambling Act 2005, pre-suppose a regulatory framework of which the individual is aware. These are situations in which the state (probably through the relevant regulator) ought reasonably to have taken steps to draw the new framework to the attention of those likely to be subject to it. The last three examples, on the other hand, concern situations in which an individual has been served with a notice or placed under a requirement – and, presumably, informed about the penalty for non-compliance. In some (but not all) of these cases, this will be sufficient to deal with any problems of ignorance of the criminal law, since and insofar as the person is informed about the relevant law before the conduct or omission that constitutes the offence.

The second type of offence commonly encountered in this context is that of giving false information. It may accompany an offence of failure to comply with a requirement, as in the following example from the Clean Neighbourhoods and Environment Act 2005. Section 28 empowers 'an authorised officer of a principal litter authority' to require a person to give name and address. Subsection (8) then provides:

'A person commits an offence if –

(a) he fails to give his name and address in response to a requirement to do so under sub-paragraph (7) above; or
(b) he gives a false or inaccurate name or address in response to a requirement under that sub-paragraph'.

Now, quite apart from the fact that the officer's demand may be accompanied by reference to the penalty for non-compliance, some might take the view that the offence under (b) is one in which there is a clear *malum in se* involved – lying. It is one thing to stand on one's supposed rights and to refuse to give name and address (which would be unsuccessful in this context, since there is no such right); it is quite another thing positively to mislead the official by giving a false name and address, and it could be argued that everyone should know that this is wrong and likely to be an offence. In this context, there is likely to be very little purchase for an argument that one was unaware that litter was regulated by 'authorised officers' with statutory powers of this kind. A lie to a public official is presumptively criminal, some would say[40] – although whether anything can be described as 'presumptively criminal' will be discussed further below.

---

[40] The Law Commission, n 37 above, para 3.123, points out that many of these offences are unnecessary since the conduct would be criminal under the Fraud Act 2006. For analysis of the Act, see D Ormerod, 'The Fraud Act 2006 – Criminalising Lying?' [2007] *Crim LR* 193.

The third typical kind of offence is that of obstructing an officer of the regulatory agency. Although the format of these offences varies a little, examples are to be found in several 2005 statutes. The Education Act 2005 gives certain rights of entry to inspectors, and these are supported by an offence (in section 24(4)) of intentionally obstructing an officer in the exercise of any of the listed functions; similarly, section 51(2) of the Serious Organised Crime and Police Act 2005 creates an offence of wilfully obstructing a designated person acting in the exercise of a power under that Act. Section 31(1) of the Commissioners for Revenue and Customs Act 2005 creates an offence of obstructing an officer without reasonable cause, a slightly different formulation. Further examples are probably unnecessary: these are situations in which either the officer is likely to explain his or her powers to the individual, or the regulatory context of the officer's intervention is apparent, before the conduct that constitutes the offence.

However, all these suggestions about the context in which the offences will arise are contingent. The defence of reasonable ignorance should be available, even if it would rarely be raised. It is possible that an individual may be unaware of, or mistaken about, the regulatory context. Since a criminal conviction constitutes a form of public censure which may be followed by punishment, there is good reason to require the state to ensure that there is adequate publicity for the introduction of new powers and new offences. We should start from the proposition that citizens should be able to plan their lives so as to avoid falling foul of the criminal law, and that leads to a requirement of fair warning. If the criminal law is to be used as a reinforcement mechanism for regulatory agencies, those agencies ought to take steps (on behalf of the government) to ensure that those involved in the relevant specialist activities are made aware of the law's existence.

(B) Serious Crimes

Having earlier criticised the concept of '*mala in se*' it may seem strange to use the term 'serious crimes' as a sub-heading. More will be said about the nature of this category towards the end of the section, but for the moment the target crimes are those for which imprisonment is often used. We now leave the year 2005 and cast our eyes more generally over recent years, considering some important changes in the criminal law that affect all of us – not just those involved in activities that are subject to regulatory schemes. A prime example of this is the Sexual Offences Act 2003. By any yardstick this was an important piece of criminal legislation. The first 71 sections all created new offences, and many of them extended the ambit of the criminal law. The aim was to modernise the law relating to sexual offences by, for example, creating gender-neutral offences and ensuring proper protection for the vulnerable. But how much of the detail seeped into popular consciousness? How many teachers of criminal law would claim to know, without referring back to the statute, many of the details of this Act? Just how have the new offences been publicised, and has that been adequate?

Let us consider a few cases. In *R v Thomas* (2006),[41] T admitted having sex with a girl of 17. She had been in foster care with T and his wife from the age of 11 to 17, but had recently moved away into separate accommodation, after which the sexual activity took place. He was convicted of an offence contrary to section 25 of the Sexual Offences Act (sexual activity with a child family member). Two important features of this offence are (i) that it applies where the child is under 18, whereas the general age of consent is 16, and (ii) that the concept of 'family relationship' on which the offence depends includes a person who 'is or has been [the child's] foster parent'. A central element in T's mitigation was that he did not know that what he was doing was a criminal offence. The Court of Appeal recognised this to the extent of reducing his sentence from four to two-and-a-half years. Leaving aside the question of whether the sentence was harsh for a man with no previous convictions and excellent references from other people fostered by him, what does this case imply about the state's responsibilities? Might it not be argued that the government had failed to discharge its obligation to publicise the changes in sexual offences law? In particular, how much publicity had been disseminated among foster carers (and former foster carers) about the wider ambit of the criminal law post-2003? To argue that such conduct involves a *malum in se* or is 'presumptively criminal' is unconvincing, since the issue is a change in the outer limits of the law. A person may well know that there is a law of sexual offences, and a law prohibiting incest or familial sex, without realising that it applies to former foster children who are over 16 but under 18.

A greater challenge for my approach is raised by the various offences of possession of a prohibited firearm, contrary to section 5 of the Firearms Act 1968. Section 5 contains a long list of types of gun, forms of adaptation of guns, and types of ammunition that fall within the prohibition and therefore the offence; the list has been amended by subsequent legislation. By virtue of section 287 of the Criminal Justice Act 2003, section 51 of the Firearms Act was amended so as to impose a mandatory minimum sentence of five years' imprisonment on persons convicted of a section 5 offence, unless the court finds 'exceptional circumstances'. In *R v Rehman and Wood* (2006)[42] both offenders had received the mandatory minimum sentence, both having unsuccessfully pleaded 'exceptional circumstances'. R had purchased a replica blank-firing handgun over the internet. The police traced him from this internet purchase and, when they came to R's house, he showed them where the gun was and said he was unaware that it was illegal to possess it. In fact, it fell within a prohibited category because it was less than 60 cm long with a barrel of less than 30 cm. His openness in purchasing the gun with his own credit card, for delivery to his own home, tends to support his story of ignorance. Lord Phillips CJ held that part of the context is that the offences have been held to impose strict liability;[43] but that the primary

---

[41] [2006] 1 Cr App R (S) 602.
[42] [2006] 1 Cr App R (S) 404.
[43] This was confirmed, after a survey of the authorities, in *Deyemi and Edwards* [2008] 1 Cr App R 25.

purpose of the legislation is to ensure that courts impose deterrent sentences on offenders, and 'if an offender has no idea that he is doing anything wrong, [the prospect of] a deterrent sentence will have no deterrent effect on him'.[44] With that, the Court of Appeal quashed the mandatory minimum sentence and substituted two years – still a substantial sentence for someone genuinely ignorant of the law. However, the Court took a different view of W's case. W was a collector of firearms, most of which were kept in locked cabinets as required. However, on searching his house the police found a number of other weapons, including a shotgun with its barrel shortened. This was in the loft, and W said he had inherited it from his grandfather. It was a prohibited weapon, but he said he did not realise this. The Court of Appeal held that in his case the mitigation was insufficient to amount to 'exceptional circumstances', largely because W had been a collector for many years and should have checked whether it was lawful for him to have this shotgun in his possession. In terms of ignorance of law, the issue in these firearms cases is that both defendants knew that the possession of firearms was restricted by the criminal law, but neither of them knew that the regulations applied to the type of firearm in their possession.

It might be argued that the defendants should have been put on notice by knowledge of the general prohibition; but this would not account for a case like *R v Beard* (2008).[45] When B's mobile home was searched for drugs, the police found no drugs but did find 66 small cartridges. These contained CS gas and were therefore prohibited ammunition contrary to section 5 of the Firearms Act, triggering the mandatory sentencing provisions. It was accepted that the cartridges could easily be mistaken for blanks, that B was unaware that their possession was illegal, and that B had no means of firing them. The Court of Appeal therefore quashed the mandatory sentence of five years and replaced it with two years' imprisonment.

These four decisions – one under the Sexual Offences Act, three under the Firearms Act – raise serious questions about the English approach to ignorance of the law. Of course the state has a duty to put in place laws that protect young people from sexual exploitation and to protect people in general from the risks created by unregistered firearms, but the highest priority should be given to the use of education and information in order to reduce the number of offences being committed. Waiting until a case arises, imposing strict liability as to knowledge of the law so as to convict the person concerned, and then following it with a disproportionate sentence so as to use this offender as a means (adequate or not) of warning others is monumentally unjust. Not surprisingly, given the general understanding of the common law, ignorance of the criminal law was apparently not raised as a defence in the above cases; whether the facts of

---

[44] Note 42 above, at 413; and see also Lord Bingham's statement that 'one important function of the criminal law is to discourage criminal behaviour, and we cannot be discouraged if we do not know, and cannot reasonably easily discover, what it is we should not do'. T Bingham, *The Rule of Law* (2010), 37–38.

[45] [2008] 2 Cr App R (S) 232.

all the cases would fit the kind of excusatory defence proposed earlier is hard to say. Yet two points should be clear. First, it is unjustifiable for the state to provide for the conviction of people who are not at fault, in the hope of deterring others from engaging in the same kind of conduct.[46] Secondly, all four defendants were people without criminal records, and still they ended up serving substantial prison terms.[47] That should raise strong alarm bells, since these are not cases involving aggression or major dishonesty.

Finally, what does the term 'serious crime', or *mala in se*, add to this discussion? It is possible to argue that there may be a 'moral core' of 'real crime', so that there are substantial elements of consensus about values as well as significant dissensus or agnosticism in other spheres.[48] However, that is not enough to establish a workable category of *mala in se* that can be used to separate crimes that people can reasonably be expected to know about from crimes that it is unreasonable to expect people to know about, not least because of the amount of discretion that would leave to the authorities.[49] Even if there is a 'functional differentiation' between 'real crime' and quasi-criminal 'regulatory offences', it cannot be 'mapped on to legal doctrine' in any secure way.[50] This is particularly so when the issues concern the boundaries of sex offences or the limits of firearms law.

(C) Positive Duties and Criminal Omissions

If we return for a moment to the survey of new criminal offences created by primary legislation, one finding was that a significant minority – 39 (or 21 per cent) in 1995 and 42 (or 26 per cent) in 2005 – are offences of omission. They penalise an individual or company for failing to do something. Offences of omission pose a special problem. The typical character of criminal offences is that they are prohibitions and are intended to operate negatively: do not assault, steal or damage, for example. Offences of omission embody obligations and require people to do positive acts, or to respond to situations in a particular way. Since the criminal law imposes fewer responsibilities on individuals to prevent

---

[46] The classic rebuttal of this utilitarian argument is by H Morris, 'Persons and Punishment' (1968) 52 *The Monist* 475.

[47] Beard alone had one previous theft conviction, but the court treated him as being of good character. Cf the sentences in the older cases, much cited on the issue of strict liability, such as *R v Howells* [1977] QB 614 (mistaken belief that gun was classed as antique no defence, fined £100) and *R v Hussain* [1981] 1 WLR 416 (lack of awareness that metal tube was prohibited article no defence, fined £100).

[48] See the fine but neglected article by P Rock, 'The Sociology of Deviancy and Conceptions of Moral Order' (1974) 14 *British Journal of Criminology* 139.

[49] Herbert Packer regarded control of official excesses as the main practical reason in favour of the principle of legality: HL Packer, *The Limits of the Criminal Sanction* (1969), 85.

[50] N Lacey, 'Legal Constructions of Crime' in M Maguire, R Morgan and R Reiner (eds), *The Oxford Handbook of Criminology* (4th edn, 2007), 184.

harm than not to cause harm,[51] and perhaps because it is widely thought that such duties are rare, it is all the more important to ensure that people are put on notice of the positive expectations that the criminal law has of them. Thus in the famous US case of *Lambert v California* (1957)[52] L went to reside in Los Angeles and was charged with the offence of being a convicted felon, and failing to register that she was residing in the city for more than five days. Her defence was that she was unaware of this law, but the court ruled that ignorance of the law was no excuse and convicted her. The Supreme Court held that this conviction violated due process: the offence penalised an omission, based on status (presence) rather than an activity, and there was nothing to alert L or anyone in her position to the requirements of the law. *Lambert* therefore demonstrates the heightened importance of re-assessing the common law's 'ignorance of law' doctrine in relation to omissions.

In order to develop those thoughts, let us explore the nature of the special problems by discussing two categories of omissions. First, we will examine some offences that can be committed by omission, focusing on the origin and nature of the duties that this involves. Secondly, we will consider general offences of omission, offences that penalise an omission rather than the causing of an outcome by omission.

(i) Offences of Commission by Omission

First, there are many duties that apply to people generally, and which are capable in English law of grounding liability for property offences, offences against the person, and more. Thus, it is theft if a person finds property and decides to keep it, without forming a belief that the owner could not be found by taking reasonable steps;[53] and it is fraud if a person fails to disclose information that there is a duty to disclose, and does so dishonestly with the required intent.[54] It is a feature of the fraud offence that the list of duties to disclose is not set out in the criminal law, and has to be sought elsewhere. It is difficult to say how widely known these duties are. But, unless they are widely known, they presumably vie in the popular consciousness with sayings such as 'finders keepers' and 'tell no secrets, tell no lies'. So it is at least possible that some people are 'ambushed'[55] by duties of which they are unaware.

This possibility also arises in relation to much more serious offences. Common law manslaughter may be committed by gross negligence in failing to fulfil a duty of care owed by the defendant to the victim. Many of these duties

---

[51] RA Duff, *Answering for Crime* (2007), 110. For discussion of the broader question of the extent to which people are culpable for not doing things, see Chapter 2 above, and J Glover, *Causing Death and Saving Lives* (1977), esp Ch 7, and AP Simester, 'Why Omissions are Special' (1995) 1 *Legal Theory* 311.

[52] (1957) 355 US 225.

[53] Theft Act 1968, ss 3(1) and 2(i)(c).

[54] Fraud Act 2006, ss 1(2)(b) and 3.

[55] The term used by Gardner, n 25 above.

of care are obligations on people in particular situations to take positive action, but where can the conscientious citizen find out about them? Two such duties are established in legislation. One well-known duty is that of the parent towards her or his child. The parent may be convicted of the discrete offence of child neglect and, where the parent causes death through failure to feed or to ensure the safety of the child, the conviction may be for manslaughter (if grossly negligent) or for murder (if there is an intent to cause death or really serious harm).[56] Another statutory duty, well known among those to whom it applies, is that of organisations to safeguard the health and safety of their employees and others affected by their activities, recently reinforced by the creation of an offence of corporate manslaughter.[57]

Beyond these statutory duties, the other duties are listed only in the criminal law books, since they have been developed by the judiciary on a case-by-case basis. The list includes relatively straightforward duties such as that of electricians to ensure the safety of their customers,[58] more controversial duties such as that of a lorry driver to ensure the safety of people who agree to be loaded into a sealed container with a view to illegal immigration (a duty that was held to exist despite their consent),[59] and manifestly controversial duties such as that of a person who accepts another into her household and assists that other by washing her when she falls ill (which was held to create a duty to take action to ensure her continued welfare).[60] These are all common law duties, created by the courts in the cases to which they were first applied, resulting in convictions for the serious offence of manslaughter and, usually, in a sentence of imprisonment.

There are two major problems with criminal liability for omissions created in this way. First, there may be nothing to put the individual on notice of the duty-situation, not least because there may be a widespread belief that in England and Wales there are few legal duties to care for one's fellow human beings.[61] The parable of the good Samaritan is an indication of what it may be morally right to do, but, we are told, not of English criminal law. This is quite a well-known difference of orientation between English and continental European criminal law. Thus the problem for the individual is that the existence of duty-situations is exceptional, since English law's general position is not to impose legal duties to care for others, and that even where the courts have considered whether to

---

[56] Children and Young Persons Act 1933, s 1. For murder by a parent's omission, see *R v Gibbins and Proctor* (1918) 13 Cr App R 134; for an unsatisfactory manslaughter decision, see *R v Lowe* [1973] QB 702 and Ashworth, n 2 above, 275.

[57] Note 28 above.

[58] *R v Prentice* [1994] QB 302.

[59] *R v Wacker* [2003] QB 1203.

[60] *Stone and Dobinson* [1977] QB 354. Much more could be said about this decision, not least because of doubts that the defendants were intellectually capable of understanding what the law was held to require. For discussion of the general issue, see J Herring and E Palser, 'The Duty of Care in Gross Negligence Manslaughter' [2007] *Crim LR* 24.

[61] Surveys suggest that the position is more nuanced: eg PH Robinson and JM Darley, *Justice, Liability and Blame: Community Views and the Criminal Law* (1995), 42–50, and B Mitchell, 'Public Perceptions of Homicide and Criminal Justice' (1998) 48 *British Journal of Criminology* 453.

impose a duty the boundaries often remain uncertain. Thus it is not clear to what extent one has a duty to care for the health of members of one's family beyond young children and a spouse or partner: at common law the existence of duties towards adult children is unclear,[62] and a similar lack of certainty attends the incidence of duties towards friends[63] and towards people who 'stay over' at one's home.[64]

The second major problem is that the list of duty-situations remains open for judicial development, so that individuals often cannot know whether their failure to intervene in a given situation will lead to liability for the serious offence of manslaughter. It is regarded as a fundamental principle that criminal legislation should not be retroactive, and that fair warning is given, yet the judicial recognition of new duty-situations in these serious cases would seem to violate this.[65] This conflict between principle and practice is evident in European human rights law: while the Strasbourg court affirms the principle of non-retroactivity of criminal laws as 'an essential element in the rule of law', the leading judgment goes on:

> 'There will always be a need for elucidation of doubtful points and for adaptation to changing circumstances. Indeed, in the United Kingdom, as in other Convention States, the progressive development of the criminal law through judicial lawmaking is a well entrenched and necessary part of legal tradition. Article 7 of the Convention cannot be read as outlawing the gradual clarification of the rules of criminal liability through judicial interpretation from case to case, provided the resultant development is consistent with the essence of the offence and could reasonably be foreseen'.[66]

Whether it could 'reasonably be foreseen' that the English judiciary would abolish the marital immunity in rape, rather than waiting for Parliament to do so, remains a matter of acute controversy.[67] Beyond that, the judgment leaves considerable scope for judges to extend the law, with correspondingly less protection for individuals from what Gardner calls 'ambush'.[68] This reduced protection is felt particularly acutely in omissions cases, where there may be nothing to put the person on notice that a criminal-law duty is likely to be imposed. The

---

[62] Compare, eg, *R v Smith* (1826) 2 C & P 449 (no duty to maintain adult brother who was mentally handicapped) and *R v Sheppard* (1862) L & C 147 (no duty towards daughter of 18, even though age of majority was then 21), with *R v Evans* [2009] EWCA Crim 650 (mother had duty towards daughter of 16, but the latter's half-sister had a duty based on other grounds – grounds which are contestable, see G Williams, 'Gross Negligence Manslaughter and Duty of Care in "Drugs" Cases' [2009] *Crim LR* 631), and Chapter 2.3(a) above.

[63] Compare, eg *R v Sinclair* (1998) 148 *NLJ* 1353 with *Lewin v Crown Prosecution Service* [2002] EWHC Admin 1049.

[64] Cf the seminal US decision in *People v Beardsley* (1907) 113 NW 1128, and the discussion of German law by GP Fletcher, *Rethinking Criminal Law* (1978), 612–13 and by M Bohlander, n 32 above, 40–45.

[65] GP Fletcher, 'Criminal Omissions: some perspectives' (1976) 24 *American Journal of Comparative Law* 703; P Westen, 'Two Rules of Legality in Criminal Law' (2007) 26 *Law and Philosophy* 229, at 268.

[66] *SW and CR v United Kingdom* (1995) 21 EHRR 363, at [3435].

[67] For analysis, see Emmerson, Ashworth and Macdonald, n 22 above, Ch 16.

[68] Note 25 above.

Law Commission ought to re-assess the approach it adopted two decades ago, when it decided that it would be best to leave the courts to develop the incidence and scope of duty-situations.[69] Now is the time for the 'appropriate study and consultation' that it felt unable to carry out then.[70]

One way of increasing notice and fair warning might be to follow German law in having a legislative statement of the categories of duty, in order to give general notice to citizens. However, the German categories of duty are very similar to those recognised judicially in England (eg 'creation of dangerous situations', 'joint dangerous enterprise or mutual trust'), and it is still for the courts to interpret them and to specify how the general standards (eg 'close personal relationship') apply to different situations.[71] Moreover, if the law were to provide a defence of excusable ignorance of criminal law, should that be available to a person who sought legal advice and was told of the *possibility* that a court would find a duty on the given facts? Is it consistent with the rule of law to require people to desist from conduct because there is a mere possibility that it may be criminalised, thereby according to the law a fairly broad chilling effect that operates to reduce the extent of individuals' liberties?

Finally, brief mention may be made of the various duties to act created by the law of accomplice liability. The courts have developed the so-called 'control principle', whereby a person who has the power to control another's actions may be held liable for aiding and abetting a crime committed by that other person if the person fails to take an opportunity to intervene and stop the commission of the offence. For example, if the owner of a car is a passenger in the car at the time when its driver is committing road traffic offences, the owner is held to be aiding and abetting if he or she makes no attempt to stop the offences.[72] The same might apply where the owner or tenant of a house knows that a visitor is committing offences and takes no steps to prevent this. How widely known are these and other duties to act that are contained in the law of accomplice liability?

(ii) General Offences of Omission

English law contains a considerable number of general or 'pure' offences of omission, which penalise failure to act in a given situation. One common law offence of this kind, more frequently prosecuted in recent years, is that of misconduct in a public office, which includes cases of failure by a police officer to intervene to prevent an offence from taking place or continuing.[73] It may be reasonable to assume that those who hold public offices are aware of their

---

[69] Law Com No 177, *A Criminal Code for England and Wales: vol 2, Commentary on Draft Criminal Code Bill* (1989), paras 7.9–7.13.

[70] Ibid, para 7.11.

[71] Bohlander, n 32 above, 40–45.

[72] *Du Cros v Lambourne* [1907] 1 KB 40 (dangerous driving).

[73] *R v Dytham* (1979) 69 Cr App R 387.

duties.[74] Similarly, it was argued in part 4 above that relatively few difficulties of awareness are likely to arise from the new omissions offences created in 1995 and 2005 because they generally take the form of 'failing to comply with a notice', a formulation that requires a notice to have been issued to the individual concerned. In general terms, therefore, the question of fair warning is taken care of by the context, which is usually a regulatory one.[75] Of broader application are various offences of omission in road traffic law, such as failing to comply with an indication given by a traffic signal[76] and, in particular, failing to stop after an accident and failing to report an accident.[77] Motorists have a duty to familiarise themselves with these duties.[78]

Rule-of-law concerns have sometimes been raised about the general offences of failure to rescue persons in peril that are common in continental European countries. Whether such an offence should be introduced into English law is not for debate here, but it is important to connect 'easy rescue' offences with the current argument. Typical is the relevant offence in German law, which penalises anyone who

> 'does not render assistance during accidents or a common danger or emergency, although it is necessary and can be expected of him under the circumstances, particularly if it is possible without substantial danger to himself . . .'.[79]

As a general omissions offence this is limited to emergency situations, and it does not require heroism or indeed any reaction beyond the individual's capabilities – in particular, the duty can be fulfilled in most situations by calling the emergency services, and the individual is not required to risk any personal danger. Critics have questioned the indeterminacy in concepts such as 'common danger' and 'emergency' and in the precise extent of the duty: the proper response is to recognise that certainty requirements should be higher for omissions offences and to examine whether the standards here ('render assistance', 'without danger') do in fact afford sufficient warning.[80]

It was assumed above that a parent's duty to care for her or his young children is widely known;[81] but there is another duty-situation of which many people may be unaware. Moreover, this offence (unlike other general omissions offences)

---

[74] Cf, however, the interpretation of this offence in *R v W* [2010] EWCA Crim 372.

[75] The Law Commission, n 37 above, Part 2, argues that regulatory approaches may be particularly appropriate where a 'target group' can be engaged; this presumably means communicating the law to members of the group.

[76] Road Traffic Act 1988, s 36.

[77] Ibid, s 170.

[78] They are stated in *The Highway Code*, paras 286–87 (accessed at www.direct.gov.uk on 12 April 2010).

[79] Section 323c, translated by M Bohlander, *The German Criminal Code* (2008), 200; on the corresponding French offence, see A Ashworth and E Steiner, 'Criminal Omissions and Public Duties: the French Experience' (1990) 10 *Legal Studies* 153; see generally A Cadoppi, 'Failure to Rescue and the Continental Criminal Law' in MA Menlowe and RA McCall Smith (eds), *The Duty to Rescue* (1993).

[80] See A Ashworth, 'The Scope of Criminal Liability for Omissions' (1989) 105 *LQR* 424.

[81] See n 55 above and accompanying text.

turns on the consequences that flow from the omission. Section 5 of the Domestic Violence, Crime and Victims Act 2004 creates the offence of allowing the death of a child or vulnerable adult in one's household, with a maximum sentence of 14 years. There was a good reason for creating some such offence, since previously there could be no conviction if a child died from injuries inflicted by either the parent or the parent's partner, and it could not be proved that the injuries were inflicted when both were present (which would make it possible to convict them both, on the basis that one would be the principal and the other would be the aider and abettor). However, the offence as drafted is much wider than necessary to cover such cases. The offence is committed where an individual is a member of the same household as a child under 16 or vulnerable adult and where that individual ought to have known that there was a significant risk of serious physical harm to that child or vulnerable adult from another member of the household. If in those circumstances the individual fails to take reasonable steps to protect the child or vulnerable adult, he or she is guilty of this serious offence.[82]

It seems perfectly possible that many people are unaware of this offence. Let us take the case of *R v Khan and others* (2009).[83] A family living in England brought a young woman of 19 from Kashmir to marry their son (her cousin). The son began to beat her, and six months after their marriage he beat her to death. Four of his relatives – his mother, his two sisters, and the husband of one sister – who lived in the same house, and who were also related to the victim, were convicted of the section 5 offence of allowing the death of a vulnerable adult in their household, and the three women were sentenced to periods of imprisonment.[84] One controversial element of the case is whether the victim was a 'vulnerable adult' within the meaning of the statute: the Court of Appeal held that she was, at least since the husband's first major attack on her three weeks before her death, and stated that the description could apply to an otherwise fit adult who is in a position of utter dependency. The other controversial element, not mentioned in the report, is whether the four family members who were convicted knew of their statutory duty to protect the victim by intervening or by summoning help. How widely known is this duty? Is it enough to suggest that it is a duty of common humanity, or does that come up against the point already mentioned, that it may be thought to be a moral duty but not a legal one? I repeat that no such point appears to have been taken in the case itself; but, again, the primary interest of the state should be in spreading knowledge about this and other duties. There is some difficulty in doing this until the ambit of the concept of 'vulnerable adult' is settled, as the Court of Appeal attempted to do here. As we saw in (i) above, this is even more difficult where the courts are free

---

[82] For analysis and discussion, see J Herring, 'Familial Homicide, Failure to Protect and Domestic Violence – Who's the Victim?' [2007] *Crim LR* 293, and J Herring, 'Mum's Not the Word: An Analysis of Section 5 of the Domestic Violence, Crime and Victims Act 2004' in C Clarkson and S Cunningham (eds), *Criminal Liability for Non-Aggressive Death* (2008).

[83] [2009] EWCA Crim 2.

[84] The man, who spent much less time at home because of work commitments, received a suspended sentence with an unpaid work requirement.

to extend the categories of duty case-by-case, as they have done in the sphere of common law manslaughter.

3.4 WHAT ARE THE STATE'S OBLIGATIONS?

Most of the discussion so far has focused on the imposition and extent of the duties on individuals, notably duties to learn about the criminal law and positive obligations to act in situations where the criminal law imposes omissions liability. Now it is time to explore and to justify the obligations on the state, and to consider how they should interact with the obligations imposed on individuals. I start from the proposition that two of the fundamental duties of the state are the duty of security and the duty of justice. As part of the justification for its existence the state should recognise a duty to provide a framework of security for its citizens, by way of laws and processes designed to protect people from physical harm. And, because the state is composed of individuals whose autonomy should be respected, the state should honour the duty of justice in the laws and procedures that it creates.

The State's duty to provide a framework for security may be presented as part of a bargain between the state and its citizens, a bargain in which a measure of security is provided in return for a measure of obedience. The right to security is therefore a core right with a corresponding duty on the state, as Liora Lazarus argues:

> 'The corollary of a "right to security" is a state duty to develop structures and institutions that are capable of responding to and minimising "critical and pervasive threats" to human security (by which I mean an absence of harm in the most core physical sense of harm to person)'.[85]

This is the narrow and focused sense in which the state has a duty of security. To what extent is an individual committed to accepting the laws that are enacted in furtherance of this duty? Three lines of argument will be considered briefly, in support of the duty of a citizen to accept the laws that are the outcome of democratic processes. One such argument is that voters consent, actually or tacitly, to the powers of the state by virtue of their involvement in the process. Another argument is that we can fairly posit a hypothetical contract as the basis of political obligation, inasmuch as citizens can be taken to have agreed to the authority of the state in exchange for the state assuring various benefits to citizens. This leads towards a further argument – that the citizen's obligations to the state stem from the acceptance, or at least from the positive seeking, of benefits provided by the state.[86] All these are in-principle arguments in favour of indi-

---

[85] L Lazarus, 'Mapping the Right to Security' in BJ Goold and L Lazarus (eds), *Security and Human Rights* (2007), 329.

[86] These are painfully clipped summaries of sophisticated arguments, elaborated and assessed (for example) by D Knowles, *Political Obligation: A Critical Introduction* (2010), Chs 7, 8 and 9. See further Chapter 2.2 above.

viduals having an obligation to obey the law (and, therefore, as already argued, having an obligation to make reasonable efforts to ascertain the law). The arguments are conditional on the state performing its part of the bargain, in terms of creating the appropriate level of security, and it is therefore for debate whether they are applicable to particular individuals in a particular jurisdiction at a given time.

These arguments do not suggest that citizens' obligations to the state are unlimited. The fundamental duty of justice requires the state to recognise certain rights of individuals in its dealings with them; notably, in the sphere of criminal law, the state should respect the rule of law and the principle of legality, so that citizens as rational agents may plan their lives so as to avoid criminal conviction. Discussing these doctrines in part 2 earlier, we noted that they are said to require that criminal laws be certain, stable and not retrospective, and that they tell in favour of insisting on culpability as a requirement of criminal liability. We then followed Fuller in emphasising a further element – that laws, and particularly criminal laws, should be adequately publicised. This stems from the same rationale as the other elements: if the law is to serve as a guide to conduct, at least to the extent of allowing citizens to apply their minds so as to avoid becoming subject to the criminal sanction, it should be reasonably accessible. It is suggested, not that knowledge of the law will always lead people not to commit crimes, but that there are some people (as in the cases discussed in part 3(B) above) who commit crimes merely out of ignorance.

This is where the two fundamental state duties – of security, and justice – come together. In order to perform its duty of security effectively, the state should take steps to ensure that fewer of the wrongs and harms it criminalises actually take place. It is better that crimes do not occur in the first place than that we convict people after they have committed them: the result should be fewer victims and fewer offenders. This resolves itself into two interlocking duties – the state's obligation to take steps to ensure greater publicity for criminal laws, and the obligation on individuals to take reasonable steps to ascertain the criminal law. For the state, one way of trying to reduce the number of crimes is to put greater energy into publicising the criminal law. This is also a political duty, since it is unjust to convict an individual, let alone to impose imprisonment, by maintaining a strict rule that ignorance of the criminal law is no excuse. The state's duty of justice indicates that it should convict only in cases of culpable ignorance of the criminal law, leaving individuals with some obligation to inform themselves reasonably (bearing in mind the state's own duty of publicity) about the contours of the criminal law.

So the argument I wish to make is (a) that the state has a duty to provide security to its citizens, which includes the creation of criminal offences in order to prevent harm and to punish wrongdoers, (b) that the offences it creates should be so framed as to impose the censure of conviction only for culpable wrongdoing, (c) that the state should recognise that citizens as rational agents may legitimately expect to use the criminal law in order to guide their conduct (indeed it should want them to do so in order to avoid criminality), and d) that therefore the state (through its duty of justice) should have the obligation to ensure that its criminal laws are not only certain, stable, prospective and based on proof of culpability, but also that they are sufficiently publicised.

3.5 SOME PRACTICAL IMPLICATIONS

These propositions now need to be linked to a more practical line of reasoning. What does it mean to require that criminal laws be 'reasonably accessible' and that they be 'sufficiently publicised'? In practice, 'reasonable accessibility' places an obligation on the State to ensure that the contents of its criminal laws are available in a form and in places to which people can have access. That access ought surely to be 'practical and effective', not 'theoretical and illusory'.[87] The notion of reasonable accessibility should not place an unfair burden on citizens, for example by requiring access to a computer and/or reasonable literacy and computer literacy.[88] There is every reason to expect people to acquaint themselves with laws relevant to their particular activities, whether it be motoring, commerce, building, or whatever. But is there sufficient reason to expect all citizens to be *au courant* with the latest activities of the legislature, let alone secondary legislation? I think not. We are a long way from an ancient Greek republic in which all citizens actively participate in law-making; we must recognise that it is quite unrealistic to expect everyone to know the criminal law under current conditions. I have argued that it is right to place some obligation on citizens – an obligation to take reasonable steps, perhaps – but it is the government that is in a position to make the real difference. The government can organise and co-ordinate the necessary mechanisms for informing citizens, and one strong reason why it should accept this responsibility is that it is in the state's interest that fewer people commit criminal offences (and that less harm is done).[89] Allowing crimes to be committed through ignorance amounts to a failure of the state's duty of security. So I propose four practical steps for consideration – a) complete accessibility of the text of criminal laws; b) availability of a simplified version of the criminal law for non-specialists; c) appropriate efforts to publicise that simplified version; and d) special attention to the education of children.

---

[87] To adopt phrases used by the European Court of Human Rights more generally; see, eg, *Artico v Italy* (1981) 3 EHRR 1.

[88] Recall the case of *R v Beard*, n 45 above; he was unable to read or write.

[89] One could propose an economic argument – that money spent on publicity may be more cost-effective than trials and punishments for those who offend; but my preference is to rely on the political argument.

(A) Accessibility of Complete Texts of Criminal Law

Finding out what is the criminal law presents a particular problem when so much legislation is secondary, by means of statutory instruments and other forms of order.[90] It is no less of a problem when legislation amending previous legislation is passed (and particularly if its commencement dates are staggered), and the official web-site fails to incorporate the latest amendments into the text of the law.[91] The Law Commission examined the problems in 2006, citing a complaint from children's organisations about the difficulty of identifying the current law through a mixture of primary and second legislation, referring to such information as 'fundamental to democracy'.[92] The government accepted the Law Commission's recommendation for a free electronic database of primary and secondary legislation, and the UK Statute Law Database (which was already being developed) is now available.[93] It does not yet include all laws: it aims to cover all primary legislation enacted since 1991 together with relevant secondary legislation, but that leaves a fair amount of law outside this particular database – not only pre-1991 laws, but also the common law. As noted earlier,[94] many offences, including manslaughter, remain governed by the common law, and are subject to judicial extension by, for example, the recognition of new duty-situations. How is the citizen expected to find out about these developments?[95]

(B) Preparing a Simplified Version of General Criminal Laws

Criminal laws aimed at particular forms of activity (often, regulatory offences) need to be explained to those involved in such activities, but our primary concern here lies with criminal laws that are generally applicable. The myriad new offences created by the Sexual Offences Act 2003 were mentioned above, and it is likely that even seven years later many people are unaware of some of the offences. Indeed, the Stern Review has recently recommended 'more publicity and information in simple language' about the 'basic elements of the Sexual Offences Act'.[96] This brings us directly to my next point – the importance of

---

[90] Failure to publish statutory instruments or other orders should afford a good defence to criminal liability: Statutory Instruments Act 1946, s 3(2), and *Lim Chin Aik v R* [1963] AC 160.

[91] This happened with the OPSI website (the Office of Public Sector Information) a few years ago, with the consequence that courts had been deciding cases under Regulations that had been superseded some five years earlier: see the strong words of Toulson LJ in *R v Chambers* [2008] EWCA Crim 2467, paras 55–62.

[92] Law Com No 302, *Post-Legislative Scrutiny* (2006), para 4.11.

[93] See www.statutelaw.gov.uk (visited 31 July 2010).

[94] See part 3(C)(i) above.

[95] The difficulties increase when a decision is unclear, often because there are multiple judgments: see Lord Bingham, n 44 above, 44–46.

[96] *A Report by Baroness Vivien Stern CBE of an Independent Review into how Rape Complaints are Handled by Public Authorities in England and Wales* (2010), 39.

informing people about the law in simple language.[97] Much criminal legislation is now difficult for lawyers to comprehend, let alone ordinary citizens;[98] if the drafting of statutes has to be so complex, efforts should be made to prepare a simplified and comprehensible version for communication to the citizenry. Two other details may be mentioned here. One is that any simplified version should give links to the place where greater detail is to be found. Awareness of the offence may be different from awareness of the relevant detail: a citizen may be aware that the Firearms Act criminalises possession of firearms without knowing that the definition extends to certain replica guns and certain forms of ammunition; one may be aware that downloading child pornography is treated as a serious offence without knowing that the definition of 'downloading' includes simply viewing. The simplified version of the law should give some examples, and then point to the need to check the details on the official web-site or (if the offence is governed by common law) elsewhere. Also relevant are cultural issues,[99] particularly in relation to foreign visitors to this country. In the old case of *R v Esop* (1836)[100] the judges ruled that a visiting sailor could be convicted of a sexual offence while in an English port, although he did not know that the conduct (lawful in his own country) was criminal here. This problem occurs now: certain forms of touching that amount to sexual assault in English law are not punishable in the laws of at least one Eastern European country, and its embassy in London has to deal with a number of cases every year in which visitors fall foul of English sexual offences law. Those who take a car to another country are usually informed of major differences in road traffic law; should there not be a one-page guide to selected English criminal laws for foreign visitors?

(C) Preparing and Implementing a Communication Strategy

Citizens need information about new criminal offences and about the ambit of the existing criminal law; and information is needed for adults and for children. Publicising new criminal offences requires a communication strategy from the department sponsoring the legislation: if the new offences concern a particular branch of industry, commerce or other activity, they require dissemination in a particular direction. Where it is the general criminal law that is being changed,

---

[97] One body of scholarship has developed the distinction between rules of conduct aimed at citizens and rules of liability and grading aimed at officials: the leading work is PH Robinson, *Structure and Function in Criminal Law* (1997), Appendix A of which contains a 'Draft Code of Conduct'.

[98] One example would be the new offences of encouraging or assisting crime, which spread the ambit of the criminal law very wide, but which cover some 20 highly technical sections of the Serious Crime Act 2007.

[99] See Power, n 30 above, and S Bronitt and B McSherry, *Principles of Criminal Law* (2001), Ch 7.6.

[100] 7 C & P 456. In *R v Hussain* [1981] 1 WLR 416, D's reaction on arrest was that the metal tube (which was held to fulfil the English definition of a prohibited firearm) was lawful in his own country and often used by children.

a broader communication strategy is required. History shows that, under certain conditions, publicity about a new law can enhance law-abidance: perhaps the best-known example is the introduction of the offence of driving with excess alcohol, with a fixed blood/alcohol ratio reinforced by breath testing, a law that was widely publicised and debated and which appears to have changed behaviour.[101] Other approaches would have to be tested for different types of crime, such as sexual offences and firearms laws, but publicity campaigns have been successful in other countries.[102] They should be regarded as a primary method by which the State carries through its duty of security. An additional difficulty, of which the Stern Report on rape reminded us, is that some criminal laws that are no longer new are still not widely and properly understood. This is not the place to propose detailed solutions: my aim is to point to a problem that should be remedied.

(D) The Special Problem of Children

There is a particular difficulty in relation to children, not least because the age of criminal responsibility remains at 10. No doubt a normal moral development should give them guidance which allows them to steer away from many forms of law-breaking, but it is not clear how far this can be expected to extend. Brooke LJ held that a prohibition in an anti-social behaviour order that required a boy of 14 not to commit any criminal offences was not only too wide but also demanded too much of a child of that age: he 'might well not know what was a criminal offence and what was not'.[103] That may be particularly true in the area of sexual offences, where there is considerable ambiguity in the reach of the criminal law. The Sexual Offences Act criminalises all kissing and intimate touching between children under 16, yet does so on the understanding that there will not be a prosecution unless there is evidence of exploitation or abuse. There are strong rule-of-law objections to that mode of law-making;[104] but if we are to have it, its implications for the realistic limits of the criminal sanction need to be spelt out to the young people concerned. The Sexual Offences Act has resulted in some convictions of young people for offences that are grossly

[101] The classic study is that of L Ross, *Deterring the Drinking Driver: Legal Policy and Social Control* (1982). A key element accompanying this particular legislative innovation was the perception of an increased probability of detection (ibid, 27–29). Simply creating a new law would probably be much less effective if the risk of being caught and prosecuted were thought to be low.

[102] On sexual assault laws in Canada, see JV Roberts, MG Grossman and RJ Gebotys, 'Rape Reform in Canada: Public Knowledge and Opinion' (1996) 11 *Journal of Family Violence* 133, at 141–42. See also M Manion, *Corruption by Design* (2005), 46–47, discussing the use of advertisements on buses, television and radio as part of the anti-corruption drive in Hong Kong.

[103] *R (on application of W) v Director of Public Prosecutions* [2005] EWHC Admin 1333. The Stern Report (n 96 above) expressed particular concern about ignorance of the law among young people.

[104] JR Spencer, 'The Sexual Offences Act 2003: Child and Family Offences' [2004] *Crim LR* 347.

disproportionate to their conduct,[105] but the real challenge is how to communicate to young people the ambit of the criminal law in these and other matters. Although schools teach 'citizenship', what is needed is a more concerted programme of education about those areas of criminal law that are likely to be relevant to them.

3.6 CONCLUSIONS

The aim of this chapter is to offer a critique of the common law doctrine on ignorance of the criminal law, with a view to moving discussions away from narrow (and unpersuasive) consequentialist arguments and opening up some wider issues of justice and political obligation. Three points have particular significance.

First, the common law doctrine that ignorance of the criminal law is no excuse has been shown to have insecure foundations. To exclude any defence based on ignorance of the criminal law is manifestly unfair, given the diverse, often technical, and changing content of the criminal law. To require actual knowledge of particular conduct's criminality would be to go too far in the other direction, since it is right to expect citizens to make reasonable efforts to find out the criminal law (so long as the state recognises its obligations too). It was argued that a defence of excusable or reasonable ignorance of the law would achieve the best alignment with fairness, bearing in mind the censure inherent in criminal conviction.[106]

Secondly, the state's duty of security requires not just the creation of laws to protect us from significant wrongs and harms, but also recognition of the state's obligations in relation to the accessibility of the criminal law and communication of its ambit to adults and to children. If the state takes proper steps to inform its citizens about the criminal law, the incidence of ignorance of the criminal law should decline, there would be fewer unfair convictions, and there might possibly be fewer crimes. The state's primary interest should be in ensuring maximum law-abidance without having to bring prosecutions, and this is in the interests of potential victims too. This obligation also flows from the state's duty of justice, respecting the right of individuals not to be convicted of offences of which it was not reasonable to expect them to have knowledge.

Thirdly, the state's duties of security and justice are particularly engaged in relation to omissions. Offences of omission are unusual in English criminal law, and are known to be so, and therefore the state must make a particular effort to draw any such offence to people's attention. The duties imposed by the courts when 'applying' the law of manslaughter have often had the impact of retro-

---

[105] Notably in the case of *G*, n 33 above, where only a minority agreed that, on the facts, convicting this boy of 15 of rape of a child under 13 was inappropriate (see the commentary at [2008] *Crim LR* 818). See further ch 7 below.

[106] Reasons for preferring this to the remedy of abuse of process were offered above: see text accompanying n 31.

active law-making on defendants, in the sense that a duty has been recognised for the first time. In the absence of any general principles stated in legislation, this raises serious questions of injustice. Similar reservations apply to the offence of allowing the death of a child or vulnerable adult in one's household, contrary to section 5 of the Domestic Violence, Crime and Victims Act 2004. And of course the same reasoning applies to my argument for the citizen's duty to take reasonable steps to understand the criminal law: it would be a positive duty of the kind that the state should take special steps to communicate.

These three points should lead the government, the Law Commission and the judiciary to re-appraise their approaches. The common law ignorance-of-law doctrine is theoretically and practically unsustainable. The criminal law, and particularly new crimes and extensions to existing crimes, must be properly communicated to the public. So much for the critical dimension of this chapter. Much more problematic is the task of devising a fair and workable response to excusable ignorance of the criminal law. Three particular difficulties may be mentioned in conclusion.

First, a defence of reasonable ignorance of the criminal law can only operate if there is a serviceable distinction between ignorance and mistakes of fact and ignorance and mistakes of law. Many of the firearms cases are close to the boundary;[107] but the thrust of this chapter has been that there are clear cases of ignorance of criminal law, such as *Thomas* on sexual offences,[108] and that it is important to focus on the principles that should apply to them.[109]

Secondly, there are still people who find a nagging attraction in the *malum in se* concept. The argument above was that there are very few *mala in se*, because in a culturally diverse country there is a range of different views about right and wrong. That argument is strong in relation to sexual offences, where the boundaries may change in a generation or from one country to another nearby, but it may be much weaker for possession of some types of firearm. Moreover, when members of a household (indeed, a family) stand by and fail to intervene as another family member repeatedly beats his wife, are we not all drawn to the argument that they must have known that it was wrong not to intervene? The answer offered here is that there is a significant distinction between knowing something is wrong and knowing that it is a (serious) criminal offence; and that this distinction is supported by English law's general and known reluctance to recognise positive duties to intervene. Our sympathies may sometimes point in a different direction, but the *malum in se* argument is too uncertain and too unruly to be relied upon in circumstances where there is excusable or reasonable ignorance of the criminal law. More difficult to accommodate is the probability

---

[107] See the cases cited at nn 42–47 above.

[108] Note 41 above.

[109] In the United States (and in Canada) discussions are dominated by the distinction between fact and law, and reasons for having congruent rules for mistakes of fact and law. Although there are undoubtedly some borderline difficulties between the categories of 'fact' and 'law', this should not be taken as a justification for neglecting, in the many clear cases, the legal and political issues highlighted here.

that many defendants may either suspect that their conduct is close to the borderline of crime or have a kind of partial ignorance, in the sense that they know there are prohibitions on firearms but do not know or are mistaken as to the details. Those cases have been treated here as falling within the ambit of reasonable ignorance, but some would prefer a narrower defence that does not extend to those who suspect that their conduct may be unlawful.[110]

Thirdly, at two crucial stages – in developing the argument for a defence of reasonable or excusable ignorance of the criminal law, and in discussing the State's duty of justice – particular emphasis has been laid on the values of the rule of law and the principle of legality. The criminal law must be certain, prospective and accessible in order to guide people's behaviour. Yet liberal criminal lawyers must note the tension that this creates: as Nicola Lacey has argued, 'criminal law confronts a serious challenge of legitimation' by proclaiming norms such as the principle of legality when it is manifestly unable to abide by those norms in many respects.[111] The compromises are evident in the arguments above in favour of an individual's duty to take *reasonable* steps to discover the law; in favour of legal specification of duty-situations that relies on broad terms such as 'joint dangerous enterprise or mutual trust';[112] in favour of the State's duty to make the criminal law *reasonably* accessible, and to take *reasonable* steps to communicate it to adults and children, and so forth. There is, however, no inconsistency in admitting that the criminal law is replete with contradictions and imperfections,[113] while pressing for greater recognition of ideals set out in part 2 above. The rule of law and principle of legality form part of what Fuller described as the 'morality of aspiration', rather than the 'morality of duty'.[114] For example, there may be various practical, political and other reasons for framing a criminal law in terms of standards (dependent on open-textured terms such as 'reasonable') at crucial points, rather than entirely by rules. The challenge then is to devise ways of rendering the standards more specific, through sub-principles or guidelines or illustrations, so as to bring the law closer to rule-of-law values.

---

[110] See, eg the arguments of WJ Stuntz, 'The Pathological Politics of Criminal Law' (2001) 100 *Michigan Law Review* 506.

[111] Lacey, n 50 above, 193.

[112] See the reference to German law, n 71 above.

[113] As demonstrated by A Norrie, *Crime, Reason and History* (2nd edn, 2001).

[114] Fuller, n 23 above, 43. However, Fuller characterised the duty to make laws accessible as part of the morality of duty, for the State, and not merely the morality of aspiration.

4

Should Strict Criminal Liability be Removed from all Imprisonable Offences?

GENERATIONS OF CRIMINAL lawyers have debated the place of strict liability in the criminal law. It is something of a paradox that criminal law textbooks emphasise the importance of *mens rea*, or (more broadly) culpability, as a moral and legal requirement for criminal conviction, and yet Irish criminal law, like English criminal law, contains many offences that depart from that standard by imposing a form of strict liability.[1] Most of these strict liability offences are supported, if at all, on the grounds that the penalty is low, that conviction carries little stigma, and that there is a strong economic argument for allowing these quasi-crimes, or public welfare offences (as they are sometimes called), to be dealt with quickly, efficiently and effectively.[2] Indeed, it is considerations such as these that have led many continental European jurisdictions to create a separate category of administrative offences, with expedited procedures and low penalties.[3] Whether Irish and/or English law should move in this direction, and create a separate category of minor offences, is not for discussion here, nor do I intend to discuss the important issues about the regulation of businesses and corporations by means of legislation that includes strict liability offences, where it is arguable that different rationales and different standards are applicable.[4] I will therefore leave aside the associated questions of social justice about the comparability of treatment of people in business as distinct from ordinary people committing offences at the same level of seriousness.[5]

Instead, I want to depart from the usual focus of debates about strict liability and turn the spotlight on serious offences. These, remarked Francis Sayre in his

---

[1] See F McAuley and P McCutcheon, *Criminal Liability* (2000), Chs 6 and 7.
[2] See the essays in AP Simester (ed), *Appraising Strict Liability* (2005), esp Ch 2.
[3] JR Spencer and A Pedain, 'Approaches to Strict and Constructive Liability in Continental Criminal Law' in Simester, n 2 above.
[4] See further, A Brudner, 'Imprisonment and Strict Liability' (1990) 40 *University of Toronto Law Journal* 738; J Braithwaite, 'Challenging Just Deserts: Punishing White Collar Criminals' (1982) 73 *Journal of Criminal Law and Criminology* 723; A von Hirsch, 'Reply to Dr. Braithwaite' (1983) 73 *Journal of Criminal Law and Criminology* 1164.
[5] See further, A Ashworth, *Principles of Criminal Law* (6th edn, 2009), Ch 5.5(a).

classic article, are 'wholly unlike public welfare offenses' and 'are subject to altogether different considerations'.[6] Sayre did not specify what those considerations are, but he implied that the usual run of arguments about quasi-crimes and the efficient disposal of cases is inapplicable here. Answers to the following questions, at least, must be found. Is it justifiable to convict a person of a serious criminal offence if strict liability is imposed as to a significant element of that offence? Is it justifiable to deprive a person of liberty, by means of a sentence of imprisonment, if the offence contains a material element of strict liability?

In choosing this topic I am, of course, aware that some related issues have been a constitutional battleground in Ireland in recent years, evoking strong reactions on both sides. I have neither the expertise nor the temerity to enter into that particular debate. What I want to discuss here relates to all common law jurisdictions, and explores the credentials of a general principle that strict liability should not be used for offences that are imprisonable. My exploration falls into four parts, with a view to yielding four central propositions.

4.1 WHAT IS STRICT CRIMINAL LIABILITY?

An essential preliminary point for discussion is the issue of terminology. The term 'strict liability' means different things to different people. In Canada there is a distinction between strict liability (where an offence provides that the defendant may prove that there was no fault, no negligence) and absolute liability (proof of no-fault irrelevant), but that distinction is not recognised in many other jurisdictions.[7] Moreover, that concept of strict liability sets itself against the presumption of innocence, by requiring the defendant to prove lack of fault, and that calls for a separate debate as to whether there is a specific and compelling justification for making an exception.[8]

In an important essay, Stuart Green has argued that the only proper concept of strict liability is a formal concept, not one of the various substantive concepts that have been put forward.[9] The formal concept that Green favours defines strict liability offences as those 'that contain at least one material element for which there is no corresponding mens rea requirement'.[10] This applies whenever it is possible to convict of an offence without proving fault as to all the material elements. Some of those offences also contain a requirement of intention or recklessness as to another element, but the point is that it is pos-

---

[6] FB Sayre, 'Public Welfare Offenses' (1933) 33 *Columbia Law Review* 55, at 75.

[7] See *R v City of Sault Ste Marie* [1978] 2 SCR 1299 and DR Stuart, *Canadian Criminal Law* (4th edn, 2001), Ch 3.

[8] For analysis of recent Irish decisions on the burden of proof, see C Fennell, *The Law of Evidence in Ireland* (3rd edn, 2009), 41–43 and 115–119.

[9] SP Green, 'Six Senses of Strict Liability: a Plea for Formalism' in Simester, n 2 above.

[10] Green, ibid, 2; McAuley and McCutcheon, n 1 above, 313. For analogous reasoning in relation to the presumption of innocence, see CJ Dickson in *R v Whyte* (1998) 64 CR (3d) 123, at 134–35.

sible to obtain a conviction without requiring fault as to all elements of the offence, since one or more of them imposes strict liability.

Green introduces a subsidiary distinction between 'constructive' and 'non-constructive' strict liability:[11] constructive strict liability arises where proof of fault is required as to an underlying wrongful element of the crime but there is strict liability as to the result element (an example would be the law of murder, under which a defendant may be convicted of murder if he intentionally causes serious injury resulting in death), whereas non-constructive strict liability arises where the *mens rea* required for the main element of the crime (usually a conduct element) does not imply any wrongdoing – for example, where the offence consists of dispensing a restricted medicine without a valid prescription, dispensing the medicine does not imply any wrongdoing. This is merely an illustrative distinction, since both kinds of strict liability fall within the formal meaning that he is advocating; but there are those who argue that strict liability is of diminished significance if fault is required as to the (underlying) wrong involved in the offence: in other words, constructive strict liability is supported on the basis that, by knowingly committing the (underlying) wrong, the offender changes her or his normative position in a way that fairly renders them liable for more serious consequences that occur, even if they had no awareness that those further consequences might result. Two obvious examples of this in Anglo-Irish law are the offence of murder, for which someone can be convicted if they merely intended to cause serious injury (strict liability as to causing death), and the offence of unlawful act manslaughter, for which someone can be convicted merely on the basis of intentionally or recklessly committing a relatively minor offence such as assault (strict liability as to causing death). There are historical reasons why the law takes this form, but I have argued elsewhere that this kind of 'moderate constructivism' is under-theorised.[12] The idea that commission of the basic wrong (eg the unlawful act in manslaughter cases) changes the defendant's (D) normative position so as to render him/her fairly liable for the death rests on nothing more than an unsubstantiated assertion, and raises the question of D's culpability in relation to that unforeseen result.[13] I recognise that constructive liability is less objectionable than pure strict liability, in the sense that constructive liability is usually based on a related element of fault, even though that fault may be morally too distant from the result (as in the law of manslaughter by an unlawful act) for it fairly to be imputed to D. The relevant point here is that such offences are rightly classified as forms of strict liability, since a person is liable to be convicted without requiring fault as to one material

---

[11] Green, n 9 above, 4.

[12] A Ashworth, 'A Change of Normative Position: Determining the Contours of Culpability in Criminal Law', reprinted as Chapter 5 below, critiquing J Gardner, *Offences and Defences* (2007), Ch 2, and J Horder, 'A Critique of the Correspondence Principle' [1995] *Crim LR* 759.

[13] Gardner's concession may be found in *Offences and Defences*, 246–47. Gardner shows that constructive liability is compatible with rule-of-law principles, since fair warning of liability is given; but it is not compatible with the fault principle.

element of the offence. However, my primary interest below lies not in the constructive variety, but in pure strict liability.

Lastly, in these preliminary definitional remarks, something must be said about risk and strict liability. Take the offence of causing death by dangerous driving: the element of causing death is one of strict liability, since the prosecution need not prove the existence of any fault specifically in relation to causing death. Such offences fall within the formal definition of strict liability, but they are much less objectionable than crimes of constructive liability, just considered. As Andrew Simester argues, such offences involve 'intrinsic risk': that is, the risk of death is intrinsic to the driver's culpability, since it is the reason why dangerous driving is criminalised and why the dangerous driving constituted a wrong.[14] There is still room for an argument that too much emphasis is placed on luck by having an offence of causing death by dangerous driving as well as an offence of dangerous driving. However, in so far as an offence of causing death by dangerous driving exists, as it does in many legal systems, it imposes formally strict liability for the death, but it does so in the context of a risk intrinsic to the wrong D is committing at the time. Although such offences fall within the formal definition of strict liability, they will be left out of the subsequent discussion because of the different considerations attending them.

This definitional discussion has therefore yielded my first proposition: *that an offence should be treated as a crime of strict liability if it provides for conviction without requiring fault as to at least one material element.* The justification for this is that it is this material element that makes the difference between conviction of this offence and either conviction of no offence, or conviction of a lesser offence (in the case of constructive crimes). This formal definition can be fulfilled where D has *mens rea* as to other elements of the offence; and, of course, it can also be fulfilled in those cases where D has *mens rea* or other fault as to the strict liability element. The key issue is whether the prosecution is required to prove fault as to all elements, or whether there is at least one element of the offence in respect of which there is no such requirement.

4.2 REASONS FOR REQUIRING FAULT FOR CRIMINAL CONVICTION

It is commonplace in legal textbooks that criminal offences, or at least serious offences, should require proof of fault. Usually this is expressed as the principle of *mens rea*: the principle that conviction should require proof that the accused intentionally or recklessly did the prohibited act, with knowledge or reckless knowledge as to any prohibited circumstances. My concern here is not to trace the historical development of these requirements,[15] or to refine the definition of

---

[14] AP Simester, 'Is Strict Liability Always Wrong?' in Simester, n 2 above, 44–46. English law does not quite measure up to this analysis, since 'dangerous' is defined in terms of causing injury or serious damage to property (Road Traffic Act 1988, s 2(3)).

[15] Impressively accomplished by McAuley and McCutcheon, n 1 above, particularly in Chs 1, 6 and 7.

the principle of *mens rea*, but rather to probe the foundations and rationale of the principle. Why has it become so influential throughout the common law world?

There are two principal arguments, which I will call the 'rule-of-law' argument and the censure-based argument. The first of these was developed by HLA Hart, who argued that it would be wrong to convict and punish anyone who had not been given 'a fair opportunity' to exercise the capacity for 'doing what the law requires and abstaining from what it forbids'.[16] The principle of *mens rea* is therefore identified as central to fairness in the criminal law, requiring advertence by the defendant to the prohibited consequences and/or prohibited circumstances.[17] The most important point is that, in so far as the criminal law only penalises people who have had a fair opportunity to avoid contravening it, it then becomes 'a method of social control that maximises individual freedom within the coercive framework of law'.[18] All of this is intimately connected with the idea of criminal law as a guide to action, and thus the principle of *mens rea* takes its place as one of the key requirements of the rule of law – alongside the requirements that the law be clear, stable, and not retroactive in its operation.[19] In this vein Joseph Raz, following Hart and Hayek, has argued that:

> 'Respecting human dignity entails treating humans as persons capable of planning and plotting their future. Thus, respecting people's dignity includes respecting their autonomy, their right to control their future'.[20]

What is unfolding here is a demonstrable connection between culpability requirements in criminal law and basic moral and political principles. The fundamental notion of human dignity entails respect for individuals as autonomous subjects, which in turn calls for recognition that people should be able to plan their lives in order to secure maximum freedom to pursue their interests. In order to facilitate this, the criminal law should operate so as to guide people away from certain courses of conduct, and should provide for the conviction only of persons who intend or knowingly risk the prohibited consequences. In other words, the principle of *mens rea* should be a precondition of criminal conviction.

It follows from this that strict liability is objectionable because it leads to the conviction of people who have not been proved to be sufficiently at fault in respect of a material element of the offence. Of course, it is accepted that a

---

[16] HLA Hart, *Punishment and Responsibility: Essays in the Philosophy of Law* (2nd edn, 2008), 152.

[17] Hart actually took the argument further, developing his views about fairness so as to support criminal liability for forms of negligence: ibid, Ch VI.

[18] Hart, n 16 above, 23. Hart developed the point further in his book, *The Morality of the Criminal Law* (1965), arguing that in a system that dispensed with the principle of *mens rea* 'the occasions for official interferences with our lives and for compulsion will be vastly increased'.

[19] J Gardner, 'Introduction', Part 5, in Hart, n 16 above.

[20] J Raz, 'The Rule of Law and its Virtue' (1977) 93 *LQR* 195, at 204; cf FA Hayek, *The Constitution of Liberty* (1960), 156–57.

person cannot be convicted of a strict liability offence if the conduct was involuntary, or if he or she had an exculpatory defence.[21] Assuming that none of these doctrines applies, it is still unfair to place the official censure of a criminal conviction on someone who has not been proved in all material respects to have *mens rea*. Otherwise, people who did something by mistake or by accident would be liable to criminal conviction; to that extent they would be deprived of the opportunity sensibly to plan their lives, and consequentially their plans and/or relationships 'may be undermined by widespread distrust or disregard fomented . . . by knowledge of one's conviction'.[22] Combined with the principle that ignorance of the criminal law is no excuse,[23] strict liability exposes individuals to conviction when they have not at all adverted to the wrongness of what they were doing. That constitutes contempt for a value (individual autonomy) which the law should respect.

Secondly, we turn to the censure-based argument. The American professor Henry M Hart argued that what distinguishes criminal from civil sanctions, 'is the judgment of community condemnation which accompanies . . . its imposition'.[24] Developing this in his expressive theory of punishment, Joel Feinberg argued that punishment has a reprobative or condemnatory aspect, and that therefore there is something 'offensive in punishing people for admittedly faultless conduct', in that it is 'arbitrary and cruel to condemn someone for something he did (admittedly) without fault'.[25] This line of reasoning recognises the seriousness with which a criminal conviction should be treated: it is the authoritative public censure of an individual for wrong-doing, usually followed by hard treatment in the form of punishment.[26] This supplies a strong reason for requiring fault, as Antony Duff argues: the coercive apparatus of the criminal law is rightly used to call people to account for their conduct, but to proceed to conviction without proof of fault as to a material element is to impose public condemnation without properly laying the foundations for it.[27] Indeed, Duff goes so far as to state that, 'strict liability is therefore both unjust and dishonest: it portrays as proven culpable wrongdoers those who have not been proved to be that'.[28] The censure-based argument therefore establishes that a requirement of fault should be a precondition of the public condemnation involved in conviction, and of liability to state punishment.

---

[21]   Accord: McAuley and McCutcheon, n 1 above, 336.

[22]   J Horder, 'Strict Liability, Statutory Construction and the Spirit of Liberty' (2002) 118 *LQR* 458, at 459–60.

[23]   I advocate the reappraisal of this doctrine in A Ashworth, 'Ignorance of the Criminal Law, and Duties to Avoid it', reprinted as Chapter 3 above.

[24]   Henry M Hart, 'The Aims of the Criminal Law' (1958) 23 *Law & Contemporary Problems* 401, at 404.

[25]   Joel Feinberg, *Doing and Deserving* (1970), 111–12.

[26]   A von Hirsch, *Censure and Sanctions* (1993).

[27]   RA Duff, *Answering for Crime:Responsibility and Liability in the Criminal Law* (2007), 231–32.

[28]   See Duff, ibid, 235.

Either separately or in combination, the rule-of-law and censure-based arguments provide convincing reasons for regarding strict liability as wrong in principle. The rule-of-law rationale links with the criminal law's function of guiding behaviour and the censure-based rationale links with the criminal conviction's function of expressing official censure. Thus, both rationales connect the criminal law with wider issues of political obligation, in the sense that they emphasise the importance of respect for individuals as rational and autonomous persons. Some have sought to pursue this reasoning to the level of human rights or constitutional doctrine. Thus, it is sometimes argued that the principle of *mens rea* may be derived from the presumption of innocence proclaimed by article 6(2) of the European Convention on Human Rights, but the prevailing Strasbourg view is that the presumption is merely a procedural or evidential principle, which does not mandate fault requirements in the criminal law.[29] However, it is of interest that when the Judicial Committee of the House of Lords was confronted with the question of whether various sexual offences imposed strict liability as to the age of the other party, it described the principle of *mens rea* as a 'constitutional principle' and found unanimously against imposing strict liability.[30] None of the judges suggested that the constitutional principle stemmed from the presumption of innocence or that it was absolute, and all recognised that it might be rebutted in appropriate circumstances.[31] The Supreme Court of Ireland has made a connection between the presumption of innocence and strict criminal liability, as well as connecting the principle of *mens rea* with other safeguards in the Constitution of Ireland.[32] However, I am not aware of any constitutional or human rights document that expressly declares the principle of *mens rea*, even though I believe that the rule-of-law and censure-based arguments make a strong case for doing so.

This leaves one further issue for brief discussion, and that is the relationship between strict liability and certain potential defences. Intoxication is often referred to as a defence, but in fact it functions largely as an inculpatory doctrine, denying a defence to those who were voluntarily intoxicated at the time of

---

[29] Compare P Roberts, 'Strict Liability and the Presumption of Innocence: an Exposé of Functionalist Assumptions' in Simester, n 2 above; A Ashworth, 'Four Threats to the Presumption of Innocence' (2006) 10 *Evidence and Proof* 241, at 253–55; and *R v G* [2008] UKHL 37, with V Tadros and S Tierney, 'The Presumption of Innocence and the Human Rights Act' (2004) 67 *MLR* 402 and V Tadros, 'Rethinking the Presumption of Innocence' (2007) 1 *Criminal Law and Philosophy* 193.

[30] *B v DPP* [2000] 2 AC 428, especially Lord Steyn at 470; *R v K* [2002] 1 AC 462, especially Lord Bingham at para 17; see also Lord Bingham in *G* [2004] 1 AC 1034, but cf the reasoning of the majority in *R v G* [2008] UKHL 37, failing to grapple with the argument from constitutional principle.

[31] Indeed, the list of such circumstances given by Lord Nicholls is so wide and malleable as to weaken the principle considerably: 'the nature of the offence, the mischief sought to be prevented, and any other circumstances that may assist in determining what intent is properly to be attributed to Parliament when creating the offence' ([2000] 2 AC 428, at 463–64).

[32] *CC v Ireland* [2006] 4 IR 66, at 80, per Hardiman J, connecting the principle of *mens rea* with the protection of liberty, with the protection of dignity, and with Art 40.3.1 on the vindication of justice. For the general constitutional significance of the presumption of innocence, see also, Hardiman J in *People (DPP) v DO'T* [2003] IR 286, and Fennell, n 8 above.

the offence (at least in respect of 'basic intent' offences).[33] In those instances, therefore, the law may be said to impose strict liability on voluntarily intoxicated people.[34] Ignorance of the criminal law operates as a defence in a few legal systems, but in others (such as Ireland and England) it is not allowed to constitute a defence[35] – which means that there is strict liability as to knowledge of the criminal law. These potential defences must therefore be considered separately in relation to the principle that liability without fault is objectionable: are they special cases, and are there sufficient justifications for recognising them as exceptions?

This discussion of the reasons for requiring fault for criminal conviction has yielded my second proposition: *that strict liability as to a material element of an offence is wrong in principle, because the rule-of-law and censure-based arguments indicate that the prosecution should be required to prove mens rea (or fault)[36] in relation to all significant elements of a crime, in order to respect the autonomy of individuals and to impose public censure only where a fair and proper foundation has been laid.*

4.3 SERIOUS CRIME: LIMITATIONS AND EXCEPTIONS

So far, I have argued that a serious offence is objectionable as a strict liability crime if it contains one material element for which proof of fault is not required. The objections have been placed on rule-of-law and censure-based grounds, emphasising the political and philosophical importance of respect for individuals as rational, autonomous persons. The argument has been conducted at a normative level, not as a description of current law (which, both in Ireland and in England and Wales, presents a much more confused picture). The next step is to examine the strength of some of the counter-arguments which are used to place limitations on, or fashion exceptions to, the position I have described as normatively ideal.

Let us take three serious crimes that raise the question. So as to keep the discussion at a general level, I am going to take three English examples, which may or may not have direct analogues in Irish law. First, there is the offence committed by anyone who 'has in his possession, or purchases or acquires, or manufactures, sells or transfers' any prohibited firearm.[37] In English law this is a strict

---

[33] McAuley and McCutcheon, n 1 above, Ch 13, and AP Simester, 'Intoxication is Never a Defence' [2009] *Crim LR* 3.

[34] Cf the argument that the law is really convicting for prior recklessness, criticised by Ashworth, n 5 above, 199–202

[35] See Chapter 3 above.

[36] This equivocation recognises the separate debate as to whether proof of negligence should be sufficient for criminal liability, which will not be pursued in detail here. Compare Hart, *Punishment and Responsibility*, Ch VI, with AP Simester, 'Can Negligence be Culpable?' in J Horder (ed), *Oxford Essays in Jurisprudence, 4th Series* (2000), and Ashworth, n 5 above, 185–89.

[37] Firearms Act 1968 (UK) s 5, as amended.

liability offence: it is committed irrespective of whether the defendant was aware that the article in his possession was a prohibited firearm, and no further intent is required.[38] Secondly, there is the offence of rape of a child under 13, which is a strict liability offence requiring no knowledge or belief about the child's age if the child is in fact under 13, and apparent consent to the act is irrelevant.[39] A third offence is that committed by anyone who sells restricted medicines or drugs without a valid prescription, an offence committed even if the prescription is a forgery and the seller is unaware of that fact.[40] These are all treated as serious crimes, in view of the maximum penalties provided – 10 years for the firearms offence, life imprisonment for rape of a child, and two years' imprisonment for the pharmacy offence. How, if at all, can these elements of strict liability be justified? Five lines of reasoning will be explored, with particular attention to the structure of these counter-arguments.

First, there is the argument from public protection. History indicates that 'the concerns of liberty and fairness which underlie the general requirement of culpability are [sometimes] dispensed with in the interests of some other social goal'.[41] There is a recurrent tension between the arguments of principle in favour of requiring fault, and the various consequentialist reasons put forward for strict liability. Public protection is probably the most frequently cited social goal in this connection, arguing that the state has a duty to provide security for its citizens, and one way of doing this is to make it easier to convict those who cause, threaten or risk harm. One problem with a justification of that kind is that it knows no limits.[42] Virtually the whole of the criminal law is there to provide security for us all – certainly the law of offences against the person, sexual offences, weapons offences and more. Yet the general principle of *mens rea* applies to many of the most significant of those offences, and arguments for strict liability are either not heard or not thought convincing. It follows that public protection alone cannot be a sufficient justification for dispensing with the requirement of *mens rea*; indeed, in so far as it is put forward as such, it is really a direct challenge to the arguments in favour of the principle of *mens rea* that were discussed in part 2 above rather than an argument for an exception. However, arguments for public protection have a certain resilience in this debate, and I will return to them at various points below.

A second reason is an abnormal difficulty of proof. Why do I load the dice from the outset by using the adjective 'abnormal'? The answer is that proving

---

[38] The authorities are legion: see *R v Howells* [1977] QB 614 and *R v Deyemi and Edwards* [2008] 1 Cr App R 25.

[39] Sexual Offences Act 2003 (England and Wales) s 5; *R v G* [2008] UKHL 37.

[40] Medicines Act 1968 (UK) s 58 (2), as applied in *Pharmaceutical Society of Great Britain v Storkwain* (1986) 83 Cr App R 359.

[41] McAuley and McCutcheon, n 1 above, 314.

[42] No less vacuous was the concept used by Lord Scarman in *Gammon v Attorney General for Hong Kong* [1985] AC 1, at 14, when he suggested that the presumption of *mens rea* could be displaced where the issue is 'public safety' – a concept of enormous breadth, rightly criticised by McAuley and McCutcheon, n 1 above, 319–20, cf n 1, 327.

fault, particularly *mens rea*, invariably causes difficulties for the prosecution. Their task would be much easier if they only had to prove causation, but it is a mark of most contemporary legal systems that this is not treated as a sufficient justification for criminal liability. Most of the elements of most serious offences in Irish law and English law require proof of *mens rea*, difficult or not. Fear of false defences is not allowed to detract from the general principle. So what we are looking for is a particular argument that it is abnormally difficult to prove knowledge that a firearm was a prohibited article, or to prove knowledge that a child was under the age of 13, or to prove knowledge that a medical prescription was invalid. When the Supreme Court of the United States was confronted with a case of possession of an unregistered automatic firearm – the defendant protesting that he was unaware that it was capable of firing automatically – the court held that, 'absent a clear statement from Congress that mens rea is not required, we should not . . . interpret any statute defining a felony offence as dispensing with mens rea'.[43] On this view, an offence serious enough to be a felony should not be lightly diluted by an element of strict liability. The reasoning is clear:

(a) possession of an unregistered automatic firearm is a felony;
(b) the defendant did not know the firearm was capable of firing automatically;
(c) therefore, the defendant did not know that registration was called for;
(d) therefore, it would be unfair to convict him of this felony in the absence of proof of awareness of this material element.

Difficulty of proof was not treated as an argument for departing from the general principle in this type of case.

Moreover, we must recall that the aim of this enquiry is to examine the justifications for strict criminal liability. Thus, it could be argued that, if abnormal difficulties of proof do exist (or if an extraordinarily acute public protection issue were to arise), the proper response is to impose a negligence requirement – for example, that the defendant did not know, and had no reasonable grounds for believing, that the gun was prohibited, the child was under 13 or the prescription invalid.[44] This is to take seriously the rule-of-law arguments developed in part 2 above, and to adopt the approach of the least restrictive alternative.[45] It amounts to a departure from the principle of *mens rea* but retains a significant element of fault in the equation, thereby keeping faith with rule-of-law principles.[46] Those who argue in favour of strict liability must therefore adduce peculiarly strong reasons for going beyond this and dispensing with all fault requirements related to this element of the three offences.

[43] *United States v Staples* (1994) 114 S Ct 1793. Possession of a firearm is sometimes viewed as a constitutional right in the United States, but this does not extend to automatic firearms.

[44] This possibility was noted by Hardiman J in *CC v Ireland* [2006] 2 ILRM 161, at 173.

[45] Another alternative would be to depart from the presumption of innocence by imposing a burden of proof on the defendant in such cases; however, the justifications for doing so are no more convincing – see Ashworth, n 29 above.

[46] This was largely why HLA Hart supported criminal liability for negligence: see fn 36.

The same counter-argument applies if, thirdly, the claims of deterrence are pressed. It is often suggested that a crime will have greater deterrent value if liability is strict: people will realise that they should steer clear of anything to do with guns and ammunition, or sexual activity with young people, for fear of incurring conviction and punishment. Some would argue that such a response creates too wide a chilling effect for individuals, curtailing their liberty of action more than is warranted,[47] but we will not pursue that reasoning here. The specific point about deterrence is our concern, and it calls for careful handling. What needs to be established is that strict liability as to whether the gun was prohibited, the child was under 13 or the prescription invalid, has a greater deterrent effect than imposing a negligence requirement (such as whether the defendant had 'reason to believe' or had 'reasonable grounds' for believing otherwise). Three arguments against this proposition may be mentioned briefly. First, in so far as deterrent theories assume rational choice by the actor, that cannot exist if a person can be convicted without having adverted to the matter at all (or, at least, without having the opportunity and capacity to do so).[48] Secondly, the state of empirical evidence to support either the individual or the general deterrent hypotheses remains impoverished: we have far more anecdotes than rigorous research. Thirdly, even if it were established that strict liability has a greater general deterrent effect, such an approach would perpetrate unfairness, by convicting innocent people in the hope of deterring others.[49] Thus, JM Kelly quoted the American jurist Jeffrie G Murphy's statement, that the deterrent theorist:

> '[M]ust say to the criminal: "We are punishing you in order to use you as an example to others and thereby to deter crime". But surely the criminal can at this point well ask the question: "What gives you the right to use me in this way? . . . Do I not have, as a rational being, a right not to be so used?"'[50]

So, even if satisfactory evidence of deterrence were produced, it would have formidable moral and political objections to overcome.

Why, in the foregoing paragraph, did I place so much emphasis on the potential role of a negligence requirement, that the defendant 'had no reasonable grounds to believe . . .'? The answer is that such a requirement allows an element of fairness to individuals (rule-of-law values and a culpability requirement) that strict

---

[47] See further Horder, n 22 above, 468–70.

[48] Preserving this possibility, without arguing it to a conclusion: see next paragraph, and n 36 above.

[49] These two arguments were accepted by the majority of the Supreme Court of Canada in *R v Hess; R v Nguyen* [1990] 2 SCR 906, holding that absolute liability as to age in sexual offences against the young violated Charter rights, since it provide that 'mentally innocent' people could be convicted and sent to prison. McLachlin J dissented on the ground that convicting such people would deter other men from having sex with young girls.

[50] JM Kelly, *A Short History of Western Legal Theory* (1992), 449, quoting from JG Murphy and J Coleman, *Philosophy of Law* (1990), 121; see also A Norrie, *Crime, Reason and History* (2nd edn, 2001), 207.

liability eliminates. In *R v Deyemi and Edwards*,[51] the defendants were found with
an article that they believed to be a large torch (since it had a lens and a bulb). It
turned out to be a stun-gun, a prohibited weapon, and they were convicted of the
strict liability offence of possession. The judge granted them both a conditional
discharge, thereby emphasising their lack of culpability. In *R v Rehman and
Wood*,[52] the first defendant (a collector of models) ordered a replica handgun on
the internet, paid for it with his credit card and had it delivered to his home. The
police traced the transaction, and called at his house, where R readily showed
them his latest purchase. The replica was classed as a prohibited firearm, unbe-
known to R, and he was convicted of the strict liability offence of possession. In
R v G,[53] a boy of 15 had apparently consensual sex with a girl he had met, and
who had told him she was 15 too. The girl, who was only 12, subsequently
reported the occurrence. The boy was advised that he had no option but to plead
guilty to the offence of rape of a girl under 13, consent being irrelevant and the
age being a matter of strict liability. His conviction was upheld. In *Storkwain*,[54]
the defendant pharmacist had supplied controlled medicines to two customers
whose prescriptions turned out to be forgeries, but the House of Lords upheld the
conviction on the ground that strict liability was necessary to ensure the highest
level of accountability. All these convictions can be said to be unfair: all four
defendants appear to have been unaware of a central element in the alleged
wrongdoing, and none of them was given the opportunity to argue that he or she
had taken all reasonable precautions, and had not been put on notice that the
criminal law was about to be broken. If these offences had been reformulated so
as to require proof that the defendant 'knew or had reasonable grounds to believe',
the defendants would have retained a fair opportunity to raise their lack of awareness, and it is questionable whether this would materially weaken the effectiveness
of the offence (and the protection of the public).

A fourth argument points to the obvious moral ambiguity of what D is doing.
The activity of becoming involved with firearms or the act of having sex with
young people is said to be morally dubious conduct attended with well-known
risks, and so the defendant cannot really complain when the risk materialises.
This is the so-called 'thin ice principle', originating in the observation of Lord
Morris that, 'those who skate on thin ice can hardly expect to find a sign which
will denote the precise spot where he will fall in'.[55]

Unfortunately, this moralistic argument is confused and unconvincing. A citizen ought to know that possession of certain firearms without registration is an
offence, but if he or she makes a reasonable mistake about the features of a
particular gun (or about the applicability of the legal categories), has she done

[51] [2008] 1 Cr App R 25.
[52] [2006] 1 Cr App R (S) 404.
[53] [2008] UKHL 37.
[54] (1986) 83 Cr App R 359 (see n 40 above).
[55] In *Knuller v DPP* [1973] AC 435, at 463.

anything morally wrong? Like Mr Rehman,[56] she knows that some guns may be lawfully possessed and others may not, and places this gun in the wrong category. If the law wanted to ban all firearms, it would do so. Since it does not, this means that possession of some firearms without registration is lawful. It seems particularly harsh to criminalise someone for doing an act reasonably believed to be lawful. Again, an adult should know that sex with young people is criminalised below a certain age, let us say 17. This means that sex with young people aged 17 or over is lawful: the legislature has not moved to criminalise older men who have consensual sex with 17-year-olds (however much some of us may deprecate that activity). What if an older man believes on reasonable grounds that a particular girl is 17, perhaps because she has shown him an identity document, but it transpires that the document was a forgery? Again, it seems harsh to criminalise someone for doing an act reasonably believed to be lawful. The age of 17 is set as the dividing line; the law recognises no moral fresco around it. If, and in so far as, the law specifies the age of 17 as the dividing line, any moral disapproval that some people may have for an older man who wants to have sex with a particular 17-year-old should not be allowed to convert a reasonable belief into an unjustified belief sufficient for criminalisation.

A more difficult problem is raised by the English offence of rape of a child under 13. Should an older man (say, in his 20s) be convicted if he had apparently consensual sex with a girl and he had reasonable grounds for believing that she was 13? That is a significantly different question because, even if she were 13, he would have been committing an offence – the offence of 'statutory rape' of a girl below the age of consent. Note that this is different from saying that his conduct was morally wrong: the point is that it was a criminal offence already, and his mistake was as to whether he was committing a more serious offence (rape of a child under 13) or a less serious offence (statutory rape). There are three possible responses to this situation. The first is to apply the undiluted principle of *mens rea* and to say that he should not be convicted of the under-13 offence if he was mistaken as to the girl's age, since he lacked the relevant knowledge. The second is to apply a broader, negligence-based fault principle and to say that he should be convicted of rape of a girl under 13, only if he did not have reasonable grounds for believing that she was 13; if he did have reasonable grounds, he should be convicted of statutory rape. The third possible response is to say that anyone who lacks reasonable grounds for believing that a girl is under 17 should be held to take the risk that she may be under 13: this is a form of constructive liability, basing liability for the more serious under-13 offence on conviction of the less serious but still criminal under-17 offence. Should we accept the third response?[57] It was argued earlier that constructive crime is objectionable (although not as objectionable as pure strict liability), on the

---

[56] See n 52 above.
[57] The speech of Baroness Hale in *R v G* [2008] UKHL 37 highlights the harm done to young people by penetrative sex at an early age, using this as an argument for strict liability. She does not consider the principled case for having a negligence standard instead.

ground that the defendant did not choose to commit the more serious offence and is being held strictly liable for a worse-than-expected result. The question in this instance, as in common law manslaughter, is whether the 'moral distance' between the underlying offence (sex with a young person under the age of consent) and the constructed offence (rape of a child under 13, with a maximum sentence of imprisonment for life) is too great.[58] In my view the moral distance is too great: in effect, we would be basing liability for a very serious offence carrying a maximum of life imprisonment on the fault relating to a much less serious offence with a lower maximum penalty. The argument for constructive liability here is weak. Those who take a different view must still provide convincing reasons as to why the law should not reserve convictions of the under-13 offence for cases where the defendant had no reasonable grounds for suspecting that the child was under that age.

Fifthly, is the public protection argument not strengthened by the seriousness of the harm that may be done by these offences? There are two responses to this proper concern. The first response is that, just as the harm to the victim becomes more serious, so the harm to the defendant of an unjustified conviction becomes greater. This is obvious on the facts of *R v G*, where the 15-year-old boy will carry the considerable stigma of this child rape conviction for many years, not having been allowed by English law to raise his lack of culpability. It also applies to cases of older men who have sex with children: the offence of rape of a child under 13 is one of the most heinous and stigmatic on the statute book, so conviction of this offence on a strict liability basis is an extremely serious matter. There will be cases in which a lack of culpability may be apparent, and juries should have no more difficulty distinguishing these rare genuine cases from false defences than they do in offences of violence generally. In sum, therefore, the 'seriousness of the offence' argument cuts both ways. The harm is very serious for the victim, but to register a conviction without culpability as to this material element is also a great injustice for the defendant. The second response to concern about the harm done to victims requires us to consider the punishment on conviction without culpability. Before considering that in part 4 below, we should formulate the third proposition: *that neither public protection, nor abnormal difficulty of proof, nor deterrence, nor the moralistic doctrine of 'skating on thin ice', nor the serious impact of the offence on the victim is sufficient reason for displacing the principle of mens rea in favour of strict liability, since conviction without culpability is a very serious matter for the defendant too; and that these and any other reasons adduced in favour of strict liability must be strong enough to defeat the argument that a requirement of negligence ('reasonable grounds for believing') should be adequate.*

---

[58] Compare Duff, *Answering for Crime* (2007), 257–60, with Ashworth, 'A Change of Normative Position: Determining the Contours of Culpability in Criminal Law', reprinted as Chapter 5 below.

4.4 IMPRISONMENT WITHOUT FAULT

It is evident from the foregoing discussion that there is considerable pragmatic, if not principled, pressure to have some strict liability offences in the criminal law. For those who, like me, subscribe to the censure-based justification for requiring fault as a precondition of criminal conviction, this is a matter for profound regret. It is not a deficiency that can be cured by the possibility of favourable treatment at the sentencing stage: a criminal conviction is an act of public censure of the individual, and it is unfair to impose this public censure unless fault has been proved. Moreover, conviction followed by a nominal sentence may tend to bring the law into disrepute, by calling into question the appropriateness of convicting a blameless person,[59] and it is unlikely to enhance the effectiveness of the law (for those who justify strict liability on consequentialist grounds).

However, reality must be faced. Some legal systems have serious offences that impose strict liability.[60] Where those strict liability crimes have a maximum sentence of imprisonment, this takes the debate to another level, since deprivation of liberty is the most severe form of punishment available in most legal systems. At this level there are two kinds of reasoning to be assessed, normative reasoning and international standards. First, we should recognise personal liberty as the essence of freedom, and as one of the bridges between individual autonomy and the ability to pursue one's conception of the good life. A sentence which deprives an individual of liberty takes away a basic and cherished right, and so should require particularly strong justification. Moreover, not only does imprisonment constitute exclusion from the community,[61] but it also subjects the prisoner to the pains and deprivations of incarceration, often including overcrowding and fear for personal safety. Thus, the normative arguments favouring the restrictive use of imprisonment must be combined with practical arguments about the state of the prisons in a particular country – and both the UK and Ireland have received some adverse comments on their prison conditions as a result of visits of the European Committee.[62] If we relate these normative/empirical reasons to the topic in hand, then as Feinberg argues:

---

[59] See, eg *R v Deyemi and Edwards*, n 38 above, where the judge gave conditional discharges.

[60] A survey of offences triable in the Crown Court in England and Wales found that some 45 per cent had a strict liability element, of which around half also had a 'due diligence' defence and the other half imposed pure strict liability. Almost all these offences had a maximum sentence of more than six months' imprisonment: A Ashworth and M Blake, 'The Presumption of Innocence in English Criminal Law' [1996] *Crim LR* 306.

[61] See, eg RA Duff, *Punishment, Communication and Community* (2001), 148–52.

[62] European Committee for the Prevention of Torture and Inhuman and Degrading Treatment, *Report to the Government of Ireland* (2007), and *Report to the Government of Ireland on the visit to Ireland* (CPT/inf, 2011, 3). For broader analysis of the development of Irish prison policy, see S Kilcommins, I O'Donnell, E O'Sullivan and B Vaughan, *Crime, Punishment, and the Search for Order in Ireland* (2004), Chs 2 and 7.

'The reason why strict liability to imprisonment (punishment) is so much more repugnant to our sense of justice than is strict liability to fine (penalty) is simply that imprisonment in modern times has taken on the symbolism of reprobation'.[63]

Reprobation (public censure) is not justified in the absence of fault. Thus the two arguments – the fundamental nature of liberty and its deprivation, and the fundamental injustice of not merely conviction but also imprisonment without fault – combine to oppose strict liability for serious (imprisonable) offences. As Sayre put it in his classic article, the possibility of a prison sentence makes it imperative not to deny a defendant the opportunity to raise lack of fault at the trial.[64]

International declarations on the use of imprisonment do not descend to this level of detail, but they point in the same direction. The United Nations has had Standard Minimum Rules for the Treatment of Prisoners since 1955.[65] When the Council of Europe agreed a revised version of the European Prison Rules in 2006, it restated the principle that, 'no one shall be deprived of liberty save as a measure of last resort'.[66] If we turn to the European Convention on Human Rights for greater detail, we find that the Convention itself is disappointingly unspecific but that the European Court of Human Rights has taken some significant steps. Thus article 5 proclaims the right to liberty and security of person, and states that, 'no one shall be deprived of his liberty save in the following cases', of which it enumerates six. The first of the six exceptions is 'the lawful detention of a person after conviction by a competent court'. That is an undifferentiated exception: it seems that any conviction suffices to make the detention lawful under article 5, without reference to the seriousness of the offence.[67] Nonetheless, the Strasbourg Court has emphasised 'the dramatic effect of deprivation of liberty on the fundamental rights of the person concerned';[68] and the court has indicated a possible further development, suggesting that a sentence that is disproportionate to the seriousness of the offence may amount to an 'inhuman' punishment contrary to article 3.[69] The English

---

[63] Feinberg, n 25 above, 111. See also Husak's argument, based on a 'right not to be punished': D Husak, *Overcriminalization: The Limits of the Criminal Law* (2008), 92.

[64] Sayre, n 6 above, 79. The reference to 'the possibility of imprisonment' lays one open to the riposte, 'what about an hour's loss of liberty, or a day's loss of liberty? That cannot be ranked as the highest possible punishment, when compared with a large fine or 150 hours of unpaid work on a community sentence'. Lippke deals with this possible objection by confining his discussion to prison sentences of six months or more, so that there can be no doubt about the significance of the deprivation of liberty: R Lippke, *Rethinking Imprisonment* (2007), 64. I propose to adopt that position here, without further argument.

[65] See www.odc.org [Last Accessed April 12, 2011].

[66] Council of Europe Recommendation Rec (2006) 2.

[67] For the similar position in the US, see SF Colb, 'Freedom from Incarceration: Why is this Right Different from all other Rights?' (1994) 69 *New York University Law Review* 781, at 791: 'Though liberty from confinement is an essential, core right of citizenship, a criminal conviction nonetheless extinguishes that right'.

[68] *Garcia Alva v Germany*, judgment of 13 February, 2001, para 39; see also *Allen v United Kingdom*, judgment of 30 March, 2010, para 47.

[69] This was suggested in *Weeks v United Kingdom* (1988) 10 EHRR 293, where W had been sentenced to life imprisonment for robbery, having threatened a shop-owner with an unloaded starting pistol and stolen 35 pence. The Strasbourg Court accepted this as a preventive sentence, subject to

Court of Appeal adopted this argument in the case of *R v Offen (No 2)*,[70] stating that a 'wholly disproportionate' sentence might contravene article 3, as well as being 'arbitrary and disproportionate' and thus in breach of article 5.

Looking more widely, the Canadian Charter of Rights and Freedoms phrases the equivalent right differently, and this has opened the way to a more specific interpretation. Section 7 states that:

'Everyone has the right to life, liberty and security of the person and the right not to be deprived thereof except in accordance with the principles of fundamental justice'.

In *Reference Re Section 94(2) of the Motor Vehicle Act (BC)*,[71] the Supreme Court of Canada held that an offence of absolute liability that is punishable with imprisonment is inconsistent with principles of fundamental justice, in that it may deprive the 'morally innocent' of their right to liberty. Thus, Canadian law insists on the link between the fault principle in criminal law and the right to liberty.

A more frequent feature of constitutional documents and human rights documents is some kind of restraint on disproportionate sentences. Often it is expressed in the form of a prohibition on 'cruel and unusual punishments', as in section 12 of the Constitution of South Africa. The same phrase in the Eighth Amendment to the Constitution of the United States of America has been interpreted as prohibiting punishments 'which, by their excessive length or severity, are greatly disproportioned to the offenses charged',[72] although recent Supreme Court decisions have construed the prohibition so narrowly as to deprive it of almost all purchase.[73] The principle has been applied conscientiously in South Africa, where it has been said to rest on the Kantian rationale that it is contrary to a person's dignity and therefore wrong to use an offender merely as a means rather than as an end in himself.[74] For example, imposing a longer-than-proportionate sentence in order to deter others falls foul of this rationale: the sentence should not be grossly disproportionate to what is deserved.

The prohibition is even more powerful if the constitutional or human rights document uses 'disproportionality' (without the adjective 'gross') as its limitation. The German Constitutional Court has derived this principle from the

---

the normal safeguards of periodic review, etc. But the court went on to say that if life imprisonment had been imposed solely as a punitive sentence, 'one could have serious doubts as to its compatibility with Article 3 of the Convention which prohibits inter alia inhuman punishment' (para 47).

[70] [2001] 1 Cr App R 372, approved by the House of Lords in *R v Drew* [2003] UKHL 25.

[71] [1985] 2 SCR 486.

[72] *Weems v United States* (1909) 217 US 349, at 371.

[73] Eg *Ewing v California* (2003) 123 S Ct 1179 (life, with a minimum of 25 years, for the theft of three new golf clubs) and *Lockyer v Andrade* (2003) 123 S Ct 1166 (twice life, with a minimum of 50 years, for two thefts involving 11 blank video tapes), where Souter J, dissenting (at 1179), exclaimed that, 'if Andrade's sentencing is not grossly disproportionate, the principle has no meaning'. For general analysis, see D van Zyl Smit and A Ashworth, 'Disproportionate Sentences as Human Rights Violations' (2004) 67 *MLR* 541.

[74] *S v Dodo* 2001 (3) SA 382, at 403.

fundamental right to human dignity in the German Constitution,[75] and this important commitment to a disproportionality limitation has recently been joined by the Charter of Fundamental Rights of the European Union, article 49(3) of which declares that, 'the severity of penalties must not be disproportionate to the criminal offence'. Despite the efforts of the then British Attorney General to sideline the Charter and its provisions,[76] this must be regarded as a significant recognition of the deep importance of a proportionality constraint upon sentencing.

That importance had already been recognised in Ireland. In *Cox v Ireland*,[77] the Supreme Court held that the Constitution requires that penalties must be neither arbitrary nor disproportionate, and this was followed in *People (DPP) v M*,[78] where the Supreme Court referred to the 'constitutional principle of proportionality'. The status of this fundamental principle was upheld in *Osmanovic v DPP*,[79] and again in *People (DPP) v McC*,[80] but the recent decision in *R v Lynch and Whelan*[81] restated the constitutional principle without reference to disproportionality, preferring the test of whether 'there was no rational relationship between the penalty and the requirements of justice with regard to the punishment of the offence specified'. However, whether the criterion is disproportionality or the requirements of justice, the question of a culpability element is surely central to the court's task.[82] Thus, if an offence of strict liability has imprisonment as its maximum sentence, does not the absence of any requirement to prove culpability support the argument that imprisonment is disproportionate to the seriousness of the offence? This train of thought may be found in the judgment of Lord Woolf CJ in *R v Offen (No 2)*:

> 'An unjustified push can result in someone falling, hitting his head and suffering fatal injuries. The offence is manslaughter. The offender may have committed another serious offence when a young man. A life sentence in such circumstances may well be arbitrary and disproportionate and contravene Article 5. It could also be a punishment which contravenes Article 3'.[83]

These words were spoken in the context of a particular English statute. Their wider significance is that Lord Woolf was using the English offence of unlawful act manslaughter (the contours of the Irish offence are very similar) as an exam-

---

[75] For discussion, see D van Zyl Smit, *Taking Life Imprisonment Seriously in National and International Law* (2002), Ch 4.

[76] Lord Goldsmith, 'The Charter of Rights – a Brake and not an Accelerator' [2004] *European Human Rights Law Review* 473.

[77] [1992] 2 IR 503.

[78] [1994] 3 IR 306, at 317, per Denham J; see also, Flood J in *People (DPP) v WC* [1994] 1 ILRM 321. For discussion of the development of the principle, see T O'Malley, *Sentencing Law and Practice* (2nd edn, 2006), 86–89.

[79] [2006] 3 IR 504.

[80] [2008] 2 IR 92.

[81] *Lynch and Whelan v Minister for Justice, Equality and Law Reform* [2010] IESC 34.

[82] O'Malley, n 78 above, 92.

[83] [2001] 1 Cr App R 372, at 395.

ple of an offence with low culpability: the only fault that is necessary for conviction is the intention to push another person. His precise point was that a sentence of life imprisonment would be disproportionate in these circumstances. The same point can be made lower down the scale of criminality, to argue that any imprisonment would be disproportionate where no fault as to a material element is required for conviction. Remember the English case of *R v Rehman*,[84] the collector of models who ordered a replica gun on the internet only to find that it was a prohibited firearm: he was not only convicted of the firearms offence but also sentenced to the mandatory minimum sentence of five years' imprisonment, reduced only to two years' imprisonment on appeal because of his lack of fault. In my view, the conviction was wrong and the deprivation of liberty even more wrong.

There is one further point that I should deal with before leaving this topic. Even if a crime has an element of strict liability, may the court at the sentencing stage take account of the degree of culpability in relation to that element? In the firearms and sex cases, as we have seen, this is often the central issue. If the prosecution adduces evidence at the sentencing stage indicating that the offender knew that the gun was prohibited or the child under age, is that not a sufficient reason for making the sentence more severe (eg by imposing imprisonment)? There are three responses to this. First, if a court receives such representations from the prosecution, it must allow the defence an opportunity to rebut them. The court should not proceed without an adversarial enquiry into this factual issue.[85] Secondly, it would be wrong in principle for the legislature to omit fault elements from the definition of an offence in the expectation that all culpability issues can be dealt with satisfactorily at the sentencing stage. If that logic were followed through, we would have a single offence of causing death, with all the issues of culpability (intent to kill, intent only to cause serious injury, provocation, etc) to be decided at the sentencing stage. That approach would be wrong because it neglects the fair labelling function of the criminal law, it devalues the criminal trial by excluding the core issue of fault, and it imposes the censure of criminal conviction on people who are not at fault. To reserve fault issues to the sentencing stage, where there is no jury and the rules of evidence and procedure are far more flexible, would be to evade the proper safeguards that form part of the criminal trial. Thirdly, there is the further danger that the use of strict liability may make an offence appear less serious than it really is. If, contrary to my arguments here, some serious strict liability offences are to remain, the proper legislative formula should be to provide two levels of offence, one criminalising the wrongdoing with an appropriate culpability requirement, and then the strict liability crime as a lesser and non-imprisonable offence.

We therefore come to the fourth proposition: *that convicting a person of a serious offence without proving fault as to a material element of that offence is*

---

[84] See n 52 above, and accompanying text.
[85] On sentencing for strict liability offences, see *R v Lester* (1975) 63 Cr App R 144, and O'Malley, n 78 above, 358.

unfair for both censure-based and rule-of-law reasons that the state should respect; and that it is even more objectionable for the state to provide the possibility of deprivation of liberty for an offence which does not require proof of culpability as to all material elements. Deprivation of liberty in those circumstances is disproportionate, since the seriousness of an offence is constituted partly by the defendant's culpability; no fair foundation for imprisonment has been laid if culpability is not required as to a significant element in the offence.

4.5 CONCLUSION

My reasoning has been essentially normative, rather than descriptive or historical. At its core is the notion of fairness, and its connection with censure-based and rule-of-law values. I have argued that it is unfair, in a political system that claims to respect the rights of individuals, to convict people of serious crimes without proof of fault as to all material elements of the offence. This goes against basic notions of personal autonomy; and it is even more destructive of personal autonomy to deprive a person of liberty, by means of a sentence of imprisonment, without such proof of fault. That is the substance of the reasoning that results in the four propositions set out above.

My other objective in putting this argument has been to provoke scholarly debate. Of course it is necessary to recognise that the stuff of law-making is compromise, and that governments and politicians often respond to what they perceive to be public attitudes, or seek to influence voters favourably. Yet – even on such controversial topics as firearms possession and sex with young people – debate about the principles has its place, not just in the universities and law reform bodies, but also among judges, legal practitioners and legislators. Its function is to test the reasons commonly put forward and to subject them to scrutiny on legal, political and moral grounds. The hope, then, is that if a particular argument cannot survive principled analysis it will be less able to influence political discussions.

The bastion of resistance against my normative reasoning is 'public protection'. I have endeavoured to expose the weaknesses in the protectionist approach: (a) that there is no satisfactory evidential basis for claims about deterrence, even if it were justifiable to punish some people in the hope of protecting others, which it is not; (b) even conceding the need for extra protection from serious crimes, this does not overcome the fairness principle that the more serious the crime is, the more unjust it is to convict someone of it (and *a fortiori* to impose imprisonment) without a requirement of fault; (c) that the idea of placing a moral fresco round the criminal law in order to convict people who believe they are doing something lawful should be rejected; and (d) that, in so far as any of these or the other counter-arguments aired in part 3 above have substance, it must be shown that a negligence-based standard (such as 'reasonable grounds for believing') is not an adequate response. In practice, there may be occasions on which the legislature concludes that there are overwhelmingly strong public protection demands – 'exceptional conditions, such as natural disasters, the outbreak of war, epidemics and the like'[86] – but even then, any change in the law should be in the direction of a negligence-based standard and not strict liability. The reason for that, as I have argued above, is that justice demands that a defendant should not be liable to conviction without the possibility of arguing absence of fault, and that imprisonment would be monstrously unfair in the absence of proof of fault.

---

[86] *Reference re Section 94(2) of the Motor Vehicle Act (BC)* (1985) 48 CR (3d) 289, at 321, per Lamer J (for the majority of the Supreme Court of Canada).

5

A Change of Normative Position: Determining the Contours of Culpability in Criminal Law

QUESTIONS ABOUT THE extent of a person's criminal liability for unforeseen consequences have long been strongly contested. The American Law Institute's Model Penal Code takes a position in section 2.03(2) on causation, setting its face against liability for results more serious than those intended and for results 'too remote or accidental to have a just bearing' on liability or on the gravity of the offence.[1] But this chapter is more concerned with the law of manslaughter, where there is a difference of approach between Model Penal Code States (where manslaughter requires proof of recklessness) and many non-Code US States and English law (in which there is a more extensive doctrine, variously called 'constructive', 'unlawful act' or 'misdemeanour'-manslaughter).[2] It is the latter form of manslaughter that is a primary focus of this chapter, examining one approach that has gained considerable support in the last decade or so – an approach that regards as the morally crucial step a person's change of normative position when he or she intentionally wrongs a person by directing conduct against a particular type of interest. This is the rationale of what John Gardner, probably the doctrine's progenitor, terms 'moderate constructivism' in the criminal law:[3] by committing an assault, for example, one changes one's normative position and thus lays oneself open to criminal liability for a more serious harm than was foreseen.

In order to assess the claims of moderate constructivism, two other approaches to the problem will be outlined – the unlawful act theory, which argues that the most significant moral threshold is crossed when a person knowingly embarks on an unlawful enterprise, and that thereafter that person may fairly be held liable for whatever consequences are caused (however unforeseen); and orthodox subjectivism, which maintains that the limits of a person's criminal liability should be determined, in principle, by what he or she intended or

---

[1] For discussion, see Markus D Dubber and Mark G Kelman, *American Criminal Law: Cases, Statutes and Comments* (2005), 399–411.

[2] For discussion, see Joshua Dressler, *Understanding Criminal Law* (3rd edn, 2001), 538–41.

[3] J Gardner, 'Rationality and the Rule of Law in Offences against the Person' (1994) 53 *CLJ* 502.

foresaw. It will be seen that these two approaches lie either side of moderate constructivism on the spectrum of liability for unforeseen consequences – unlawful act theory indicating a wider scope for criminal liability, and orthodox subjectivism insisting on a much narrower scope. Recognising that the influence of the various approaches has waxed and waned in the history of the common law, the purpose of this chapter is not to chart historical developments[4] but rather to re-assess the foundations of moderate constructivism.

5.1 UNLAWFUL ACT THEORY

Perhaps the best known manifestation of unlawful act theory is the doctrine propounded by Sir Edward Coke in the seventeenth century: that if a man shoots at another's chicken and by mischance kills a person, this is murder, 'for the act was unlawful'.[5] Although it is doubtful whether Coke's doctrine was an accurate rendering of the law as it then stood,[6] it was influential for many years, and even when it had been overtaken by the narrower felony-murder rule (restricting liability for murder to persons who killed accidentally in the course of committing a felony), it continued to exert an influence in the law of manslaughter on both sides of the Atlantic.[7] On this approach it is the commission of any crime against another that is taken to supply sufficient culpability to justify extended liability: by deciding to commit such an offence, the defendant crosses a significant moral and criminal threshold, and is rightly held not only causally responsible but also morally responsible for resulting harm, since it would not have resulted if D had not crossed the criminal threshold. Thus, once on the wrong side of the criminal law, it is appropriate that D should be answerable for any resulting harm that can be said to have been caused by him or her.[8]

This unlawful act theory remains part of the current English law of homicide through the doctrine of unlawful act manslaughter, and in some non-Code US States in the form of misdemeanour-manslaughter.[9] The 'unlawful act' that must be proved as the basic offence upon which a conviction for manslaughter can be constructed must be a crime requiring proof of *mens rea*, and is usually an assault on another, but it appears that it need not be an offence against the

---

[4] See, for example, KJM Smith, *Lawyers, Legislators and Theorists: Developments in English Criminal Jurisprudence 1800–1957* (1998) and, more briefly, J Horder, 'Two Histories and Four Hidden Principles of Mens Rea' (1997) 113 *LQR* 95.

[5] Coke, 3 Inst 56; at this time, and certainly for the purposes of the law of manslaughter until the early nineteenth century, the 'unlawful act' could be a tort or other civil wrong – see, eg, RJ Buxton, 'By Any Unlawful Act' (1966) 82 *LQR* 174. In the present context, the discussion will be limited to unlawful acts that were crimes.

[6] JM Kaye, 'The Early History of Murder and Manslaughter' (1967) 83 *LQR* 569, at 593.

[7] See Buxton, above, n 5, for discussion.

[8] The rules of causation have a significant limiting effect in English law at some points, but they will not be discussed here: see further AP Simester and GR Sullivan, *Criminal Law: Theory and Doctrine* (2nd edn, 2003), Ch 4.2; A Ashworth, *Principles of Criminal Law* (5th edn, 2006), Ch 4.5.

[9] Above, n 2.

person.[10] So long as it is also a 'dangerous' act,[11] then it can form the basis for a conviction of manslaughter.[12] While critics of this form of manslaughter argue that the gap between the fault involved in the unlawful act and the death resulting is much too great to justify liability for a serious offence, its supporters would point to the inherent criminality of what the defendant was doing and to the fact that this criminal venture caused the victim's death. The defendant had knowingly crossed the criminal threshold, and should therefore be labelled in such a way as to make clear the responsibility for the final outcome. It is true that there are few examples of this basis for criminal liability beyond the law of manslaughter, and that people in general rank such forms of homicide low on the scale.[13] However, the enormity of the harm done often creates tremendous emotional effects: it certainly requires an apology from the harm-doer, and often the payment of compensation, but whether it is right to convict the harm-doer of a homicide offence is the point of dispute. Some might say that it is an acceptable compromise to apply the label 'manslaughter' to what has been done, and then to impose a sentence that attributes only reduced significance to the fact that death has been caused.[14]

5.2 THE NUB OF SUBJECTIVISM

Subjectivist justifications for culpability focus on the elements of choice and belief, and so may be found at the opposite end of the spectrum of liability for resulting harm. Starting from respect for the moral autonomy of all individuals, subjectivists argue that criminal liability should not be imposed in respect of a given harm unless D intended to cause or knowingly risked causing that harm (the principle of *mens rea*). Similarly, D should be judged on the facts as he or she believed them to be (the belief principle). By respecting these principles, criminal liability is tied as closely as possible to what D intended, knew or

[10] Smith and Hogan, *Criminal Law* (edited by D Ormerod) (11th edn, 2005), Ch 15.3. Cf the recommendations of the English Law Commission in Law Com No 304, *Murder, Manslaughter and Infanticide* (2006).

[11] *R v Church* [1966] 1 QB 59.

[12] It should be noted that there is also a separate head of manslaughter in English law, manslaughter by gross negligence, which may apply to some of these fact situations. Neither that, nor American forms of reckless manslaughter, are discussed further here, in order to focus on the points at issue.

[13] B Mitchell, 'Public Perceptions of Homicide and Criminal Justice' (1998) 38 *British Journal of Criminology* 453, at 457–58, and also in Appendix A of the English Law Commission's Consultation Paper 177, *A new Homicide Act for England and Wales?* (2005).

[14] The leading sentencing decision was *R v Coleman* (1991) 13 Cr App R (S) 508 [now superseded by *Attorney General's Reference No 60 of 2009 (Appleby)* [2010] 2 Cr App R (S) 311]. Compare the offence of causing death by driving while uninsured, disqualified or unlicensed, introduced by the Road Safety Act 2006 (UK). The introduction of the offence is a response to the deep emotions felt by victims' families in these cases, and is supported by reference to prohibited drivers' greater risk of involvement in 'accidents'. This offence does not require any fault in the manner of the defendant's driving: it is constituted by the defendant's decision to drive when prohibited from doing so, and the fact that death happens to result.

believed when involved in the relevant behaviour. Such states of mind do not exist in some unattached manner, however. The intention is to produce a particular consequence, or the belief is as to a particular fact or circumstance. Proper respect for those two principles therefore leads to a third, the principle of correspondence: that in relation to each component of the conduct element in an offence the requirement of fault should be at the equivalent level. Thus, if there were a crime with a conduct element of 'causing serious injury', the correspondence principle would require that the fault element should be intention or recklessness as to causing serious injury and not as to some lesser degree of harm.[15]

All the subjectivist doctrines are phrased as strong principles, and few contemporary subjectivists would regard them as absolutes. There may well be sufficiently compelling justifications for departing from the principle of *mens rea*, or the belief principle, or the correspondence principle, in a particular set of circumstances. For example, one can adhere generally to the belief principle and yet argue convincingly in favour of requiring reasonable grounds for a belief in certain sets of circumstances in which D can be said to be on notice or subject to high standards of accountability – two examples would be sexual encounters, where reasonable grounds for a belief in consent may properly be required,[16] and the use of lethal force by the police or other trained personnel,[17] where there are strong arguments for a general requirement of reasonable grounds, albeit leavened by exceptions for urgency, etc. Moreover, although subjectivists would not accept that negligence should be an alternative fault element for all offences, they can support some offences of negligence, subject to certain conditions (for example an incapacity exception, and suitable rule-of-law protections such as due notice).[18]

Underpinning the subjectivist doctrines is a notion of autonomy based on the capacity to reason and to exercise will power. The argument is that, if a legal system is to claim moral authority over its subjects and to respect their autonomy, it should adhere to rule-of-law principles in its criminal law, by ensuring fair warning, maximum certainty of definition, subjective requirements for criminal liability,[19] and so on. This insistence that persons should be able to know the legal implications of their conduct may be said to provide a kind of 'costing system' for those choices. By these means, as HLA Hart put it:

[15] See further V Tadros, *Criminal Responsibility* (2005), 93–99.

[16] See, eg, A Ashworth, *Principles of Criminal Law* (1st edn, 1991), 303–5.

[17] A Ashworth, *Principles of Criminal Law* (above, n 8), Ch 4.6.

[18] As, perhaps, in the offence of gross negligence manslaughter (above, n 12). For general discussion, see, eg, AP Simester and GR Sullivan, *Criminal Law: Theory and Doctrine* (above, n 8), Ch 5.5; Ashworth, *Principles of Criminal Law* (above, n 8), Ch 5.5(f) and (g); V Tadros, *Criminal Responsibility* (2005), 95.

[19] John Gardner argues that the case for subjective requirements for liability does not flow from the concept of moral autonomy: that concept is only concerned with the capacity to exercise rational will, which makes them responsible agents but does not conclude the question of responsibility for particular conduct or result: J Gardner, 'On the General Part of the Criminal Law' in A Duff (ed), *Philosophy and the Criminal Law: Principle and Critique* (1998), 243–44.

'First, we maximize the individual's power at any time to predict the likelihood that the sanctions of the criminal law will be applied to him. Secondly, we introduce the individual's choice as one of the operative factors determining whether or not these sanctions shall be applied to him . . . Thirdly . . . we provide that, if the sanctions of the criminal law are applied, the pains of punishment will for each individual represent the price of some satisfaction obtained by breach of the law'.[20]

References to 'price' and a 'costing system' come close to the precepts of an economic theory of criminal law, but Hart was not subscribing to modern 'rational choice' theory and all its implications.[21] His point was that only by emphasising choice and predictability can the criminal law show proper respect for the individual as an autonomous reasoning person.

These autonomy-based arguments do not, however, appear to deal convincingly with all sets of circumstances. It must be accepted that (a) the law's concept of intention encompasses many cases of sudden reaction or rage that leave little room for reasoning of the kind presupposed by the subjectivist paradigm;[22] (b) that some or many people who use violence may have little appreciation of the extent of the harm or injury they will cause; and (c) that some or many people who use violence will know little of the criminal law's ladder of offences against the person. These points can be conceded without abandoning the subjectivist paradigm. Many cases of violence will not involve sudden reaction or rage, and some of those who commit it will have a good idea of what degree of harm they will cause (eg by use of a weapon or a shod foot) and may have an (albeit hazy) idea that the criminal law grades its offences against the person by, for example, distinguishing between assault and grievous bodily harm. In all these cases it is right for the criminal law to reflect the choices made by the defendant, by means of the principle of *mens rea*, the belief principle and the correspondence principle. In other cases, certainly those falling within (b) and (c), it is surely fairer for the criminal law to respond *as if* the defendant had foreseen the foreseeable unless there is any reason to hold otherwise.

This stands in sharp contrast to the principle underlying unlawful act theory – that, as soon as one puts oneself on the wrong side of the law, one must be prepared to be held liable for whatever consequences one causes, since crossing the criminal threshold is morally the most significant step. Subjectivists, on the other hand, argue that the extent of criminal liability should be measured by the extent of the harms intended or actually foreseen by the defendant. The moral significance of conduct increases by degrees according to what the defendant intends or knowingly risks. On this view, criminal liability for causing really serious harm should be based on an intention or recklessness as to causing that level of harm, and it is wrong for liability for an offence of recklessly causing

---

[20]   HLA Hart, *Punishment and Responsibility* (1968), 47.

[21]   See, for example, R Posner, 'An Economic Theory of Criminal Law', (1985) 85 *Columbia Law Review* 1193.

[22]   Eg the troublesome case of *R v Parker* (1976) 63 Cr App R 211, where D slammed down and broke a telephone receiver in a momentary fit of temper.

serious harm to be based on the lesser culpability requirement of knowingly taking a risk that some injury (not necessarily a serious injury) might result.[23] In principle, therefore, and subject to any justifiable exceptions, the principle of *mens rea*, the belief principle and the correspondence principle may be regarded as maximising the choice of individuals about how they wish to organise their lives and as enabling them not only to choose whether to risk criminal conviction but also to choose whether to risk conviction in respect of harm of a particular kind or degree.[24]

5.3 MODERATE CONSTRUCTIVISM, AUTONOMY AND THE RULE OF LAW

We have noted that the notion of respect for individual autonomy underlies subjectivism in its modern form, but John Gardner argues that there are other concepts of autonomy that are more relevant. In particular, he argues in favour of a notion of 'personal autonomy',[25] consisting in 'a life shaped substantially by the successive choices of the person leading it' but conditioned by the situations in which one finds oneself. This notion of personal autonomy is a more substantive idea, focusing not simply on the capacity for autonomous decision-making but rather on shaping one's life through making choices from among the options available at a given time and place. Gardner identifies this notion of autonomy as central to 'Western post-industrialised cultures', so that the promotion of personal autonomy requires the availability of a wide range of activities.[26]

The criminal law may be seen as a restraint on personal autonomy, in the sense that its purpose is to close off certain options, on pain of conviction and punishment. In this connection, Gardner writes, 'the value of personal autonomy turns respect for the rule of law into an obligation . . . for modern governments', and thus requires the criminal law to conform to some fundamental principles:

> 'Respect for the rule of law ensures that, so far as possible, people will be able to predict their collisions with the law in order to be able to steer their lives around it. In the criminal law, the rule of law militates in favour of clear and certain offence definitions, good publicity, and conformity between announced rule and adjudicative standard. The same considerations also militate in favour of devices that allow those who are about to cross the threshold into criminality to be put on notice that they are doing so'.[27]

---

[23] This is the current English law in relation to section 20 of the Offences Against the Person Act 1861.

[24] Hart (above, n 20), 23–24, as developed by DAJ Richards, 'Rights, Utility and Crime' (1981) 3 *Crime and Justice: an Annual Review* 274.

[25] Gardner (above, n 19), 241.

[26] Ibid, 242–43.

[27] Ibid, 243.

Among the devices for putting people on notice would be giving clear warnings or giving special training to those wishing to engage in particular activities. Also in this category fall subjective requirements of criminal liability: Gardner argues that requiring subjective *mens rea* 'means that, assuming one knows the law itself, one also knows that a violation of it is now a possibility, because such knowledge is built into the very definition of the crime'.[28] This accords well with Gardner's (Aristotelian) concept of personal autonomy as active well-being, placing the emphasis on responsibility for a particular action that is bound up with making a particular choice at a given time and place. At this point it appears to coincide with the (neo-Kantian) view of the orthodox subjectivists, insofar as both autonomy-based approaches lead to rule-of-law principles and subjective requirements of criminal liability.[29] However, while moderate constructivists tend to subscribe to a form of subjectivism, they argue (in contrast to orthodox subjectivists) that it does not necessarily lead to doctrines such as the correspondence principle.

Thus it is at this stage that the two autonomy-based approaches diverge. Supporters of the neo-Kantian view tend to argue, as we saw earlier, that the subjective requirements should be co-extensive with the conduct and/or outcome specified in the definition of the offence (the correspondence principle), and they therefore oppose constructive liability, whereby fault as to a lesser harm can ground liability in respect of a more serious harm. Gardner disagrees:

> 'the requirement of subjective *mens rea* introduced by the obligation to respect the rule of law is a requirement that does not necessarily extend to every element of an *actus reus*. So long as the law builds in an element of subjective *mens rea* at the point where people enter the realm of criminality, it matters very much less from the rule-of-law perspective that they may then commit a variety of different crimes with that same *mens rea*, some more serious than others. They were, after all, put on warning that this could happen by the fact that the law to that effect was correctly promulgated, publicised, and so on'.[30]

In this passage the argument is that all that the rule of law requires is the giving of a fair warning, and some evidence of the agent's awareness of crossing the threshold into crime (of that type, presumably).[31] What, then, can be said about requiring subjective fault merely in this limited sense? Gardner asserts that this has sufficient significance:

> 'By committing an assault one changes one's normative position, so that certain adverse consequences and circumstances that would not have counted against one but

---

[28] Ibid.

[29] It will be recalled that Gardner holds that the subjective requirements do not flow from the neo-Kantian concept of autonomy: see above, n 19.

[30] Gardner (above, n 19), 244.

[31] It will be noticed that in the passage quoted Gardner expresses himself broadly: the phrase 'enter the realm of criminality' might appear to support the criminal threshold theory. The context suggests that he is advocating moderate constructivism based on families of offences, as we discuss below.

for one's original assault now count against one automatically, and add to one's crime'.[32]

Thus committing an assault – with the required subjective fault requirement – constitutes a change of position of such normative significance that it can justifiably, on this view, ground liability for more serious consequences that were not within contemplation. Similar arguments are found in the writings of Jeremy Horder ('the fact that I deliberately wrong V arguably changes my normative position *vis-à-vis* the risk of adverse consequences of that wrongdoing to V, whether or not foreseen or reasonably foreseeable'),[33] Andrew Simester and Bob Sullivan ('by entering into an agreement or joint enterprise, S changes her normative position [and] her new status has moral significance'),[34] William Wilson (anyone who intends 'to expose another to the serious risk of death' crosses the moral threshold appropriate to liability for murder),[35] and Chris Clarkson ('those who attack their victims in the sense of assaulting them intending or foreseeing some injury . . . alter their normative position relevantly to bring themselves within the family of violence').[36] Reasoning of this kind seems to indicate not just different and more condemnatory labels in respect of the harm that results in these situations but also higher penalties to reflect the (unforeseen) harm.[37] Some searching questions must therefore be asked about the doctrine. What does this change of normative position consist of, and why is such significance attributed to it? Does it depend on an *intentional* crossing of the threshold, or can it be extended to cases of the knowing or intentional creation of risk, or even negligence? According to what parameters is the scope of the risk determined?

5.4 THE IDEA OF CHANGE OF NORMATIVE POSITION

Thus far, the reliance of moderate constructivists on the concept of 'changing one's normative position' has been more salient than their explanations of the concept, and we must now explore it further. First, what is the normative position that is being changed? The argument appears to be that a person who intentionally attacks another breaks away from the ordinary relationship between citizens in a morally significant way; but what is this ordinary relationship, and how does it relate to the boundaries of criminal liability? The general starting point in tort law is that we have a duty of care in many situations, and should

[32] J Gardner, 'Rationality and the Rule of Law in Offences against the Person' (1994) 53 *CLJ* 502, at 509.

[33] J Horder, 'A Critique of the Correspondence Principle' [1995] *Crim LR* 759, at 764.

[34] AP Simester and GR Sullivan, *Criminal Law: Theory and Doctrine* (2nd edn, 2003), 226.

[35] W Wilson, 'Murder and the Structure of Homicide' in A Ashworth and B Mitchell (eds), *Rethinking English Homicide Law* (2000), at 40.

[36] CMV Clarkson, 'Context and Culpability in Involuntary Manslaughter' in A Ashworth and B Mitchell (eds), *Rethinking English Homicide Law* (2000), at 159–60.

[37] It is not clear how John Gardner's insistence on a form of proportionality in sentencing relates to this: see J Gardner, 'Crime: in Proportion and in Perspective' in A Ashworth and M Wasik (eds), *Fundamentals of Sentencing Theory* (1998), at 37 and 47.

only be liable for the consequences (damage, injury) if we have negligently or intentionally breached that duty. In criminal law it is unclear what the relevant normative position is, but one might say that there is a duty not knowingly to wrong another by injuring their protected interests, either by way of an attack (which is essentially harmful) or by way of endangerment (which is potentially harmful).[38] But, as noted above, there was a time when, if death resulted from the commission of any unlawful act, that would amount to murder, or (in the nineteenth century, at least) to manslaughter.[39] Unlawful act theory could be said to have been based on a version of 'change of normative position', in the sense that the commission of an unlawful act might be thus interpreted. But it is a version that moderate constructivists reject, as is implicit in the adjective 'moderate'. To represent the historical development crudely,[40] the relevant normative position for the crime of murder went from the commission of any unlawful act, to the commission of a crime, and then the commission of a felony. The original doctrine was particularly severe, although it persisted in the law of manslaughter until well into the nineteenth century. The trend across four centuries is to require a more substantial and relevant normative position to be changed.

What is it that now changes a person's normative position in offences against the person? The clearest answer, given by Horder,[41] is that it is the element of intentionality. A person who intentionally attacks another crosses the relevant moral threshold, and thereby nullifies (or perhaps forfeits the protection of) the restrictive principles that would normally prevent us being held criminally liable for consequences accidentally or unforeseeably caused.[42] Presumably those restrictive principles still mean that it is unfair to render a person who simply crosses the criminal threshold (by committing any offence) liable for *any* resulting harm – thus marking the difference from unlawful act theory – but they cease to apply in respect of more serious crimes of the same kind:

> 'If . . . my unlawful act is meant to wrong V, its relevance is normative, and not merely evidential. Its deliberateness changes my relationship with the risk of adverse consequences stemming therefrom, for which I may now be blamed and held criminally responsible, irrespective of their reasonable foreseeability'.[43]

Part of the reasoning here is that we should concern ourselves not so much with the intention to harm another but rather with the intention to wrong another, ie to bring about a certain harm in a certain way. Horder gives the example of D deliberately discharging a gun close to V in order to frighten V. That is an intentional assault, but if it unexpectedly causes psychiatric harm to V, that converts it (in the current English law) into the more serious offence of assault occasioning actual bodily harm (maximum sentence, five years) rather than common

---

[38] See the discussion of attack and endangerment by RA Duff, *Criminal Attempts* (1996), 364–65.
[39] Buxton (above, n 5).
[40] See the writings of Smith and of Horder (above, n 4) for fuller analysis.
[41] Horder (above, n 33), 764.
[42] Except for the principles of causation, as noted at n 8 above.
[43] Horder (above, n 33), 764.

assault (maximum sentence, six months). D intended to wrong V in a particular way, and therefore changed his normative position in relation to V and V's well-being, and is rightly held criminally liable for the further and more serious consequence of psychiatric harm, however unforeseeable it was.[44]

We must return, however, to the fundamental question, of why D's normative position has been changed in this way and with this effect. First, it should be noted that moderate constructivism appears to be based on a cognitivist foundation: this seems implicit in the reliance on intentional (sometimes rendered as 'deliberate') action as the trigger. It is therefore no less vulnerable than orthodox subjectivism to criticisms of the unreality of applying it to impulsive conduct or acts done in temper.[45] Secondly, it also seems to be implicit that it is not sufficient that D has intentionally committed *any* offence (as in unlawful act theory), and that instead the offence committed must be of the same 'family' as the resulting harm. For example, if D throws a brick through a window, intending to commit criminal damage to property, that would surely not be taken to change D's normative position in relation to subsequent harm to V, who is injured when the brick lands on a computer, causing it to catch fire and then forcing V to flee the premises, in the course of which the injury occurs. Some would wish to say that D changed his normative position in respect of resulting damage or destruction of property, and some might wish to add that it should not matter whether the resulting damage is caused by a different method (eg an unexpected fire). The danger of relying on a restrictive principle such as a 'family of offences' is that it is open to manipulation on other grounds: there can be nuclear and extended families,[46] and English criminal law already has experience of the kindred notion of the 'same type' of offence being stretched for other ('policy') reasons.[47] However, this is not to suggest that moderate constructivism has no effective limits: the key difference between it and the unlawful act approach is that, even if intentionally committing an offence amounts to a change of normative position, it does not do so generally and indeterminately – so as to hold the person liable for any resulting harm of any description. This is inherent in what Horder describes as 'the malice principle':

> 'When D wrongfully directs his conduct at a particular interest of V's, such malice justifies criminal liability for harm done in consequence to that interest, whether or not D foresaw that harm to the interest of the degree V suffered would result'.[48]

The significance of this limiting principle will be discussed further below.

[44] It is also argued that a key element in explaining the structure of property offences is the intention to wrong another (in which the concept of dishonesty plays a major part), although the problem of liability for unforeseen consequences has less legal significance there. Compare Gardner (above, n 32), at 510–11, and Horder (above, n 33), at 762, with the counter-arguments of B Mitchell, 'In Defence of a Principle of Correspondence' [1999] *Crim LR* 195.

[45] Noted in part 2 above.

[46] Cf Gardner's differentiation between assaults and violence (above, n 32), 522.

[47] Cf *R v Bainbridge* [1960] 1 QB 219, *Maxwell v DPP for Northern Ireland* [1978] 3 All ER 1140, and the discussion by Ashworth, *Principles of Criminal Law* (above, n 8), Ch 10.4.

[48] Horder (above, n 5), at 96.

Discussion of the ways in which the concept of 'change of normative position' has been applied to offences against the person has not yet brought us to a persuasive justificatory account. We are told that for D to commit a common assault on V changes D's normative position vis-à-vis V in such a way as to render D liable for greater harm than D foresaw when he committed the assault, but we are not told why this is. It is certainly not a simple forfeiture theory, of the kind that appears to underpin the unlawful act approach – that once one has (to adopt Gardner's words in another context) 'entered the realm of criminality' one may be held criminally liable for whatever harm results, even if it is of a different kind from that intended or knowingly risked. For the moderate constructivist, simply crossing the criminal threshold is not morally significant enough. But entering the same family of offences, as by committing a common assault, is said to be sufficiently morally significant to justify holding D liable for some more serious offences against the person: intentionally wronging a person by attacking a particular interest is claimed to be a fair basis on which to hold the attacker criminally liable for unforeseen (and possibly unforeseeable) resulting harm. The orthodox subjectivist's principle of fairness, insisting on correspondence between the level of harm D chose to cause or risk causing and the level of harm for which D is held criminally liable, is rejected. The orthodox subjectivist's position is supported by the argument about choice, predictability and fairness. We must enquire further into the implications of moderate subjectivism in the hope of finding the justificatory arguments on which it relies.

5.5 DETERMINING THE EFFECT OF A CHANGE OF
NORMATIVE POSITION

We turn next, then, to the extent of criminal liability: even granting that, if D attacks V, D changes his normative position in relation to V, to what extent should that render D criminally liable for further (unintended) harms that D happens to cause? Antony Duff argues that there is a stark difference between attacks (where D intends to injure V's interest) and endangerment (where D knowingly creates a risk that V's interest will be harmed): the attacker cannot plausibly claim to be relieved if the harm does not ensue, whereas the endangerer can claim to be relieved if the risk does not materialise since the causing of harm was no part of the plan.[49] But this leaves open the question at issue here: if an attacker causes more harm than intended, should that fact alone lead to liability for a more serious offence? One of John Gardner's examples is the relationship between common assault and the more serious offence of assault occasioning actual bodily harm, already mentioned in part 4 above. Both offences have the same *mens rea* requirement – intention or recklessness as to

---

[49] RA Duff, 'Whose Luck is it Anyway?' in CMV Clarkson and S Cunningham (eds), *Criminal Liability for Non-Aggressive Death* (2008), 61.

touching another without consent – but the second offence penalises those assaults that result in 'actual bodily harm' with a much higher maximum sentence than the first (five years' imprisonment, compared with six months for common assault). Gardner argues that, by assigning this more serious label and higher penalty if certain consequences ensue, the law announces that assaulting another 'also exposes one to secondary risks, risks of additional liability, which one would not have faced but for one's commission of the original crime'.[50] Thus a person who changes normative position by intentionally assaulting another faces the possibility of liability for causing actual bodily harm or indeed of liability for assaulting a police officer in the execution of his duty (if the victim turns out to fit that description). Neither outcome need be foreseeable: for Gardner, as mentioned earlier,[51] the justice of this additional liability is constituted by the facts (i) that the law gives notice of the higher liability and (ii) that the two offences may be said to form part of the same family. As to the former, Gardner sets great store by the fact that people have been 'put on notice' by the law's clear statement (since 1861, at least) that this higher liability may be imposed if the outcome is more serious than D anticipated. Fair warning and notice are important components of the rule of law, but they are not capable of supplying substantive moral justification for a particular head of liability. Giving fair warning of an unfair rule does not turn it into a fair rule. For example, subjectivists (including, one assumes, most moderate constructivists) oppose strict criminal liability in principle, and argue that there must be fault requirements before conviction and punishment can be justified. Would moderate constructivists support a law that argued that, once a person intentionally assaults another, he or she should be strictly liable for whatever consequences ensue, whether foreseeable or not? If notice were given of this draconian law, would that render it more justifiable? Surely not, but this is a case in which both of Gardner's conditions are fulfilled: notice has been given, and the offences are part of the same family.

At this point one would expect some further kind of limiting principle to be introduced – perhaps a proportionality principle, to ensure that any enhancement of liability is not out of all proportion to the defendant's fault[52] – but Gardner fails to specify how far the effects of the change of normative position extend. He argues that to ask whether there are any boundaries to criminal liability, once a person has changed normative position by crossing the moral threshold, is to start the enquiry from the wrong end. If there has been a killing, ie a death caused by D's conduct, then that is where we should begin – by enquiring about D's responsibility for that killing of V and not about D's responsibility for the consequences of his assault on V. On this view, subjectivists who

---

[50] Gardner (above, n 32), 508.

[51] See nn 22 and 25 above, and text thereat.

[52] Cf Gardner's discussion of a proportionality principle (above, n 37) with A von Hirsch and A Ashworth, *Proportionate Sentencing* (2005), esp at 20–21.

adopt the neo-Kantian view outlined above, and focus on a concept of moral agency according to which what we do is (morally speaking) that and only that which we will, are 'stacking the cards at the very outset, before questions of responsibility even arise'. Thus:

> 'all the hard work now has to be done by moderate defenders of constructive liability, who face the uphill struggle of showing why (on policy grounds) liability should be upgraded from assault to manslaughter, rather than the downhill slope of showing why, in view of the fact that the killing was accidental, the liability should be [for] manslaughter rather than murder (intended killing being the paradigm)'.[53]

The difficulty with this is that it might equally be said that starting with the killing stacks the cards at the outset. In fact, the root problem is unchanged and remains part of the extensive and intricate debate on moral luck.[54] The agent who causes death has a moral duty of apology, perhaps a duty to pay compensation (depending on the circumstances), but the question whether there should be *criminal* liability for causing the *death* turns on further issues, not least one's conception of the proper function and scope of the criminal law. Even if one accepts that the law should mark the death with a special offence, it does not follow that the label should be such a serious one as manslaughter.[55] Moreover, it is unclear whether Gardner is able properly to claim that his starting point is that D killed V, when the change of normative position on which he places such weight is surely an assault, and nothing more. This, after all, is how he explains other examples – the assault changes D's normative position so as to render him properly liable for the more serious offence of assault occasioning actual bodily harm.[56] In respect of the homicide case relevant to the above quotation, Gardner concedes that 'the killing was accidental', and so we still need to resolve the question whether D's intention to commit an assault or battery against V should be a sufficient fault element for conviction for manslaughter when V's death was unforeseeable and was a statistical freak, a true accident, albeit one caused by D's conduct. In other words, there should be less focus on how the cards are stacked – let it be conceded that the enquiry is about responsibility for the causing of a certain death[57] – and more attention to the conduct that constitutes the change of normative position, and its proper implications.

[53] Gardner (above, n 19), at 239. For a version of the same argument, see his 'Crime: in Proportion and Perspective' (above, n 37), at 45, rejecting the 'extremely restrictive account of human agency' that confines enquiries about an actor's blameworthiness to evaluating the actor's perspective *ex ante*, and arguing instead for an approach that views blameworthiness in respect of the activity (or result) that the actor has brought about.

[54] Eg in S Shute, J Gardner and J Horder (eds), *Action and Value in Criminal Law* (1993), essays by RA Duff and A Ashworth, and Introduction; see also V Tadros, *Criminal Responsibility* (2005), 92–93.

[55] Cf n 17 above. The 'causing death by . . .' formula may be thought less stigmatic than the term 'manslaughter'.

[56] See the text above at nn 31 and 48.

[57] See RA Duff, 'Acting, Trying and Criminal Liability' in Shute, Gardner and Horder (above, n 54), and V Tadros, *Criminal Responsibility* (2007), 97–98.

While Gardner identifies no limiting principle other than the restriction to the same family of offences, Horder argues in his historical survey that a principle of proportionality has been at work in this field:

> 'Where D acts maliciously towards V, and causes worse harm than anticipated, the greater the injury intentionally done to V, the greater the crime for which D may be criminally liable respecting the harm actually done, whether or not that harm was anticipated by D; but the harm done must not be disproportionate to the harm intended, if criminal liability for the harm done is to be justified'.[58]

This operated largely as a restrictive principle, ensuring that there was not too great a 'moral distance' between the harm anticipated and that for which D was held liable. Thus Horder shows how the narrowing of the 'unlawful act' doctrine in the English law of manslaughter and other developments in the nineteenth century reflected the influence of such a principle.[59] It is not clear what the measure of proportionality should be, but Horder's own discussion of it tends to suggest that where there is a ladder of graded offences against the person, liability for the offence next above the harm anticipated may fairly be regarded as not too morally distant. In English law this would support convictions for assault occasioning actual bodily harm (up to five years imprisonment) based on a mere intention to assault (six months), convictions for inflicting grievous bodily harm (up to life imprisonment) based on an intention to cause some lesser physical injury,[60] and convictions for murder based on an intention to cause grievous bodily harm. Clearly much depends on the structure of the relevant law and the number of gradations of offences against the person. However, it is significant that unlawful act manslaughter is an absentee from this list: Horder notes the considerable moral distance between a mere assault and the causing of death,[61] although in this particular context the principle's ambit and its ability to perform a restrictive function remain somewhat unclear.[62]

To illustrate some of the issues we may take the case of *R v Williams*,[63] where D pushed V and slapped her once, with the result that she fell backwards and cracked her head on a heater, which severed an artery and caused her death. Accepting D's plea of guilty to manslaughter, the judge commented that V's

---

[58] Horder (above, n 5), at 96.

[59] Ibid, at 107 and 111–12.

[60] Cf Horder's criticism of the decision in *R v Mowatt* [1968] 1 QB 421 (ibid, at 112); and also the remarks in Horder (above, n 33), at 763 and 766.

[61] Cf Horder (above, n 5), at 115 and fn 106, with Horder (above, n 33), at 764 and 769, although in fn 25 he raises the possibility that manslaughter 'is too damning as a label to represent one's criminal responsibility here', and tentatively suggests a label such as 'causing death by intentional attack'.

[62] The Law Commission, in Law Com No 304, *Murder, Manslaughter and Infanticide* (2006), paras 3.46–3.49) proposes a form of unlawful act manslaughter that would slightly narrow the existing law by requiring that D killed someone by committing a criminal act while aware that it involved a serious risk of causing some injury.

[63] [1996] 2 Cr App R (S) 72.

death 'was fortuitous and, in a sense, accidental'.[64] There is, in principle, a whole range of possible fault elements in such a case. To take four, D could have been (i) walking past V when he tripped over, pushing her against the heater; (ii) leaving the house after burgling it when he encountered V and in his surprise tripped over, pushing her against the heater; (iii) assaulting V by pushing and slapping her once, as in *Williams* itself; or (iv) attacking her with punches and kicking her in the abdomen, causing her to fall against the heater.[65] In which of these scenarios does D change his normative position, or cross a moral threshold, sufficiently for liability for manslaughter? Of course there is a labelling issue here, and we should assume that the crime of manslaughter is understood to be a lower grade of homicide than murder, requiring a lesser degree of fault. Case (i) can be eliminated swiftly, on the ground that D did not intend to assault V or indeed to commit any wrong against V. Perhaps, in order to retain our focus, we can also deal swiftly with case (iv): kicking V in the abdomen suggests an intention to cause at least moderate injury, if not serious injury, and might therefore be regarded as a sufficient fault element for a crime of manslaughter. But what about cases (ii) and (iii)? Is it satisfactory to say that case (iii) ought to be sufficient for manslaughter because D has intentionally assaulted V, thereby changing his normative position in relation to harms that might result to V (including death)? We noted earlier that, when Gardner considered the distinction between the offences of common assault and assault occasioning bodily harm, he argued that committing an assault was a sufficient change of normative position to justify holding D liable for any actual bodily harm that might result, and that the law puts people on notice about that. Can that argument be extended to manslaughter, even if, to adopt Gardner's imagery, one asks the question by travelling 'downhill' from D's responsibility for causing V's death?

In relation to case (ii), can one say that D has sufficiently changed his normative position by intentionally committing a crime against V (burglary), so that it is fair to hold him criminally liable for any resulting harms? One obvious difference between cases (ii) and (iii) is that the crimes of burglary and assault form part of different families of offences. That is a restrictive consideration that points away from the unlawful act approach, which allows the intentional commission of *any* crime to constitute a sufficient change of normative position or crossing of a moral threshold,[66] and we saw earlier that Horder's formulation of the malice principle restricts it to conduct wrongfully directed at a particular type of interest. So, if we return to case (iii), the key question is how the moral connection between a death caused by D and D's intentional assault on V is to be established. If D intended nothing more than a common assault, and if the possibility of causing death was statistically very low (as it must be if a simple

---

[64] The Court of Appeal reduced the sentence from five to two-and-a-half years, so as better to reflect the accidental nature of the death.

[65] Cf *Attorney General's Reference No 43 of 1995 (Burnett)* [1996] 2 Cr App R (S) 74.

[66] Horder (above, n 33), 764, argues that the doctrine would be too crude without some such restriction.

assault is intended), is it merely a question of putting D on notice of the risk of a manslaughter conviction[67] if death should by mischance ensue? If notice alone were sufficient, that would raise the question whether due notice could convert case (ii) into a morally satisfactory foundation for a manslaughter conviction. The haziness of the notion of 'families of offences' was mentioned earlier; the restrictiveness of the malice principle, as formulated by Horder, would not have to be accepted by those who adopt a robust view of morally significant thresholds; and the ambit of the proportionality principle (and the related concept of moral distance) remains vague, lacking in articulated rationale and clear limits. Thus Horder's own view appears to be that there is too great a moral distance in case (ii):

> 'So, when I unlawfully kill another, I should not be convicted of manslaughter, if what I foresaw – or what should have been obvious – was that only some harm would result from my conduct. For the moral distance between the foreseen or foreseeable form of harm (actual bodily harm) and the harm actually done (killing) is too great to justify a manslaughter conviction: "manslaughter" would not be representative as a label in these circumstances'.[68]

One infers that Gardner would take a different view, or at least adopt a different analysis. But this example demonstrates not only that there is a need for greater coherence in the trio of purportedly restrictive criteria of 'families of offences', the malice principle and the proportionality principle, but also that those principles need to be applied and justified in relation to both the label of the offence for which conviction is indicated and the level of sentence to which the offender then becomes liable.

One limiting principle not advocated by proponents of moderate constructivism, although it lies close to their concerns, is the idea of scope of risk. If a particular consequence of D's action or 'attack' lies outside the scope of foreseeable risk, as determined by common experience or (if available) statistics, that ought to be taken to indicate that it would be unjust to hold D liable for that consequence. Thus one might argue, in the context of English law, that the causing or occasioning of actual bodily harm lies within the scope of the risk created by a common assault, but that the causing of death lies outside it. This is a view 'uphill' from the assault rather than 'downhill' from the killing, but that is legitimate when we are discussing the significance of the change of normative position itself (ie the consequences of an attack). Whether this limiting principle would be more restrictive than the somewhat ill-defined notions of proportionality and moral distance already discussed is difficult to determine; but the idea of scope of foreseeable risk has at least the merit of linking blame to probability, and avoiding the imposition of blame for the highly improbable. Such an approach might be used to confirm the provisional view taken of case

---

[67] Or other homicide offence: see Horder's suggestion at n 61 above, and also n 54 above and text thereat.

[68] Horder (above, n 33), 769; cf his possible qualification, at n 61 above.

(iv) above: intentionally kicking V in the abdomen may be taken to be the deliberate infliction of fairly serious injury, substantially more serious than a mere common assault, and creating a greater risk of death, thus making a stronger case for constructive liability for a serious offence such as manslaughter.[69]

5.6 CHANGE OF NORMATIVE POSITION BY ACTING KNOWINGLY

How does moderate constructivism apply to offences that turn on knowledge rather than on intention? In the English case of *R v Forbes*,[70] D had tried to bring into the country video recordings of two films. He said that he knew the videos were prohibited goods, but thought that they contained adult pornography, whereas in fact they contained child pornography. The House of Lords upheld his conviction for knowingly evading a prohibition on importation, and held that it was immaterial that he did not know the precise contents of the videos. Subjectivists would oppose the kind of offence that results in conviction despite the fact that D lacked knowledge of a key feature of the goods imported, ie that they contained child, rather than adult, pornography.[71] What position would the moderate constructivist adopt? Much depends on whether D could be said to have 'changed his normative position' by deciding to contravene a prohibition on importation. Unlawful act theory might support the conviction on the ground that any decision to smuggle goods into the country should render D liable for the consequences, whatever they might be. Moderate constructivists might reach for their concept of a 'family of offences' as a limiting principle here, but that raises the question whether adult and child pornography belong to the same family. It could be argued that the law (through its special provisions for child pornography) indicates otherwise, and many of those who use adult pornography would resist its classification within the same 'family'. If the concept of 'family of offences' proves sharp enough to distinguish between these two forms of pornography, the moderate constructivist would join the subjectivist in arguing against liability for this offence.[72]

---

[69] Reasoning based on 'scope of risk' may intelligibly be used to justify an offence such as causing death by dangerous driving, since causing death lies within the scope of the risk that the lesser offence of dangerous driving warns against. But it is straining the concept to apply the same reasoning to the new offence of causing death by careless driving, introduced by the Road Safety Act 2006 (UK).

[70] [2002] 2 AC 512.

[71] It should be noted that one consequence of D's conviction, in addition to 6 months' imprisonment, was that he was placed on the sex offender's register (now, subject to notification requirements) in virtue of involvement in child pornography. [See *R (on application of F) and Thompson v Secretary of State for the Home Department* [2010] UKSC 17, holding the notification requirements to be incompatible with Article 8 because there was no provision for review of individual cases.]

[72] D's admissions would amount to a confession of an attempt to evade a prohibition in respect of the films he thought he was importing.

A more awkward question concerns knowledge of age in sexual offences. In *R v G*[73] the defendant pleaded guilty to rape of a child under 13, having admitted the sexual intercourse but maintaining (as the girl conceded) that she told him she was 15. The law insists on strict liability as to the age of a person under 13, no knowledge as to this being required. Unlawful act theory would support a conviction, on the basis that G knew he was committing a crime (since she was under 16). Moderate constructivism might follow the same approach: by deciding to have sex with an under-age partner G changed his normative position, and the different offences (rape of a child under 13, sexual activity with a child under 16) belong to the same family. If it were countered that there is too great a moral distance between intentionally engaging in sexual activity with a girl under 16 (maximum sentence of five years, for an offender under 18, G being 15 himself) and rape of a girl under 13 (maximum sentence of life imprisonment), this confirms the questions raised earlier about the uncertain structure and content of the notions of proportionality and moral distance employed as limiting principles here. Subjectivists would oppose strict liability as to age, although they too would have to face questions about the circumstances in which they might regard it as justifiable to depart from a purely subjective approach in order to protect the vulnerable. That issue was broached in Chapter 4 above.

5.7 MODERATE CONSTRUCTIVISM RE-STATED

Has this discussion brought us any closer to an understanding of moderate constructivism? There seem to be three essential features of the position. First, the trigger for liability must be intentional conduct that may be said to amount to a change of normative position *vis-à-vis* the consequences of that conduct. It seems that the same approach may be taken to knowing conduct, arguing that where a person embarks on conduct with a prohibited form of knowledge, that may amount to a change of normative position that renders the person liable for unforeseen circumstances and consequences. (Some may well wish to take this line of reasoning further and apply it to endangerment, so that where a person knowingly creates a risk of a certain kind, and the consequences are more serious than anticipated, the original creation of the risk may count as a relevant change of normative position.) Secondly, the intentional or knowing conduct must be the commission of a crime that belongs to the same family as the (unforeseen) elements for which liability is in question. And thirdly, there must be a measure of proportionality, or no great moral distance, between the intended wrong and the harm resulting. The last two elements are, in effect, limiting principles.

---

[73] [2008] UKHL 37. Cf the article by J Horder, 'How Culpability Can, and Cannot, be Denied in Under-Age Sex Crimes' [2001] *Crim LR* 15.

Is this a sufficient justificatory account of moderate constructivism? The second and third features described above are both limiting principles (and are used in the same way in section 2.03(2) of the *Model Penal Code* on causation),[74] and so the main justificatory force must be found in the first feature (perhaps combined with the second). Why should the intentional or knowing commission of a crime of the same family render a person criminally liable for the unforeseen consequences of the conduct, which might otherwise be described as 'accidental'? No good reason has been given for this, other than the assertion that there has been a change of normative position, and that begs the question. What is required is a reason for saying that, given that the basis for liability is the subjective and cognitivist requirement of intentional conduct, the extent of the liability should be governed not by what the actor intended or foresaw (as subjectivists, applying the correspondence principle, would insist) but rather by events outside the actor's contemplation. There might be arguments for grounding such liability on a species or degree of negligence (as is done in manslaughter by gross negligence), but such arguments have not been found in the accounts offered by moderate constructivists.[75] It may be true that moderate constructivists tend to differ from many orthodox subjectivists in their view of the proper impact of moral luck on the criminal law, maintaining that the starting point should be the fact that D is responsible for causing the unanticipated and unforeseeable death and not, as many orthodox subjectivists would argue, the fact that D intended nothing more than a minor assault. But it is difficult to see why this difference should play such an important role in this particular debate: what D intended to do is also the basis of liability for moderate constructivists too, since that is where they find the significant change in D's normative position, and so it is right to focus on the moral quality of that act in relation to consequences that flow from it. No convincing argument has yet been produced by moderate constructivists to explain why the change of normative position inherent in D's original intentional conduct should be accorded such far-reaching moral and legal significance.[76]

---

[74] See n 4 above.

[75] Of the kind, for example, found in Jeremy Horder's 'Gross Negligence and Criminal Culpability' (1997) 47 *University of Toronto Law Journal* 495, an article that also criticises the cognitivist focus of orthodox subjectivism.

[76] John Gardner's book, *Offences and Defences: Selected Essays in the Criminal Law* (2007), includes reprints of his essays discussed above, and also includes a 'Reply to Critics', with comments on this chapter at 246–48.

6

The Unfairness of Risk-Based Possession Offences

6.1 RISK-BASED POSSESSION OFFENCES

I T IS A commonplace that in recent years the criminal justice system has come to put increasing emphasis on risk rather than on simply responding to past events: in policing, in pre-trial procedures, in the criminal law, in sentencing, in release procedures and in post-release supervision, we increasingly see risk-reduction and public safety being referred to as priorities.[1] In this article I want to engage with one small pocket of that movement – that constituted by risk-based offences of possession – and to examine its implications for criminal law doctrine.

Possession offences are one of the most ubiquitous forms of crime in modern systems of criminal law. They comply, much more fully than many other crimes, with rule-of-law requirements such as fair warning and certainty of definition. However, I will argue that some of the current forms of possession offence fall so far outside normal criminal law paradigms as to require serious re-assessment. To substantiate this claim, I will need to examine not only the contours of the offences but also the paradigm doctrines of the criminal law.

The authoritative survey of criminal offences of possession and their role by Markus Dubber is well known.[2] Taking a wide sweep, he identifies several changes in the structure and method of the criminal law through the last two centuries, arguing that possession offences came to be used in the 20th century in the way that vagrancy statutes were used in the 19th. The change of structure is manifested in a burgeoning of offences penalising the creation of a risk of harm, and much less emphasis on result-crimes that penalise the culpable causing of a particular consequence. The change of method takes the form

---

[1] See eg P O'Malley, *Risk, Uncertainty and Government* (2004); R Ericson, *Crime in an Insecure World* (2007), and L Zedner, 'Fixing the Future: The Pre-Emptive Turn in Criminal Justice' in B McSherry, A Norrie and S Bronitt (eds), *Regulating Deviance: The Redirection of Criminalisation and the Futures of Criminal Law* (2009).

[2] MD Dubber, 'Policing Possession: the War on Crime and the End of the Criminal Law' (2001) 91 *Journal of Criminal Law & Criminology* 829; see also MD Dubber, 'The Possession Paradigm' in RA Duff and SP Green (eds), *Defining Crimes: Essays on the Special Part of the Criminal Law* (2005).

of offences created in order to bolster the police power (in terms of regulating public order and controlling the dangerous) rather than offences that simply penalise wrongs culpably done against others. My emphasis here will be on the former change – the rise of what Douglas Husak terms 'non-consummate crimes'[3] and what Andrew Simester and Andrew von Hirsch refer to as 'non-constitutive crimes',[4] in the context of what Lucia Zedner describes as a movement from crime to pre-crime.[5] In much liberal theory the core of criminal liability is represented as culpable wrongdoing[6] – the paradigm of a criminal offence is where X culpably wrongs Y in a way that is of public concern – whereas these non-consummate and non-constitutive offences may be committed prior to, and without, anyone being wronged or harmed. These offences therefore seem to create a challenge to prevailing criminal law theory, in the sense that the restrictions on liberty they impose by criminalising people at a much earlier stage call for strong and specific justification.

The reason for this apparent extension of the criminal law is prevention. This is a term often used in the same context as risk and danger, and it is usually associated with utilitarian or consequentialist rationales. Risk and danger may refer to situations created by individuals (as in offences of dangerous driving or reckless endangerment), or they may be adapted so as to refer to particular individuals as presenting an unacceptable risk or being a 'dangerous person'. The references to particular individuals usually occur at the sentencing stage, in terms of special forms of incapacitative sentence or restraining order aimed at such persons. But the idea of creating special offences aimed at preventing wrongs or harms by penalising conduct before the wrong or harm is actually perpetrated seems attractive, not only for the obvious consequentialist reasons, but also on a retributive rationale. Although preventive rationales are at the core of consequentialist theories, the prevention of harm is also to be found at the core of retributive justifications for punishment. It would not be persuasive for a retributivist to suggest that the purpose of the criminal law is simply to declare the most serious wrongs and to provide for the conviction and punishment of those who culpably commit them, as if the prevention of such wrongs were of no concern. Since these wrongs are identified as sufficiently serious to justify criminalisation, it is important also to prevent their occurrence. The 'backward-looking' justification for making these wrongs punishable gives good reason for supporting the 'forward-looking' objective of preventing such wrongs from

---

[3] D Husak, 'The Nature and Justifiability of Non-consummate Offenses' (1995) 37 *Arizona Law Review* 151.

[4] AP Simester and A von Hirsch, 'Remote Harms and Non-Constitutive Crimes' (2009) 28 *Criminal Justice Ethics* 89. They use the term 'non-constitutive' to refer to offences in which 'the ultimate harm that justifies such crimes is remote from the crime itself; 'constitutive crimes' are those where the very harm that justifies criminalisation is part of the definition of the crime (eg murder).

[5] L Zedner, 'Pre-Crime and Post-Criminology' (2007) 11 *Theoretical Criminology* 261.

[6] See eg J Gardner, 'Wrongs and Faults' in AP Simester (ed), *Appraising Strict Liability* (2005), and Simester and von Hirsch, n 4 above.

being perpetrated. In principle, therefore, the retributivist has an interest in the taking of anticipatory or preventive measures for this purpose, although whether that supplies a justification for non-consummate offences (or, for example, for other forms of regulatory intervention) will be assessed below in relation to particular examples.

The focus here will be on a sub-set of possession offences. As Dubber has documented,[7] there is an enormous range of possession offences, and they differ in the purposes they are intended to fulfil. Drug offences are probably the most frequently prosecuted form of possession offence: while they raise some of the problems discussed below, they will not be the focus of this study. Another group of crimes may be termed 'past-regarding' possession offences, since their rationale is that possession of, say, stolen goods or of child pornography links the possessor to a previous crime (eg theft, or child abuse), in the sense that the possession may fairly be taken as an endorsement of that earlier offence. But the focus of this article will be upon a third group, which may be termed 'risk-based' possession offences. These offences – for example, unlawful possession of a handgun, burglary tools, or a concealed weapon – link the defendant to the creation of a risk or danger. Their rationale is said to be to penalise the creation of a risk of serious harm, be it the risk of burglary, of terrorism, or of death or injury. Central to the enquiry are handguns, and so it is necessary to give a brief description of the controversial and contrasting approaches of different jurisdictions in the US and England and Wales to firearms. Broadly speaking, the United States recognises a citizen's right to bear arms, but there are significant and substantial excluded categories (minors, felons, illegal aliens, drug users, those convicted of various domestic violence offences, and others). People in these categories may not possess a gun: this is ostensibly on grounds of increased risk, although the categories are drawn much more widely than is consistent with enhanced risk: in relation to 'felon-in-possession' laws, for example, those who have committed offences of violence might indeed present an enhanced risk, but not fraudsters or thieves. Another important aspect of US laws is that certain types of firearm are excluded from the citizen's general right to bear arms, such as grenades and automatic weapons, the possession of which is prohibited. In many US jurisdictions there are also controls on the buying and selling of guns, and sentence enhancements for those who commit offences with guns are widespread.[8] In England, by way of contrast, no constitutional right to bear arms is recognised, and the possession of a firearm is unlawful unless the owner has a licence.[9] The licensing system is much more restrictive than in the US, and the number of deaths involving firearms is far lower than in the US, even taking account of population size. Nevertheless, there is concern in England about the availability

[7] Dubber (2001), n 2 above.
[8] JB Jacobs, *Can Gun Control Work?* (2002), 19–35.
[9] Firearms Acts 1968–1997 (UK).

of guns to those minded to commit crimes with them, and this concern helps to sustain the far-reaching offences of firearm and ammunition possession that underpin the British licensing system.[10]

Given these strong social reasons in both countries for having laws that restrict firearm possession, why should there be difficulties in justifying them in terms of the doctrines of the criminal law? Two major difficulties are explored below. The first, in part 2, is that possession offences appear to flout several basic tenets of the criminal law – that liability requires an act by the defendant, that liability should be for an act unless the situation gives rise to a positive duty that the defendant fails to fulfil, that in principle *mens rea* should be required for liability, that the prosecution should bear the burden of proving guilt beyond a reasonable doubt, that the law of attempts should set the limits of inchoate liability, and that a person should only be liable for what he or she causes, encourages, assists or otherwise becomes normatively involved in. Consideration of the application of these doctrines will raise questions, incidentally, about the contours of liberal criminal law theory. The second difficulty, examined in part 3, is that possession offences seem not to satisfy the criteria for creating offences of endangerment. In part 4 we will briefly consider the implications of possession offences for sentencing, before attempting a re-assessment in part 5.

6.2 POSSESSION OFFENCES AND CORE DOCTRINES

Typical of the structure of risk-based offences of possession in English law would be those of possessing a firearm without a valid certificate, and of carrying in a public place any firearm (whether loaded or not) or imitation firearm. A more far-reaching example is the offence of possessing an article 'in circumstances which give rise to a reasonable suspicion that his possession is for a purpose connected with the commission, preparation or instigation of an act of terrorism'.[11] A typical offence in the US would be one of possession of a firearm by an ineligible person: the federal offence of possession of a handgun by a convicted felon carries a maximum sentence of 10 years' imprisonment. New York goes further and requires anyone to obtain a licence if they wish to carry a gun in public, allied to an offence of possession of a firearm in public without a licence.[12] Another common US example would be the possession of burglar's tools, which is penalised in most States.[13] The question I want to ask now is: in

---

[10]   For the current law, see *Blackstone's Criminal Practice, 2011*, B12.

[11]   Terrorism Act 2000 (UK), s 57(1); see also the offence under s 58 of the same Act, possessing a document likely to be useful to a person preparing an act of terrorism, analysed in *R v AY* [2010] EWCA Crim 762.

[12]   Jacobs, n 8 above, 33–35.

[13]   W Stuntz, 'The Pathological Politics of Criminal Law' (2001) 100 *Michigan Law Review* 506, at 538.

what ways, and to what extent, do offences in this form depart from the core doctrines of the criminal law?[14]

(A) The So-Called Act Requirement

Penalising possession may appear to run afoul of what is known as the act requirement in criminal law – that criminal responsibility must be based on a voluntary act. However, before we can conclude that this is the reality as well as the appearance, we need to analyse the matter further. The nature of the act requirement is contentious. The basic distinction seems to be between penalising an act (voluntary conduct by the defendant, permissible) and penalising a status or state of affairs (such as illness or addiction, impermissible).[15] But that raises the question whether the true requirement is of a 'voluntary act', which Michael Moore calls a 'bodily-movement-caused-by-a-volition'.[16] If that is the requirement, it is one that is violated by several familiar forms of offence and situation, notably offences of omission (discussed in part 2(B) below). An alternative approach is to adopt the 'control requirement', which states that people should only be held responsible for that which lies within their control.[17] This is a more inclusive approach, and it succeeds, without too much stretching, in encompassing crimes of possession. Along these lines is the stipulative definition of possession in the Model Penal Code:

> 'Possession is an act . . . if the possessor knowingly procured or received the thing possessed or was aware of his control thereof for a sufficient period to have been able to terminate his possession'.

This deems possession to be an act if either of those two sets of circumstances is proved, the former being an act done prior to the possession, the latter being a failure to carry out an obligation imposed by the definition itself.[18] Both sets of circumstances may be said to fulfil the control requirement,[19] even though it is not the act of acquisition that is being penalised as such, and the duty to

---

[14] For earlier discussions, see Dubber (2001), n 2 above, 915–18; Husak, n 3 above and D Husak, 'Gun and Drugs: Case Studies on the Principled Limits of the Criminal Law'(2004) 23 *Law and Philosophy* 437; Simester and von Hirsch, above n 4; DJ Baker, 'The Moral Limits of Criminalizing Remote Harms' (2007) 10 *New Criminal Law Review* 370 and DJ Baker, 'Collective Criminalization and the Constitutional Right to Endanger Others' (2009) 28 *Criminal Justice Ethics* 168.

[15] In *Robinson v California* (1962) 370 US 660 the US Supreme Court held that it was unconstitutional to criminalise addiction, that being a mere state of affairs.

[16] M Moore, *Act and Crime: The Philosophy of Action and its Implications for Criminal Law* (1993), Ch 1.

[17] D Husak, 'Does Criminal Liability Require an Act?' in RA Duff (ed), *Philosophy and the Criminal Law: Principle and Critique* (1998), and RA Duff, *Answering for Crime: Responsibility and Liability in the Criminal Law* (2007), 99 and 106–7.

[18] American Law Institute, *Model Penal Code* (1985), Part 1, 224.

[19] The English offence of possession for terrorist purposes relies on presumptions, rather than stipulations, to reduce the potency of the act requirement: Terrorism Act 2000 (UK), s 57(3).

divest creates an omissions offence. More will be said about the link with omissions in (B) below, but it must be noted that Duff regards the second part of the Model Penal Code definition as over-extending the act requirement. He favours an 'action presumption' – that in principle people should only be criminally responsible for the actualisation of a result of practical reasoning – and this leads him to conclude that simply failing to move or dispose of articles introduced by someone else should not be regarded as possession.[20]

On his way to these conclusions Duff remarks that a theoretical *actus reus* requirement that extends to offences of possession should be found because 'theorists agree that criminal responsibility for possession should not be ruled out in principle'.[21] This is problematic in that it looks like backwards reasoning: it more or less concedes that stretching is required if possession in some of its forms is to be regarded as an act rather than a state of affairs. It also casts an interesting shaft of light on criminal law theory. To what extent is criminal law theory normative, and to what extent descriptive? One might think that there would be little use (but still some curiosity?) in a criminal law theory that was philosophically persuasive but excluded many forms of criminal offence that legislators have found serviceable. On the other hand there would be little use in a criminal law theory that simply mirrored the contours of the forms of criminal law commonly enacted. To be brief on a subject of great complexity, I would argue that criminal law theory must take up a critically reflective position, with its roots in moral, political and social theory. It must examine whether certain assumptions about responsibility are acceptable or objectionable in principle. If they are found to be objectionable, then it cannot be a significant consideration that most criminal law theorists find some form of *modus vivendi* with possession offences. If the arguments in favour of the control principle are convincing, and that principle happens to encompass possession offences, so be it. But it should not be an argument in favour of the control principle that it does succeed in including possession offences. The control principle is either philosophically more plausible than the 'voluntary act' requirement or it is not.

I will return to the debate about the shape and limits of criminal law theory in part 5 below. For the moment, I conclude that the effort to bring offences of possession within the act requirement involves considerable stretching. It is much more natural to state that such offences penalise a state of affairs rather than an act. Whether the possessor is responsible for that state of affairs seems to depend partly on a mental element not yet discussed. It may be true that in most cases the possessor will have done some act in order to acquire the article, or have failed to remove it, but that will not always be true. There will be some

---

[20] Duff, n 17 above, 107. See also PR Glazebrook, 'Situational Liability' in PR Glazebrook (ed), *Reshaping the Criminal Law* (1978), 111, and also at 118, that Parliament should never 'provide that a person who has neither done anything nor been at fault in not doing something should incur criminal liability'.

[21] Duff, n 17 above, 106.

cases where someone else has brought the article into the possessor's house or car without the possessor's knowledge.[22]

(B) Possession as an Omission

The Model Penal Code definition has the effect of creating a duty-situation that partly constitutes possession. A person who is aware of the presence of a prohibited article on property that she or he controls (eg clothing, bag, dwelling, car) and who has sufficient opportunity to 'terminate possession' has a duty to take steps to do so. This duty is sensitively phrased, since it does not arise until the person has been 'aware of his control thereof for a sufficient period to have been able to terminate his possession': the duty is only triggered if there is awareness of the article's presence, and the duty requires only what is possible. But it is a duty nonetheless. Accepting that omissions liability is unusual and that the imposition of a duty requires special justification, how robust are the reasons here? Many of the real-life situations concern the finding of drugs on a person's property, which is not a central concern of this discussion; here, we should assume that the article is a handgun and that the putative possessor is a person not entitled to have it. We further assume that that person becomes aware of its presence, and knows that this is unlawful. Why should that person have a duty to do something about it, particularly if she or he is not responsible for its arrival?

Three possible analogies may be briefly considered. First, there is a well-known duty-situation where a person causes danger unknowingly or accidentally, and is held to have a duty to prevent the danger from going further.[23] The justification for this duty is that the person was responsible for causing the danger in the first place, albeit unwittingly, and so should have a duty to take remedial action; but the causal link on which that argument relies is not present here. Secondly, and more controversially, some jurisdictions recognise a duty of easy rescue. Can we say that the presence of a prohibited weapon presents a danger and that it is right that a person who becomes aware of its presence should take steps to neutralise that danger? The problem with this is that, even in a jurisdiction that does have a duty of easy rescue in criminal law, application of such reasoning here is clearly an extension – because no direct danger to an individual is assumed, whereas in the easy rescue cases there is direct danger. So this analogy will not be pursued further. Thirdly, some legal systems impose a duty on the owner of property to ensure that an offence is not committed on or with that property. An example from English law would be the owner of a car, who is a passenger while another person is driving the vehicle dangerously and says nothing to discourage such criminal driving: English law holds the owner criminally liable as complicit in the

---

[22] For discussion of the complicated English case-law on this, see Simester and Sullivan's *Criminal Law: Theory and Doctrine* (4th edn, 2010), 161–63.

[23] *R v Miller* [1983] 2 AC 161.

driver's offences.[24] Similar reasoning could be used to support the property owner's duty to inform the authorities of the presence of the prohibited weapon, or to neutralise it. However, the reasoning is controversial in itself, since it effectively co-opts the citizen as a law enforcement officer simply because he or she owns a particular house, car or other property. Thus none of the three analogies is strongly persuasive, and we have not moved significantly forwards from the question why a person who becomes aware of the presence of a prohibited firearm should have a duty in relation to that firearm. When, if at all, should citizens be under a duty, on pain of criminal conviction, to take steps to reduce a potential threat to public safety?

To the extent that there is a duty arising from awareness (as under the Model Penal Code), what should it require the person to do? Dubber makes the point that simply divesting oneself of the article is likely to be a crime, since it will amount to distribution of weapons, explosives, drugs or whatever.[25] However, the duty should surely be to hand over the article to the authorities, particularly where it is a dangerous article. English law provides for a justificatory defence of necessity for a person who is in possession of a prohibited drug while trying to deliver it into lawful custody or to prevent another from misusing it;[26] and the courts have extended the common law defence of necessity to similar situations involving firearms.[27] Thus if the doctrine of constructive possession is to impose a duty, it should be not simply to divest oneself of the dangerous article but to take reasonable steps to ensure that the article is delivered into lawful custody and its threat neutralised. But all of this is based on the assumption that there are adequate grounds for imposing the duty in the first place. The question is whether citizens are rightly constituted as their fellow citizens' keepers in this respect, singling them out for a duty because of their control and knowledge, to the extent of convicting them of a crime for failing to take steps to neutralise a possible danger. Opponents might argue that this is in reality a form of guilt by association, likely to be used chiefly against marginalised groups. Others would regard that as an enforcement issue, and as secondary to the question whether the justifications for imposing a duty on *de facto* possessors are strong enough to support the invocation of the censuring institution of the criminal law, a question to which we will return.

(C) The Culpability Requirement

Standard criminal law doctrine states that a person should not be liable to conviction without proof of fault, because that would be to impose state censure undeservedly and to fail to respect persons as thinking, planning individuals.

---

[24] *Du Cros v Lambourne* [1907] 1 KB 40; see ch 2.3(iii) above.
[25] Dubber (2005), n 2 above, 104.
[26] Misuse of Drugs Act 1971, s 5(4)(a) and (b).
[27] *R v Pommell* [1995] 2 Cr App R 607; for US cases, contrast *People v EC* (2003) 761 NYS 2d 443 with *United States v Teemer* (2005) 394 F 3d 59.

Criminalising possession may appear to run counter to this doctrine of *mens rea* in two respects. First, the definition of possession has only a restricted mental element; secondly, some possession offences do not require proof of a further intention. Starting with the definition of possession, some might question whether this should be regarded as part of the *mens rea* at all, since it seems to fall into the classical definition of *actus reus*. However, some elements commonly viewed as *actus reus* requirements do have a mental or culpability component in them, and possession is an example.[28] Possession is not simply a state of affairs (or, even, an act): the Model Penal Code definition refers to 'knowingly' procuring or receiving the article, or otherwise being 'aware' of control. Even if the effect of this is to insert culpability elements into the *actus reus*, that should not be regarded as a problem, since the division between *mens rea* and *actus reus* is simply an analytical tool which should not stand in the way of principled argument. More to the point is the reality in the United States that these apparent culpability elements are often diluted in practice by the operation of presumptions, such as the presumption that one possesses an article if one is present in a particular room or vehicle. The doctrine of constructive possession in many US jurisdictions reduces the role of culpability significantly.[29] Similar reductions in any culpability requirement operate in the English concept of possession: the leading authority on possession is not absolutely clear in its implications, because different points are made in different judgments, but the general drift is that knowing possession of a container (in this case, a box) is presumed to be knowing possession of its contents, but that presumption may be rebutted if it appears that the person believed that the contents were of an entirely different nature and had no reason to suspect otherwise.[30] The prevalence of presumptions and of doctrines of constructive possession shows that legislatures and courts are not comfortable with allowing culpability requirements to take their normal course, ie proof of knowledge by the prosecution beyond reasonable doubt. No doubt fear of false defences is a major factor in this; but that fear exists wherever an offence requires intention or knowledge to be proved, and if there are grounds for special concern, that can be minimised by employing a 'reasonable grounds' requirement.[31]

Having shown that the concept of possession itself has at best a diluted culpability element, what about *mens rea* requirements proper? There appears to be a plethora of offences in UK and US jurisdictions that penalise possession with intent. Possession of drugs with intent to supply is the obvious one, but in

---

[28] Simester and Sullivan, n 22 above, 161.

[29] For discussion of the details, see eg MD Dubber and MG Kelman, *American Criminal Law: Cases, Statutes and Comments* (2005), 263–72.

[30] This is a tentative distillation of the House of Lords judgments in *Warner v Commissioner of Police for the Metropolis* [1969] 2 AC 256. Warner's story (not accepted by the courts) was that he believed the box contained scent. In fact it contained drugs.

[31] As in the offence of possessing unsafe consumer goods for supply, contrary to s 10 of the Consumer Protection Act 1987, which provides the defence that the possessor 'neither knew nor had reasonable grounds for believing that the goods failed to comply with the general safety requirement'.

the UK we have possession of a firearm with intent to injure, possession of a firearm with intent to cause fear of violence, and so forth. These offences may be thought to make up for the defects of principle in the definition of possession by their insistence on proof of a further intent. The problem is that the prosecutor does not need to use them, because they are underpinned by a general offence of possessing a prohibited firearm, which carries a minimum sentence of five years and a maximum of 10 years' imprisonment. That general offence requires nothing more than proof of simple possession, which, as we have seen, often amounts to constructive rather than knowing possession.[32] Moreover any ignorance or mistake of law seems to be irrelevant to this offence, as it is generally.[33] Thus the most-prosecuted English firearms offence is effectively a crime of strict liability. It can be said to run counter to the general principle of *mens rea*, although this must be seen in the context of a significant gulf between theory and practice. Numerically, most offences in English law are strict liability offences, and even if we turn to the most serious offences that are triable in the Crown Court (similar to the US classification of felonies) some 40 per cent have a strict liability element.[34] It would be highly unusual for anyone to suggest that strict criminal liability is an appropriate paradigm that is justified in principle. Some scholars would accept strict liability for minor or regulatory offences, but would still insist on seeing this as a departure from an important general principle.[35] Others oppose it on the ground that negligence should be sufficient to achieve the policy ends of those who support strict liability, and that imprisonment should never be available as a penalty for an offence of strict liability.[36] In relation to *mens rea*, then, some of the most-used possession offences diverge from what is often presented as the paradigm, but that itself is a site of considerable ambivalence in criminal law theory.

(D) The Presumption of Innocence

Reference to the operation of presumptions shows that the burden of proving all the elements of possession offences does not always rest on the prosecution. The presumption of innocence has a central place in both European human rights law and US constitutional law; it is declared in Article 6(2) of the European Convention on Human Rights, and it also arises from the 'due process' clause of the Fourteenth

[32] See the English examples above at n 30 (drugs) and n 11 (terrorism). This is also why Fletcher regards such offences as objectionable, since they embody a presumption of guilt: GP Fletcher, *Rethinking Criminal Law* (1978), 198–99.

[33] See the discussion of the New York case of *State v Marrero* (1987) 507 NE 2d 1068, by PH Robinson and MT Cahill, *Law Without Justice: Why Criminal Law Doesn't Give People What they Deserve* (2006), 28–31; more generally, see Chapter 3 above.

[34] A Ashworth and M Blake, 'The Presumption of Innocence in English Criminal Law' [1996] *Crim LR* 306.

[35] The prevailing view among the contributors to *Appraising Strict Liability*, edited by Simester, n 6 above.

[36] For discussion and analysis, see Chapter 4 above.

Amendment.[37] But the presumption is subject to exceptions, and the debate therefore turns to the justifications for departing from the presumption of innocence in relation to a particular offence. Among the justifications generally advanced are two that will be mentioned briefly here. First, it is said that where public protection is important because the offence is serious – and this would apply to handgun possession, if not to all cases of possessing burglar's tools – that is a strong reason for requiring the defendant to bear the burden of proof. This is utterly unpersuasive: just as the offence becomes more serious, so the consequences of wrongful conviction for the defendant become more serious, and therefore the balance of reasons for placing the burden of proof is unchanged or even worsened. The presumption of innocence affirms that the state, with its great power and in relation to the censure and punishment that flows from criminalisation, should exercise the power to punish only after it has adduced sufficient evidence to prove the guilt of an individual.[38] Secondly, it is argued that the defendant should bear the burden of proving matters that lie 'peculiarly within his own knowledge'. Although Wigmore denounced this idea as unhelpful,[39] it re-surfaces from time to time for the pragmatic reason that it makes life less difficult for prosecutors. The underlying argument seems to be that an element should be proved by the party for whom its proof is easier; but that is not a principle to which the criminal law generally subscribes – otherwise all culpability requirements would have to be proved by the defendant, not the prosecutor. There is no particular reason why it should apply to possession offences more than to regular offences requiring *mens rea*, such as homicide, to which it certainly does not apply. So, insofar as possession offences place the burden of proof on the defendant (or have presumptions with this effect), they are inconsistent with prevailing doctrine.

(E) The Limits of Inchoate Liability

In paragraph (B) above we noted that the criminal law generally disfavours omissions offences, and requires special reasons for creating a duty-situation reinforced by the criminal sanction. A similar reluctance is found with inchoate offences such as conspiracy and attempts. Thus the limits of the inchoate offence of attempt have been the subject of constant controversy and debate among criminal lawyers. Two issues of principle stand out: first, at what point, beyond the first overt act, is it fair to impose liability for an attempt? And secondly, should an intention to commit the full offence be required for all inchoate offences, or might some lesser mental state be sufficient? English law and US

[37] The leading decision is *In re Winship* (1970) 397 US 358.

[38] For elaboration, see A Ashworth, 'Four Threats to the Presumption of Innocence' (2006) 10 *International Journal of Evidence and Proof* 241, and A Stumer, *The Presumption of Innocence* (2010).

[39] H Wigmore, *Treatise on Evidence* (P Tillers, (ed), 1985), 2486; cf the argument based on duties of citizenship put forward by RA Duff, 'Strict Liability, Legal Presumptions and the Presumption of Innocence' in Simester, n 6 above, 141.

laws tend to resolve these questions slightly differently, but we need not catalogue the divergences here. The relevant point is that these issues are widely
regarded as crucial to determining the frontiers of attempts liability. Thus, on
the *actus reus* of attempt, the Model Penal Code requires proof of a 'substantial
step' towards committing the full offence,[40] whereas English law requires proof
of a 'more than merely preparatory' act.[41] There is a difference, but more significant is the consensus that any overt act is not enough – the person must show
greater engagement on the road to committing the full offence than that, not
least because of all the possible contingencies short of completing the substantive offence. On the *mens rea* of attempt the Model Penal Code specifies 'the
kind of culpability otherwise required for commission of the [substantive
crime]', usually intention with or without the alternative of recklessness,
whereas English law requires intention for all attempts, although that can be
combined with recklessness as to circumstances if that suffices for the full
offence.[42] There is a difference between the two approaches, but more significant
is the consensus that a subjective mental element should be proved in relation to
the substantive offence. This consensus is also maintained in most jurisdictions
in relation to impossibility: English law and most US jurisdictions hold that the
offence of attempt is committed even if it is impossible to commit the full
offence by the means chosen, so long as the defendant's intention is established.

There are good reasons for criminal lawyers to agonise over these issues; reasons that relate to respect for an individual's liberty and autonomy.[43] Simply
doing any overt act with the required intention should be insufficient for criminal liability: this would reduce liberty by requiring us to forego options that may
be valuable to us and which may well be harmless, would condemn people even
though perpetration of the wrong of the substantive offence remains subject to
various contingencies, would deny people the opportunity to change their
minds (whether through repentance or failure of courage) before taking a deci-
sive step towards causing harm, and would also risk arbitrariness by giving the
police considerable power over individuals. To convict of an attempt should
require both a proximate act and a high level of culpability and commitment.

These are important patterns of principled reasoning; yet amazingly they dis-
appear when the discussion turns to offences of risk-based possession, despite
their being much more remote from the actual causing of harm, and often not
requiring proof of any subjective element in relation to the potential ultimate
harm.[44] Why do the principles governing attempts not apply to possession? Why

---

[40] Model Penal Code, s 5.01(1)(c).

[41] Criminal Attempts Act (UK) 1981, s 1(1).

[42] See Model Penal Code, s 5.01.1; Criminal Attempts Act (UK) 1981, s 1(1).

[43] The leading study of attempts is RA Duff, *Criminal Attempts* (1996); for a briefer overview, see
A Ashworth, 'Attempts' in J Deigh and D Dolinko (eds), *Oxford Handbook of the Philosophy of
the Criminal Law* (2011).

[44] Cf the discussion of this aspect of the writings of Günther Jakobs by D Ohana, 'Trust, Distrust
and Reassurance: Diversion and Preventive Orders through the Prism of *Feindstrafrecht*' (2010) 73
MLR 721, at 726.

do criminal lawyers stop talking about 'substantial steps' and proof of culpability when they turn to possession offences? Why should we not reject crimes of possession as too remote from the substantive offence, particularly those possession offences that do not require a further intent? We should note that the Model Penal Code includes some forms of possession within criminal attempts: it sets out seven forms of conduct that 'if strongly corroborative of the actor's criminal purpose, shall not be held insufficient as a matter of law' as substantial steps in relation to an attempt, the fifth and sixth of which refer, respectively, to possession of materials specially designed for unlawful use and to possession of relevant materials at or near the intended place of the crime.[45]

These provisions aim to narrow the distinction between criminal attempts and offences of possession, but they do not remove it. There are many possession offences which do not require proof of a further intention, and which might be committed in a situation that was not 'strongly corroborative' of a particular criminal purpose. Moreover in English law the possession of materials for crime would not itself amount to a 'more than merely preparatory act': it is far more likely that having the materials would be regarded as preparatory, and that a more proximate act would still be required.

So the conundrum persists: why do the reasons of principle that oppose liability for attempts at a point before a 'substantial step' or 'more than merely preparatory act' not apply to negative liability for offences of mere possession? Is it that we are not serious about those requirements? That is hardly likely, given their connection with the arguments of principle that underpin the law of attempts. Is it that criminal lawyers have simply failed to notice the inconsistency? I have more respect for my colleagues than that. So is it that criminal lawyers believe that there are some countervailing factors that justify taking a different approach to possession offences? This has not been articulated. One possibility is that, because possession offences are often absolutely clear about what they prohibit, their general compliance with the rule-of-law requirements of fair warning and reasonable certainty is thought to compensate for their other deficiencies (as contrasted with the indeterminacy of the 'substantial step' or 'more than merely preparatory' tests for attempts). In relation to the risk-based possession offences being discussed here it could be the risk to public safety, stemming from the potential danger to life or limb from use of the weapon, which is taken to overwhelm the principled arguments that normally hold sway. But the most salient fact is the failure of many commentators to engage with mainstream doctrines on criminal attempts when discussing risk-based possession offences, despite the obvious incompatibility.

---

[45] Model Penal Code, s 5.01(2)(e) and (f).

(F) Liability for the Possible Future Acts of Others

Underlying possession offences is a concern about what harm might be done to others with the prohibited article. The source of that danger is unspecified. Usually the risk is thought to be that the future harm might be done by the possessor, in which case the offence of possession would be an extended form of inchoate offence, as discussed in the previous paragraphs. In some cases the risk might be that the future harm might be done by some other person, and we turn to that possibility here. In principle one individual is not criminally liable for the acts of another individual unless the first person joins in, assists, encourages, incites or causes the other's acts. The basic principle is that each of us is responsible only for what we do (cause), and that we should therefore not be liable for the results of the intervening choices of other people, since they are separate choosing persons.[46] Accepting that basic principle, can we identify a plausible link between D's possession and the act of another who may subsequently use that article if, say, D leaves it (gun, explosives, or other weapon) visible on the back seat of his car? That act is not an incitement or encouragement, since those terms indicate some form of oral, or at least verbal, suggestion of what further act might be done. Nor does it amount to causing the other to act, or joining her or him in some combined enterprise. Leaving a prohibited article around, making it available to others, cannot really amount to more than assisting another. Even that is stretching the point, unless it can be established that there is an intention to assist. A wide range of acts, wholly innocent or otherwise, can be construed as helping another to some extent; but it would only be fair to hold D liable for assisting another if D additionally had an intention to assist, or at least was aware that the act would assist another.[47] This would be the normal requirement of the law of criminal complicity: there must, as Andrew Simester and Andreas von Hirsch put it, be some sort of 'normative involvement' by D in the other person's subsequent choice.[48]

We therefore see that, insofar as one rationale for risk-based possession offences is to criminalise D's possession on the basis of what other people may do with the prohibited article (not even, what they have done with it), such criminal liability diverges strongly from normal paradigms. D's conduct in having the article with him is treated, in effect, as the creation of an opportunity that might not otherwise exist, and that is the ground for criminal liability. Dubber, perhaps by way of caricature, suggests that it is D's association with the dangerous article that is the ground for criminal liability. Thus, by having

---

[46] A von Hirsch, 'Extending the Harm Principle: Remote Harms and Fair Imputation' in AP Simester and ATH Smith (eds), *Harm and Culpability* (1996), 266–67; see also Baker (2007), n 14 above, at 372–73.

[47] I leave out of account here the problem of D's liability for doing an act that foreseeably encourages another to commit an offence: see the discussion of Glanville Williams' views by Baker (2007), n 14 above, 383–86, and also in Baker (2009), n 14 above, 179–81.

[48] Simester and von Hirsch, n 4 above, at 99.

the article with her or him, D is taken to share the article's dangerousness: indeed, as Dubber reminds us, presence while an offence is being committed is not sufficient to establish criminal complicity, but in possession offences there is often a presumption that everyone present in a car or room has possession of all the articles contained in it.[49] Of course there cannot be complicity between D and an inanimate object, no matter how 'dangerous' that object is. But Dubber's purpose is to demonstrate how far offences of possession have travelled from the paradigm. Insofar as they hold one person liable for what another person might do, without any requirement of normative involvement in that other's activity, they are entirely inconsistent with normal rules of imputation.

6.3 POSSESSION AS A FORM OF ENDANGERMENT

The message of part 2 above is clear: many current forms of possession offences stand outside the normal paradigms of the criminal law. Insofar as there is a voluntary act requirement in criminal law, they seem to fail this, or to be included only by stretching. Whether possession offences can be re-worked as offences of omission remains to be seen, but they have not typically been so regarded. The definition of possession involves a heavy constructive element, and no further *mens rea* is required for many possession offences. Reverse burdens of proof are common for possession offences, creating departures from the presumption of innocence that do not seem to be supported by convincing reasons. Possession offences go beyond the normal principles of imputation in criminal law, insofar as they hold people liable for creating an opportunity for acts by independent others. And, above all, the criminal law takes an understandably restrictive approach to inchoate offences, which penalise people before the harm has eventuated; but possession offences provide for people to be convicted at a significantly earlier stage, despite the obvious inconsistency with the principles applicable to inchoate offences. Yet, notwithstanding all these objections, risk-based possession offences are a major feature of many criminal justice systems, created in significant numbers (eg possession of illegal firearms, other weapons, burglary tools, counterfeiting equipment, and so on) and frequently enforced.[50] Can strong justifications for these offences be found?

As a preliminary point, we must recall that the focus here is on risk-based possession offences, a particular sub-group typically relating to handguns, explosives, other weapons and burglary tools. The rationale for offences of this kind must be preventive. Possession itself involves neither the infliction nor the threat of harm: it is criminalised in order to prevent possible harm to others arising from the potential misuse of the dangerous objects. This rationale draws upon the importance of public safety, in terms of protection from death or

[49] Dubber (2001), n 2 above, at 864, 896.
[50] Some American figures are given by Dubber (2001), n 2 above, 835–36, suggesting that one-fifth of prison sentences in New York in 1998 were for possession offences (mostly drugs).

serious injury, which must be high on the list of priorities of the state; it also draws upon the dangerousness of the article, in terms of its potential to be used to cause death or serious injury. These considerations are familiar in debates relating to endangerment offences, or what some call 'proxy crimes'.[51] We are concerned here, not with crimes of concrete endangerment where someone actually has been put in danger, but with crimes of abstract endangerment – cases where a dangerous situation has been created but there is no need to show that anyone was put in actual danger. There are two ways in which such a dangerous situation may come about: first, the person's possession of the weapon creates the risk that he or she may use it offensively, to cause unjustified harm; secondly, the person's possession of the weapon, notably by leaving it in an accessible place, creates the risk that another may use it offensively.

Our principal concern here is with the former situation, where the possession is held to create a risk that the possessor will subsequently use the weapon offensively. Simester and von Hirsch, adapting Feinberg, set out the harm principle in the following schematic form:

'Step 1: Consider the gravity of the eventual harm, and its likelihood. The greater the gravity and likelihood, the stronger the case for criminalization.

Step 2: Weigh against the foregoing, the social value of the conduct, and the degree of intrusion upon actors' choices that criminalization would involve. The more valuable the conduct is, or the more the prohibition would restrict liberty, the stronger the countervailing case would be.

Step 3: Observe certain side-constraints that would preclude criminalization. The prohibition should not, for example, infringe rights of privacy and free expression'.[52]

Applying this schema to cases of illegal gun possession, the first step is crucial. Although the risk of a firearm being used offensively seems to be statistically low,[53] the eventual harm is as grave as can be – death. Much therefore depends on how heavily that grave outcome is weighted as against the low probability of its occurrence.[54] Some light may be cast on this in the second step, when one asks what valuable options may be sacrificed by criminalisation. One is the possibility of keeping or carrying the weapon for self-defence (or the defence of others): that is legally justifiable in a fairly narrow set of situations, but there is the attendant danger that possession of the weapon will act as a form of over-stimulation and may lead to the use of the weapon in situations outside the boundaries of justification. Such uses may occur in the home, as where the gun's possessor uses it in a domestic dispute, or in a public place. These are difficult calculations, depending to some extent of the prevailing

---

[51] This terminology is employed by M Moore, *Placing Blame: A Theory of the Criminal Law* (1997), 783–84, and by L Alexander, K Ferzan and S Morse, *Crime and Culpability: A Theory of Criminal Law* (2009), 310–11.

[52] AP Simester and A von Hirsch, *Crimes, Harms and Wrongs* (2011), Ch 4.2.

[53] See D Husak, *Overcriminalization: The Limits of the Criminal Law* (2008), 172.

[54] Cf Husak's first two limiting principles for offences of risk-creation, ibid, 161–62.

culture (ie whether guns are often carried, or whether, as in the United Kingdom, this is relatively rare). Step 3 has some relevance in the United States, where there is a general constitutional doctrine of the individual's right to bear arms, albeit that some individuals are deprived of this right. However, the critical issue appears to be the link between guns and death, both in the particular and in the general statistical sense (an estimated 12,000 homicides per year perpetrated with guns in the United States).[55] In practice, it seems that this link overwhelms all the other arguments. Thus, rather than waiting until the possessor has reached the stage of an attempted crime, the criminal law intervenes in these instances at the very stage of possession. It does so because the consequences could be fatal, and human life is the supreme value that the law should strive to protect.

Is this reasoning likely to prove strong enough to justify offences of weapon possession? Michael Moore contends that these grounds for criminalisation fail to reach the required level:

> 'Such crimes are defended on the preventive ground that they isolate a convenient point in time from which it is predictable that some moral wrongs will occur, and such wrongs can thus be efficiently prevented by preventing the earlier, non-wrongful act . . . The problem with this defence of "wrongs by proxy" is that it gives liberty a strong kick in the teeth right at the start. Such an argument does not even pretend that there is any culpability or wrongdoing for which it would urge punishment; rather, punishment of a non-wrongful, non-culpable action is used for purely preventive ends. We rightfully eschew such preventive incapacitation generally in our punishment theories, and we should not allow such practices to enter unwittingly because disguised as supposedly independent crimes'.[56]

Moore's argument is that retributive theory requires it to be shown that the possessor deserves punishment for wrongdoing. What his critique fails to capture is the question of the nature and remoteness of the permissible link between the possession and the wrong. Since the rationale is to prevent death, there is clearly a wrong 'involved'. The need is for an argument that shows that it is the possessor's responsibility to guard against the dangers outlined earlier (overexuberant use of the weapon at a subsequent time); or, to put it in Simester and von Hirsch's terms, that the possibility of those future acts can fairly be imputed to the possessor now, at the stage of mere possession.[57] Is it right to criminalise a person now for the possibility that in the future they may change their mind and use the article offensively? Some may protest that a person who brings a concealed weapon into a public place must already have decided that he or she is prepared to use it to cause harm. That is problematic on at least two grounds: first, that the possessor may undergo a change of mind; and secondly, that the possessor may have decided only to use the weapon justifiably (eg in self-defence),

---

[55] *New York Times*, 27 September 2010, A10.
[56] Moore, n 51 above, 784.
[57] Simester and von Hirsch, n 52 above, Ch 4.4(B).

and so may be argued to be carrying the weapon for a lawful purpose.[58] The relevance of a possible change of mind is fundamental, as Duff affirms:

> 'to criminalize my conduct is to criminalize me on the basis of what I might go on to do: what connects my present conduct to the prospective criminal harm is not my intention to do that harm (which would be a morally relevant connection), but an empirical prediction about what people might do – a prediction whose use in this way denies my responsible agency by treating me as someone who cannot be trusted to guide his actions by the appropriate reasons'.[59]

Therefore, strong as the practical arguments may be for such offences as easy to prosecute, risk-based possession offences of this kind cannot be supported as endangerment offences.

Thus far we have been discussing the primary basis for criminalising possession of firearms and dangerous articles – that the possessor may use them to cause unjustified harm. But there is also a secondary basis. These may be termed crimes of indirect abstract endangerment, in the sense that 'harm would ensue only in virtue of the intervening actions of others'.[60] As Duff comments:

> 'Whether and when we have good reason to criminalize such indirect endangerment depends on what view we should take of our responsibilities in relation to the conduct of others: whilst we cannot plausibly deny that we have some general responsibility to guard against the direct risks of harm that our conduct creates, there is more room for argument about whether, when or how far we should be expected to attend to the risk that our conduct will give others the means or opportunity to do harm'.[61]

Let us explore what Duff refers to as the 'room for argument'. The principled starting point, as von Hirsch points out, ought to be a recognition of 'the separateness of persons as choosing agents. It is that other person who has made the culpable choice of doing harm, not the original actor'.[62] Thus, if there is evidence that the possessor has left the weapon in a particular place in order to encourage another person to use it, that might fairly be treated as an offence of possession with intent to assist in the commission of an offence. But in the absence of any such direct link between possessor and subsequent user, the focus ought surely to be any duties that might properly be imposed on the possessor. We might agree that anyone who deals lawfully with explosives and nuclear materials is rightly placed under strong safeguarding duties and procedures at all times: to impose such duties does not seem inappropriate in view of

---

[58] The second point might lead to the conclusion in some high-crime neighbourhoods that everyone might be justified in carrying a weapon because everyone might justifiably fear attack; this would create a serious problem for law and legitimacy, among other things.

[59] Duff, n 17 above, 165; cf D Ohana, 'Desert and Punishment for Act Preparatory to the Commission of a Crime' (2007) 20 *Canadian Journal of Law and Jurisprudence* 113, at 123, arguing that a responsible legislator would take account of the probability of a renunciation (presumably, by regarding it as improbable in most cases?).

[60] Duff, n 17 above, 163–65.

[61] Ibid, 164.

[62] Von Hirsch, n 46 above, 267.

the enormous scale of the potential harm that could result from misuse of those materials, and an offence of negligently failing to guard such materials as required would seem to be appropriate. Firearms are not quite in the same category, but given their lethal potential and the detailed regulatory provisions applicable to them, it is not difficult to construct a plausible argument (in the UK at least) to the effect that possessing firearms in circumstances and places outside those regulations ought to give rise to a duty to safeguard them from others. If we accept this duty to safeguard firearms, there is a *prima facie* argument in favour of criminalising a negligent breach of that duty.

It remains true that there is a considerable difference between explosives, in terms of their massively destructive potential, and handguns. Explosives are more likely to be used to cause multiple deaths, and to present a deeper challenge to community safety and state legitimacy, than a gun. But liberal theorists must remain concerned about 'whether we may legitimately coerce [one person] to give up options merely because others might later misbehave'.[63] Simester and von Hirsch argue that this is not a strong enough justification for criminalising the creation of danger unless the possessor is sufficiently 'normatively involved' in the subsequent conduct of the other person. The possessor must 'in some sense affirm or underwrite the intervening actor's subsequent choice', as by advocating that behaviour, encouraging it, giving advice about it, or supplying a product designed for such behaviour. In relation to that last category, they argue that 'to supply a tool is to condone the use of that tool for its core function', which amounts to normative involvement in that use. As Simester and von Hirsch approach the precise topic of this article, they indicate that it lies close to the limits of justifiable criminalisation:

'Other cases will be borderline because of uncertainty about the core nature of a thing's functions. Handguns, perhaps, are in this category. To the extent that their core use is uncertain, the case for prohibiting their supply is also borderline, and may well differ across societies. Effectively by constitutional fiat, the possession and use of handguns is deemed prima facie legitimate within the U.S. It seems hard to claim, therefore, that their core use is in mounting wrongful attacks on people or their property. By contrast, the social understanding of handguns in the U.K. associates their use much more closely with violence and wrongdoing; perhaps reflecting the traditionally more crowded nature of domestic housing, which permits few opportunities for recreational use. Insofar as this is true, their supply can be more clearly understood as associating suppliers with the wrongdoing they facilitate'.[64]

Much would depend on the degree to which the concept of 'core use' can be nuanced: whereas US constitutional law is said to recognise the possession of handguns as legitimate, this does not apply to people with an excluded status, where felon-in-possession offences presume that the core use would be dangerous. In respect of that group of people, therefore, US law is on a par with

---

[63] Simester and von Hirsch, n 4 above, 99, also citing Duff, n 39 above, 64.
[64] Simester and von Hirsch, n 4 above, 101–2.

UK law. Simester and von Hirsch's reasoning focuses on the supply of an article such as a handgun to another, and in order to confine the law's reach to unacceptable cases they propose the inclusion of an ulterior mental element in the offence – for example, supplying a gun to another, knowing that there is a substantial risk that the other's use will be unlawful.

The discussion so far has focused on the relationship between the possession and the ultimate harm (death, in the case of guns). A different perspective would be to consider whether it would give rise to harm if possession were not criminalised. The law of attempts would remain, but law enforcement agencies would not be empowered to intervene until a person had done a 'more than merely preparatory' act or taken a substantial step towards causing direct harm.[65] It could be argued that in some situations this would leave law enforcers impotent to prevent the occurrence of a major harm – by requiring them to wait until the gun was about to be used, which could leave only a split second in which to intervene. This suggests a pragmatic and harm- and wrong-related reason for criminalising possession;[66] but it does not weaken the argument in the previous paragraph for requiring proof of intent or absence of reasonable grounds.

In conclusion, then, it has been argued that risk-based possession offences are most appropriately conceptualised as offences of endangerment. However, in terms of liberal criminal law theory, that does not mean that principles of responsibility and imputation no longer apply. On the contrary, those principles must be kept in the foreground, as the English Law Commission has recently argued:

> 'Fault elements in criminal offences that are concerned with unjustified risk-taking should be proportionate. This means that the more remote the conduct criminalized from harm done, and the less grave that harm, the more compelling the case for higher-level fault requirements such as dishonesty, intention, knowledge or recklessness'.[67]

On this basis there seem to be two possible endangerment-based grounds for criminalising the possession of weapons, taking account of the gravity of the possible harm. The first is to criminalise such possession in order to remove the risk that the possessor will decide to use the weapon offensively. Thus, when English law penalises a person who has an unlicensed firearm in her or his house,[68] as well as the person who takes a gun into a public place, it does so in order to prevent an unacceptable danger of death or serious harm. However, offences of simple possession are objectionable because they presume an offen-

---

[65] See n 45 above and accompanying text for the situations in which possession may of itself amount to a substantial step under the Code.

[66] Cf the nuanced discussion by Simester and von Hirsch, n 52 above, Ch 3.2.C.

[67] Law Commission, *Criminal Liability in Regulatory Contexts*, Consultation Paper 195 (2010), Proposition 10 (para 4.61), summarising the argument in Part 4 of the paper.

[68] The offence is committed even if the possessor does not realise that the gun is prohibited, thinking that it is an antique or is a permitted article: see *R v Howells* [1977] QB 614 and *R v Hussain* (1981) 72 Cr App R 143.

sive intention, and do not require proof of it. The primary offence should penalise the possession of a prohibited firearm with intent to commit, or to assist in the commission of, a crime (which would, in effect, require the prosecution to negative innocent use).[69]

Secondly, this might be under-pinned by a broader offence drafted along similar lines to the general 'health and safety' offence in English law, such as failing to take reasonable steps to ensure that a dangerous object is properly secured. That would be an offence of negligence and, as such, it would not appear to reduce the possessor's options too greatly (in terms of liberal theory). There would also be room for a third offence – an offence of failing to comply with licensing requirements, which would be a regulatory offence of simple possession, not carrying liability to a prison sentence. All these offences should be subject to a defence of reasonable mistake or ignorance of law, to cater for cases where the defendant was reasonably ignorant that the article was prohibited.

6.4 IF POSSESSION IS CRIMINALISED, HOW SHOULD IT BE SENTENCED?

The obvious answer for a retributivist is that sentence should be based on the degree of culpability of the possessor, which depends on the nature of the offence of conviction. If the offence is one of possessing a prohibited firearm with intent to commit crime, or without reasonable excuse, this should be treated as a preparatory or pre-inchoate offence. This means that the sentence ought to be distinctly less than the sentence for an incomplete attempt that is stopped before the offender comes close to committing the substantive offence. The projected harm may be death or serious injury, but its remoteness ought to lead to a substantial reduction from that for, say, attempted wounding. In the kind of case where the offence is one of negligence – ie where the possessor failed to safeguard the prohibited object – the sentence should be even lower, and should take full account of the remoteness of the possession from any harm or threatened harm. Since it is not a case of supply, which should be a separate offence, its gravamen is the creation of a risk that another will seize and misuse the gun. The magnitude of that risk will depend on the circumstances in which the gun was found.

These arguments point strongly in the direction of re-appraising the English approach to sentencing for possession of a prohibited firearm. The minimum sentence is five years' imprisonment unless there are exceptional circumstances, but there is no defence of ignorance or mistake as to the law. The result is that people are liable to be convicted of the strict liability offence of simple possession, even though they may be ignorant that they have a prohibited article, and

---

[69] Accord: Ohana, n 59 above, 136.

deprived of their liberty.[70] This is far too severe a regime for an offence of simple possession; it constitutes an unacceptable departure from criminal law doctrine and proportionality in sentencing.

The argument here is that sentence ought to be based solely on desert. Examples of this approach for offences of indirect abstract endangerment would be the response to exceeding the speed limit or drunk driving, offences justified by their potential danger to life and limb. Speeding is the more remote from the ultimate harm, and is usually punished with a financial penalty, often with the consequence of loss of driver's licence for those who persist. Drunk driving is thought to be closer to the ultimate harm and to involve more serious misconduct, but it is usually punished fairly low on the scale, by financial penalties and sometimes a short custodial sentence (particularly in Scandinavian countries). The point here is that these sentences are significantly lower than those required by British legislation for simple possession of a firearm. Can this be justified by the relative distance from the ultimate harm and the relative culpability of the offenders? Can it be said that possessing a gun is a less ambiguous indication of wrongful intentions? Surely not, since there is the awkward question of possession for self-protection. Are the punishments for drunk driving too low, rather than those for illegal gun possession too high? This is an important question in its own right. For the present, the argument is that the mandatory minimum sentence of five years' imprisonment for simple possession of a prohibited firearm or ammunition is much higher than can be retributively justified; that a moderate fine would under-value the seriousness of an offence other than simple unlicensed possession[71]; and that, certainly if an offence of failure to safeguard a firearm were introduced, a middle ground (not routinely involving custodial sentences) must be developed.[72]

6.5 CONCLUSIONS: POSSESSION OFFENCES AND CRIMINAL LAW DOCTRINE

Offences of simple possession are to be found in many modern legal systems. They have the great rule-of-law merits that usually they are clearly defined and give fair warning of the reach of the criminal law. But they fail to meet many of the standard requirements of the criminal law: they do not require a voluntary action; they do not always require awareness and/or intention; they often depart from the presumption of innocence; by penalising people on the basis of what they might subsequently decide to do, they do not measure up to the require-

---

[70] Eg *R v Deyemi and Edwards* [2008] 1 Cr App R 25; *R v Rehman and Wood* [2006] 1 Cr App R (S) 404; *R v Beard* [2008] 2 Cr App R (S) 232 and the discussion in ch 4.4 above.

[71] Three decades ago, moderate fines for the offence were not unusual: see *R v Howells* and *R v Hussain*, n 68 above.

[72] See Jacobs, n 8 above, 220.

ments for inchoate offences; and they also criminalise people on the basis of what other individuals might decide to do.

One response to this catalogue of apparent failings is to suggest that the standard requirements of the criminal law are not standard: they are ideals, but we recognise that in fact legal systems depart from them. This takes us back to the argument, in part 2, about the relationship between possession offences and the so-called voluntary act requirement of criminal offences. If possession offences do not fit, we asked, should we therefore adjust the paradigm and devise a wider requirement that can accommodate these offences? This is surely not the right manoeuvre, since theoretical robustness and consistency are more important than an absolute fit with reality. We must recognise that certain policies may operate as political imperatives, for reasons of local tradition or beliefs about public opinion or politicians' fears. Thus William Stuntz argues that a major reason for the spread of possession offences is that they are much easier for prosecutors and police to use:[73] that is why those groups lobby for such offences, and why legislatures enact them, particularly in anti-terrorist statutes. If that is so, they should simply be cast as pragmatic exceptions or departures from the general doctrine.

This cannot be said where the exceptions exceed the number of applications of the 'standard', as with strict liability offences in English criminal law. The criminal law textbooks and theoretical writings argue that *mens rea* or a fault element is a basic requirement of criminal liability, but Parliament has enacted and continues to enact many more offences with elements of strict liability. The textbooks refuse to alter their presentation in the face of this reality, because they are making a normative point rather than a descriptive one: the argument is that rule-of-law values and respect for the autonomy of the individual in the context of state censure and punishment establish a conclusive case for requiring fault as a condition of criminal conviction, and therefore that the legislature is wrong to enact strict liability offences, particularly where imprisonment is a possible sanction. In other words, we should not sacrifice sound principles simply to enable one common outlying type of offence – possession offences – to be brought within the justificatory scheme.

It was suggested in part 2(B) and part 3 that the most convincing justification for possession offences is to regard them as offences of abstract endangerment, grounded in an omission to carry out the duty of care and protection imposed on someone who knowingly has control of a dangerous object. This throws a great deal of weight on appropriate expectations of an autonomous individual in that position. Should a person be liable to conviction for what he or she might subsequently do with a particular article? Or, *a fortiori*, for what someone else might do with that article?

---

[73] Stuntz, n 13 above, 558: 'Proving burglaries may be costly; proving possession of burglars' tools will be much easier (and the latter charge will therefore tend to generate more guilty pleas)'.

'In any liberal conception of the state, people have a fundamental right to be treated as separate individuals, as autonomous moral agents who are distinctively responsible for, and only for, the consequences of their own actions . . . That, at least, is the starting point'.[74]

For what reasons might one move from this starting point? One relevant consideration may be the nature of the country with which one is dealing, its social and legal traditions. What degree of priority should be assigned to individual liberty, as compared with the community-based imposition of duties on citizens to take precautions with dangerous articles that could be used to kill or maim? The danger presented by a loaded gun is considerable, but this refers to its potential use, so that mere possession remains remote from the apprehended harm or wrong. Standard doctrine would respond by requiring at least proof of an intention to commit some further harm. If the pressure for political compromise is irresistible, then, as Christopher Slobogin has argued,[75] this may be an appropriate point for the criminal law to borrow from the principles applicable to incapacitative measures such as civil detention, and to demand that possession offences be enacted only if and insofar as they require proof of the probable danger of the article being used to cause serious harm. If as criminal lawyers we are not seriously committed to limits of this kind, then we must reflect on our commitment to principle more generally. In view of their practical on-the-street effects and the substantial sentences to which they can now lead, many risk-based possession offences are unfair in their present form. In particular, simple possession is an insufficient foundation for anything more than regulatory liability, and a substantial sentence for that is unjustifiable.

---

[74] Simester and von Hirsch, n 4 above, 98.
[75] C Slobogin, 'A Jurisprudence of Dangerousness' (2003) 98 *Northwestern University Law Review* 1, at 58–62.

7

Child Defendants and the Doctrines
of the Criminal Law

I N RECENT YEARS the question of the proper approach of the criminal
law to child defendants has been debated extensively, both in Europe and
beyond. Despite the existence of a number of international conventions,
there are still considerable divergences of approach among legal systems that
appear similar in some other respects. There are well-known differences between
Scots law, which sets the age of criminal responsibility at eight years[1] but in
practice deals with the overwhelming majority of accused under the age of 16 in
Children's Hearings and consigns those aged 16 and over to the adult criminal
courts, and the law of England and Wales, which sets the age of criminal responsibility at 10 and deals with the vast majority of prosecuted children under 18 in
the youth court. Internationally, the contentious issues include how to determine whether a child is capable of understanding and participating in criminal
proceedings, how to determine whether a child has sufficient capacity to be held
criminally liable for what he or she has done, and to what extent children who
are tried and found guilty of offences should be subjected to different sentencing regimes from older offenders. Some of these issues will be touched upon
obliquely below, but the focus of this essay is upon the interactions between the
defendant's youth and the doctrines of the criminal law. Thus the central question here concerns the effect of youth on defences such as duress, provocation,
diminished responsibility and ignorance of the law, on consent, and on intention and recklessness. In view of the breadth of the field this is merely an explor-
atory study; but I offer it as a modest tribute to Gerald Gordon, whose
ground-breaking and theoretically sophisticated works on Scots criminal law
have had an influence on me and on many others beyond his native land.

By way of preparation for this study, part 1 examines some relevant characteristics of childhood, part 2 discusses the question of children as moral agents,
and part 3 outlines some actual and possible responses to misconduct among
the young. These three opening sections are merely brief discussions of complex
issues, intended to sketch the background for part 4 on general defences, part 5
on consent, and part 6 on fault requirements. The fundamental question is

---

[1] Since the essay was first published, a provision has been enacted in section 52 of the Criminal
Justice and Licensing (Scotland) Act 2010 to raise the age to 12.

whether the criminal law should be more flexible in its assessment of child defendants and, if so, how this would best be accomplished.

7.1 CHILDHOOD

The concept of childhood is as controversial as its implications.[2] Even its definition is contested, since there are various purposes for which it may be defined. One might pragmatically take the age of majority (18 in the United Kingdom and many other countries) as the end of childhood, accepting that there may be considerable differences in 'responsibility' (howsoever defined) between most 12-year-olds and most 17-year-olds. For present purposes it may be sufficient to identify three major respects in which children typically exhibit features that indicate reduced culpability, as compared with adults.[3] First, their cognitive abilities tend to be under-developed:[4] they may have limited understanding (for example, of the impact of their conduct on others) and, in particular, little experience of applying the understanding they do possess to new situations. Secondly, their emotional controls tend to be under-developed:[5] this means that their responses to situations may be self-centred, and may tend to override any awareness of the vulnerabilities of others. Thirdly, they tend to be more easily led than adults, being more likely to be swept along by the encouragement or 'daring' of others, particularly in a group situation. Much more could be written, and has been written, about these and other typical characteristics of children. Clearly they may vary according to the chronological age of the child, the child's maturity, and the culture and socio-economic circumstances in which the child has grown up.

7.2 CHILDREN AS MORAL AGENTS

In the light of these three typical deficiencies, how can we determine whether a particular child should be respected as a moral agent, ie whether her or his choices satisfy a threshold of rationality and therefore should be as determinative as the choices of an adult? It might be thought that the easiest step to take would be to assert that this should be a question not of chronological age but rather of relative maturity, to which chronological age may be an imperfect

---

[2] See eg D Archard, *Children: Rights and Childhood* (2nd edn, 2004); J Fionda (ed), *Legal Concepts of Childhood* (2001).

[3] Following F Zimring, 'Toward a jurisprudence of youth violence' in M Tonry and M Moore (eds), *Youth Violence: Crime and Justice, a review of research*, vol 24 (1998), 447–501.

[4] See eg T Grisso and RB Schwartz (eds), *Youth on Trial: A Developmental Perspective on Juvenile Justice* (2000) 158–59, cited by the Law Commission of England and Wales' Consultation paper, *A new Homicide Act for England and Wales?* (Law Com Consultation Paper No 177, 2005), para 6.81.

[5] See the evidence cited in Law Commission, *A new Homicide Act* (ibid), para 6.82.

guide.[6] Thus the famous *Gillick* test of competence to take decisions about contraception was said to require 'sufficient understanding and intelligence to enable [the child] to understand fully what is proposed', and 'sufficient discretion to enable [the child] to make a wise choice in his or her interests'.[7] Details of the test are further developed in the *Gillick* judgments and in subsequent decisions,[8] and versions of it now apply quite widely across child law and medical law. There remains, however, a tension about its application to decisions to refuse treatment rather than to accept it,[9] and about the fact that assessments of children's competence are inevitably carried out by adults who may have particular views.[10]

Children may express their opinions in a forthright manner, and may be able to reason logically and to draw conclusions from premises. As Bingham LJ stated in a case concerning the right of a child aged 11 to litigate on his own behalf, decision-makers should listen to the views of children affected by their decisions, but it should be borne in mind that a child:[11]

'is, after all, a child. The reason why the law is particularly solicitous in protecting the interests of children is that they are liable to be vulnerable and impressionable, lacking the maturity to weigh the longer term against the shorter, lacking the insight to know how they will react and the imagination to know how others will react in certain situations, lacking the experience to match the probable against the possible'.

Thus Lord Bingham cautioned against accepting articulate children's views as determinative. At the age of 11 such caution may be the proper response, whereas many children at age 14 or 15 will have a degree of maturity that should be accorded some respect. The difficulty is that the different age limits selected by the law for different purposes do not appear to be consistent, and have no flexibility. The age of majority – the age at which a young person can vote and can enter into binding contracts – is 18. A young person can marry at 16, a decision that ought to require long-term understanding. One implication of the flexible *Gillick* test is that the consent of a child of 15 may be relevant when a doctor takes decisions about the child's 'best interests', even though in English

---

[6]   On this, see C McDiarmid, *Childhood and Crime* (2007), Ch 3.

[7]   *Gillick v West Norfolk and Wisbech Area Health Authority* [1986] AC 112, at 184 and 187 respectively. For discussion, see M Brazier and E Cave, *Medicine, Patients and the Law* (4th edn, 2007), Ch 15, esp 400–407 and J Herring, *Medical Law and ethics* (2nd edn, 2008), 166–70 and 185–87.

[8]   See M Freeman, 'Rethinking *Gillick*' (2005) 13 *International Journal of Children's rights* 201.

[9]   Cf the case reported in *The Times*, 11 November 2008 (where a girl of 13 was determined to refuse a transplant operation).

[10]   For references on this and related issues, see H Keating, 'The "responsibility" of children in the criminal law' (2007) 19 *Child & Family Law Quarterly* 183, to which I acknowledge my indebtedness. For varying assessments of the reliability of children as witnesses, see F Raitt, 'Robust and raring to go: judges' perceptions of child witnesses' (2007) 34 *Journal of Law and Society* 465.

[11]   *Re S (a minor) (Independent representation)* [1993] 2 FLR 437, at 444. For further relevant discussion, see A Cleland, 'Children's voices' in J Scoular (ed), *Family Dynamics: Contemporary Issues in Family Law* (2001).

law the age of consent to sexual activity is 16. In other words, parliament regards children under that age as generally not competent to take decisions on sexual matters in their own (long-term) interests. Much more could be written about the different age thresholds in British law, but these few remarks should be enough to illustrate the nature of the problem.

7.3 THE STATE'S RESPONSE TO CHILDREN'S BAD BEHAVIOUR

How ought the state (eg the legislature, children's services and the criminal justice system) to respond to bad behaviour by children, ie to behaviour that would certainly constitute a criminal offence if the perpetrator were aged 18 or over? In the discussion above[12] emphasis was placed on limitations on the understanding and control possessed by children, and on the ease with which they may be led. This would suggest that, in normative terms, the state should not expect such high standards from children as from adults, and should respond in ways that reflect the state's obligation to assist the proper development of children and not in ways that are likely to be counter-productive or repressive.[13] The state's obligation to support the development of children by promoting the best interests of the child and attending to her or his welfare is uppermost in international instruments such as the United Nations Convention on the Rights of the Child.[14] This positive obligation is heightened where criminal liability is the issue, given that this involves public censure and punishment. Two threshold tests need to be examined before a child should be held accountable in a criminal court: the test of sufficient understanding of the proceedings, and the minimum age of criminal responsibility.

First, it may be contrary to human rights to hold a criminal trial of a young child in a solemn proceeding. Thus the European Court of Human Rights has twice held that the trial of a very young child in the English Crown Court is likely to violate the Article 6 right to a fair trial unless there are major amendments to the normal procedure, in order to ensure that the child is able to participate effectively in the proceedings.[15] There is an obvious parallel here with the question of the fitness of a mentally disordered person to plead to the

---

[12] See parts 1 and 2 above.

[13] See A von Hirsch, 'Reduced penalties for juveniles: the normative dimension' in A von Hirsch, A Ashworth and J Roberts (eds), *Principled sentencing: readings on Theory and Policy* (3rd edn, 2009), 374–82.

[14] UN Convention on the Rights of the Child (1989) art 3 ('the best interests of the child shall be a primary consideration'); UN standard minimum rules for the Administration of Juvenile Justice (1985) ('to further the well-being of the juvenile and her or his family'); see the excerpts and discussion in von Hirsch, Ashworth and Roberts (eds) (n 13 above), 355–65.

[15] The Strasbourg Court's decision in *T and V v United Kingdom* (2000) 30 EHRR 121 is well known, but the more powerful judgment in *SC v United Kingdom* (2005) 40 EHRR 226 places even greater emphasis on effective participation and understanding, and its implications are that trials of younger children ought invariably to take place in a youth court and not in the Crown Court.

indictment. The two issues – fitness to plead on grounds of mental disorder,[16] and the ability of a child to participate – came together in the Scots case of *HM Advocate v S*,[17] where the trial of a boy of 13 was not allowed to proceed. Lord Caplan stated that the boy 'should not be expected to sit passively, like an object, while adults take exclusive control of his defence'. Thus, irrespective of the minimum age of criminal responsibility, the particular child must have sufficient understanding to be held accountable in a court of law, which means that the court proceedings should be adapted so that he or she is able to follow and to participate effectively in those proceedings, or the trial should not be allowed to proceed. The decision must depend on an assessment of the particular child, as in *HM Advocate v S*, and not on a set age limit.

Secondly, there is the question of the minimum age for criminal responsibility – the affirmation that it is wrong and unfair to resort to the criminal law beneath a certain age, and that bad behaviour by younger children should be the concern of the social services rather than the criminal justice system. In Scots law the defence of nonage applies only under the age of eight,[18] although there is now a provision raising it to 12;[19] in the law of England and Wales the minimum age is 10.[20] Although none of the international instruments specifies a minimum age of criminal responsibility, the United Kingdom has received considerable criticism from international organisations for having such low minimum ages, significantly below the minimum age in comparable countries such as France (13), Germany (14) and Spain (16). In October 2008, the UN Committee on the Rights of the Child set out various criticisms of the operation of youth justice in the United Kingdom, the first of which was the low ages of criminal responsibility in Scotland and in England and Wales.[21]

Although the minimum ages are higher in most other European countries, they all appear to have a fixed age of criminal responsibility, and do not adopt a variable age that depends on the differing degrees of understanding and maturity of children – in other words, a *Gillick*-type test is universally thought inappropriate for the criminal law. Yet the idea of holding a preliminary inquiry into the child defendant's level of 'responsibility' was adopted in England and Wales

---

[16] On which now see s 53 of the Criminal Procedure (Scotland) Act 1995, inserted by the Criminal Justice and Licensing (Scotland) Act 2010.

[17] Unreported, 9 July 1999. Available at: www.scotcourts.gov.uk/opinions/845a_99.html. The case is also discussed extensively by McDiarmid (n 6 above), at 59–60, 99 and 136–38.

[18] Criminal Procedure (Scotland) Act 1995 s 41; Chalmers and Leverick, *Criminal Defences*, Ch 9.

[19] *Report on Age of Criminal Responsibility* (Scot Law Com No 185, 2002) and the Criminal Justice and Licensing (Scotland) Act 2010 s 52. Cf the changes in Irish law discussed by U Kilkelly, *Children's Rights in Ireland* (2008), 537.

[20] Children and Young Persons Act 1963 s 44. There was provision in the Children and Young Persons Act 1969 to raise the minimum age to 14, but this was never brought into force. See AE Bottoms, 'On the decriminalization of English juvenile courts' in R Hood (ed), *Crime, Criminology and Public Policy: Essays in Honour of Sir Leon Radzinowicz* (1974), 319.

[21] UN Committee on the Rights of the Child, *Consideration of Reports Submitted by States Parties under Article 44 of the Convention, Concluding Observations: Great Britain and Northern Ireland* (2008). Available at: www2.ohchr.org/english/bodies/crc/docs/AdvanceVersions/ CrC.C.GBr. CO.4.pdf.

while the doctrine of *doli incapax* formed part of the law: when the defendant was aged 10 to 14, the prosecution had to prove that he or she was aware that the conduct alleged was 'seriously wrong', and only if that was established could the case proceed to conviction. Now, this doctrine may well have operated in a crude and unsatisfactory manner, but as late as 1990 the government commended it as making 'proper allowance for the fact that children's understanding, knowledge and ability to reason are still developing'.[22] The much-cited critique by Glanville Williams turned largely on the claim that the doctrine acted against children's best interests by acquitting them and thereby excluding them from supportive sentences;[23] however, it also saved some children from detention. The doctrine of *doli incapax* was a kind of developmental test, not far from the *Gillick* model. This is not to suggest that *doli incapax* should necessarily be restored,[24] but it does demonstrate that despite having the virtues of speed and simplicity, a fixed age may not be the most just or only workable solution.

In practice, Scots law mitigates the effect of its low minimum age through the system of Children's Hearings, which means that very few children find themselves prosecuted in the criminal courts. The vast majority of children under 16 are dealt with in the hybrid civil-criminal environment of the Children's Hearings, but after their 16th birthday most children are tried and sentenced in the adult courts.[25] The effect of this arrangement is to mitigate the effect of the low minimum age of criminal responsibility for almost all accused persons younger than 16, although the point of principle remains important for the 150 or so children under 16 prosecuted in the criminal courts each year.[26] In England and Wales the demise of the doctrine of *doli incapax*[27] has left young children open to the full rigours of the criminal law from the age of 10, provided that the article 6 requirement for a fair trial is met.

Finally, however, the sentencing provisions to which young offenders are subject are much attenuated, even if open to variable interpretations. In the context of England and Wales, the Criminal Justice and Immigration Act 2008 states that, when sentencing a person under 18, a court must have regard to (a) the principal aim of the youth justice system, which is the prevention of offending by children and young people; and (b) the welfare of the offender. The Act also

---

[22] Home Office, *Crime, Justice and Protecting the Public* (Cmd 965, 1990), para 8.4.

[23] G Williams, 'The Criminal Responsibility of Children' [1954] *Crim LR* 493, quoted by eg Lord Lowry in *C (A Minor) v DPP* [1996] 1 AC 1.

[24] The House of Lords has confirmed that the whole doctrine – the presumption and the defence, insofar as they differed – was abolished by s 34 of the Crime and Disorder Act 1998: *R v JTB* [2009] UKHL 20, on which see F Bennion, '*Mens rea* and defendants below the age of discretion' [2009] *Crim LR* 757.

[25] At the time of writing, two specialist youth courts dealing with 16- and 17-year-olds were operating in Scotland as a pilot scheme. No decision has yet been taken on whether or not to extend their operation, despite an evaluation having reported in 2006: G McIvor et al, *Evaluation of the Airdrie and Hamilton Youth Court Pilots* (2006).

[26] Chalmers and Leverick, *Criminal Defences and Pleas in Bar of Trial* (2006), para 9.02.

[27] See n 24 above and accompanying text.

required the court to have regard to (c) four other purposes of sentencing, notably punishment, reform and rehabilitation, protection of the public, and reparation to those affected by the offence.[28] However, this provision has not been brought into force – probably because of the argument that it would exclude deterrence as a lawful purpose when sentencing young offenders[29] – and this failure to implement the statute is regrettable. A first offender pleading guilty in England and Wales is normally, unless the offence is very serious, made subject to a referral order, which places the child in the hands of a youth offending team for three to 12 months. A child aged between 12 and 14 cannot be sentenced to deprivation of liberty unless he or she is a 'persistent offender'; that restriction does not apply to those aged 15, 16 or 17, but the normal maximum custodial sentence for any offender under 18 is two years. However, despite the reduced maxima for young offenders, England and Wales uses custody for young offenders at a rate that is internationally very high, and well beyond that of most other European countries.[30]

7.4 THE EFFECT OF CHILDHOOD ON GENERAL DEFENCES TO CRIMINAL LIABILITY

If the defendant is a child under 18, what should be the effect of her or his youth on the normal requirements of a defence or partial defence to criminal liability? Before considering the answers to this question in the context of duress, provocation, diminished responsibility and ignorance of the law, we may reflect on the rationale for defences of this kind. The first three are predominantly excusing conditions, and, according to John Gardner, the gist of such excuses is whether the defendant lived up to society's expectations in the normative sense: did this person exhibit as much self-restraint, resilience, and so on 'as we have a right to demand of someone in her situation'?[31] Gardner discusses the problem of those who may lack the capacity to measure up to society's expectations, and his various formulations of the 'normative expectations' approach to excuses are consistent with a lowering of expectations for young people beneath a certain

---

[28] Criminal Justice and Immigration Act 2008 s 9, inserting s 142A into the Criminal Justice Act 2003; see now Sentencing Guidelines Council, *Overarching Principles: Sentencing Youths* (2009).

[29] Criminal Justice Act 2003 s 142 includes the same list of sentencing purposes for adults, plus deterrence. The Canadian legislation, like the unimplemented s 142A, has a list of sentencing purposes for young offenders that omits deterrence (which is on the list of purposes for sentencing adults), and the Supreme Court of Canada decided in *R v BWP* [2006] SCC 27 that the implication is that deterrence is not a lawful purpose when passing sentence on a young offender.

[30] The UN Committee on the Rights of the Child pointed out the high number of children deprived of liberty in England and Wales, suggesting that detention is not always applied as a measure of last resort, as international conventions require: see the Committee's Report (n 21 above), para 77(c). [The figures have now improved a little, the average population in youth custody being 27 per cent lower in 2010–11 than in 2000–01: see: www.justice.gov.uk/downloads/statistics/youth-justice]

[31] J Gardner, 'The gist of excuses' in *Offences and Defences: Selected Essays in the Philosophy of Criminal Law* (2007), 121 at 124.

age, for the reasons given in part 2 above. He discusses 'normative expectations' in terms of the roles people fulfil, and so argues that the law should expect teenagers to have the self-control, steadfastness and knowledge that 'they ought to have if they are fit to call themselves proper, self-respecting teenagers'.[32] Whether reference to the 'role' of being a teenager is the most illuminating way of expressing the point may be doubted; but Gardner is surely right to insist that the question of what the law should expect of children and/or teenagers is a normative question that should be informed by the characteristics set out in part 1 above. To some extent, he observes, it may not be morally unacceptable for a teenager to be more 'impulsive, passionate, heedless'[33] than we would expect of an adult. In the light of this, what is the law's proper approach to excusatory defences that may be raised by young defendants?

(A) Duress

Duress is a general defence to criminal liability in English law. In essence, the defence is available where a person acts under threats of death or serious harm to self or family, in circumstances in which a person of reasonable firmness would give way and to which the person had not contributed by joining a gang that used violence.[34] The test of the 'person of reasonable firmness' may be modified in response to certain conditions, two of which are youth and clinical mental disorder (as held in *R v Bowen*).[35] Thus it is integral to the law of duress, as it has developed in English common law, that less firmness and control is expected of a child than of an adult. This reflects the fact that children tend to have under-developed controls, as described in part 1 above. It seems that the test varies according to chronological age rather than the degree of maturity of the given child – ie the test would be 'a child of 14 of reasonable firmness' – but the inclusion of clinical mental disorder as a variable that may be taken into account leaves room for the argument that, where there is evidence that a particular child is less mature than normal for her or his age, the test should be lowered to account for the reduced level of maturity.

A major problem for this analysis is the rule of English law that the defence of duress is unavailable in cases of murder or attempted murder.[36] This means that where a child is subjected to duress in order to make him or her participate in a killing, this defence cannot apply at all. Thus in *Wilson*[37] a boy of 13 helped his father to kill a neighbour, by fetching an axe at the father's request and by joining in the violence, striking the victim's head with a metal pole. The boy's

[32] Gardner (ibid) 170.
[33] Gardner (ibid) 170.
[34] See Ashworth, *Principles of Criminal Law* (6th edn, 2009), Ch 6.3.
[35] [1996] 2 Cr App R 157.
[36] *R v Howe* [1987] AC 417; *R v Gotts* [1992] 2 AC 412.
[37] [2007] EWCA Crim 1251.

evidence suggested that he was not provoked (he denied loss of control) and that he was not suffering from diminished responsibility (he said that he knew what he was doing, and may even have encouraged his father to make the attack). Duress being unavailable, the essence of the defence was that the boy did not intend to cause death or really serious harm, since he was being 'swept along' by his father's uncontrolled aggression and was therefore incapable of forming the necessary intent. Neither the trial judge nor the Court of Appeal found this denial of intent convincing, and the murder conviction was upheld. We will return to this case below, but two matters require discussion at this stage.

First, if the defence of duress had been available on the murder charge, there was probably sufficient evidence for it to be left to the jury. It might be said that, when the father was already involved in a violent attack, his command to his son to fetch the axe implied a threat of serious harm if he did not: the son's evidence was that he was too frightened of his father to disobey. According to *Bowen*, the applicable standard would be that of a 13-year-old child of reasonable firmness. So the defence might have succeeded, in which case the boy would have been acquitted entirely. Secondly, it is unclear whether English law allows a simple defence of 'no *mens rea*' when its effect is to circumvent the limitations on a general defence. If the essence of the defence was that the boy lacked *mens rea* because he was 'swept along' by his father's aggression, could the judge deem such a defence to fall within (1) duress or (2) provocation and thus insist on applying the tests of the appropriate defence to them? One decision says not: *R v Clarke*,[38] where the defendant, charged with shoplifting, argued that she took the relevant articles in a fit of absent-mindedness brought on by depression. The trial judge ruled that this had to stand or fall as a defence of insanity, but the Court of Appeal reversed this and held that a plea of lack of intention is open to those who fall outside the M'Naghten rules[39] because they retain the power of reasoning but in moments of confusion or absent-mindedness fail to use their powers to the full. If this remains good law, it suggests that a plea of lack of intent grounded on the evidence that the boy was 'swept along' by his father's aggression should have been put before the jury. The defence of duress being unavailable on a murder charge, there appeared to be nothing to prevent a straightforward argument of lack of intent. Indeed, since the *Woollin* formula is that, where a person foresees the forbidden consequence as virtually certain, the jury is only 'entitled'[40] to find intention, this may be an instance where a jury might decide not to exercise its entitlement.

In its consultation paper on homicide, the Law Commission of England and Wales demonstrated its consciousness of these issues by raising two questions

---

[38] (1972) 56 Cr App R 225.

[39] Which govern the defence of insanity in English law: see *M'Naghten's Case* (1843) 10 Cl and Fin 200.

[40] *R v Woollin* [1999] 1 AC 82, on which see Ashworth, *Principles of Criminal Law* (above, n 34), Ch 5.5(b).

for consultation. First, it recognised as a 'potential injustice' the inability of juveniles to argue duress in a murder case:[41]

'Capacity to withstand duress is increased with maturity and it would be unjust to expect the same level of maturity from a twelve-year-old as from an adult. *Bowen* also states that youth is a relevant characteristic for the purpose of whether or not the defendant could have been expected to resist the pressure of a threat in cases other than murder. A ten-year-old whose moral character is not fully formed should not be expected in all the circumstances to resist the temptation to kill in order to avert a threat to himself'.

The Commission consulted on the idea of a special provision for duress affecting juveniles and young persons. The Commission's proposals in this regard appear to have met with little enthusiasm from respondents,[42] but the Commission did go on to recommend that duress should become a defence to murder, and that youth should remain a relevant factor in deciding how a reasonable person would have responded to the threats. Despite the Commission's proposed reversal of the burden of proof,[43] this would be an advance on the position in *Wilson*, where the boy could not argue duress at all.

The second question raised by the English Law Commission was whether the law should go further and provide a partial defence of developmental immaturity, which would prevent a conviction for murder (or for first-degree murder)[44] for any killing in which a child was involved. Put another way, the distinction between murder and manslaughter would be abolished for offenders under 18: there would be a single offence, perhaps termed 'culpable homicide', with sentencing at the court's discretion:[45]

'The argument in favour of this solution is that it may be hard to tell whether very young offenders had a proper appreciation of the moral significance of their actions, in a way that engages the fine distinctions between murder and manslaughter'.

This particular argument relates specifically to 'very young offenders', in respect of whom it is surely compelling; but there are those who would oppose its application all the way up to the 18th birthday, which raises again the appropriate chronological dividing line between young offender and adult. In the end, the Law Commission decided not to pursue this approach, and opted instead for an enlarged doctrine of diminished responsibility (described in (C) below).

---

[41] Law Commission, *A new Homicide Act* (n 4 above), para 7.72.

[42] Law Commission, *Report on Murder, Manslaughter and Infanticide* (Law Com No 304, 2006), para 6.142.

[43] On which, see A Ashworth, 'Principles, Pragmatism and the Law Commission's recommendations on homicide law reform' [2007] *Crim LR* 333, at 340–42.

[44] The Law Commission recommended the creation of a three-tier structure for the law of homicide: offences of first-degree murder, second-degree murder and manslaughter. Only first-degree murder would attract a mandatory life sentence (Law Commission, *A new Homicide Act* (n 4 above), para 2.23).

[45] Law Commission, *A new Homicide Act* (n 4 above), para 6.87.

In relation to the Scots defence of coercion, there seems to be little doubt that the standard of the 'ordinary sober person of reasonable firmness' is to be modified for child accused. Sir Gerald Gordon noted a passage from Anderson which refers to threats 'of such a nature as to overcome the resolution of an ordinarily constituted person of the same age and sex as the accused',[46] although he made no comment on the reference to age and sex. The appeal court in *Cochrane v HM Advocate*[47] was more specific, holding that:[48]

'the test does not . . . apply a single standard to all cases. It recognises that what may reasonably be required of ordinary people will depend on their age; a child cannot be expected to react like an adult'.

However, that case did not involve a young accused. More uncertain is the question of whether Scots law would admit coercion as a defence to murder. The point remains without authority, which has the probable benefit that if a Scots court were confronted with a case such as *Wilson* it would be able to consider the justice of the matter in the round.[49]

(B) Provocation

Leaving the details aside, we may say that the partial defence of provocation is characterised by two factors: (1) an uncontrolled reaction to a perceived wrong, (2) in circumstances where a reasonable person might also have been provoked.[50] The second factor establishes an objective standard: we are entitled to expect a reasonable standard of self-control from citizens, even in the face of gross provocation. The standard required by English law is lowered in the case of young defendants, however. The leading case of *DPP v Camplin*[51] involved a boy of 15 who reacted to taunting by a man who had raped him by taking up a chapati pan and striking the man on the head, killing him. In the House of Lords, Lord

[46] GH Gordon, *The Criminal Law of Scotland* (2nd edn, 1978), para 13.25, citing AM Anderson, *The Criminal Law of Scotland* (2nd edn, 1904), 16. This passage is omitted from the third edition of Gordon, by which time there was more reported case law on the coercion defence (specifically *Cochrane v HM Advocate* 2001 SCCR 655 and *Thomson v HM Advocate* 1983 JC 69).

[47] 2001 SCCR 655.

[48] Para 21.

[49] See n 37 above and accompanying text for discussion of *Wilson*. For general discussion of how scots law should deal with coercion defences in murder cases, see Gordon, *Criminal Law* (above, n 46), at para 13.29; Chalmers and Leverick, *Criminal Defences* (above, n 26), paras 5.27–5.31.

[50] Gordon, *Criminal Law*, Ch 25; Chalmers and Leverick, *Criminal Defences*, Ch 10; Ashworth, *Principles of Criminal Law*, Ch 7. The partial defence of provocation has been replaced in England and Wales by one of 'loss of control' under the Coroners and Justice Act 2009. Although there will be some significant changes to the defence (primarily in relation to the qualifying triggers), these do not affect the discussion that follows. The defence retains the equivalent of a 'reasonable person' test, in that it is available only if 'a person of D's sex and age, with a normal degree of tolerance and self-restraint and in the circumstances of D, might have reacted in the same or in a similar way to D' (s 54(1)(c)).

[51] [1978] AC 705.

Diplock held that the proper test was that of the reasonable 15-year-old confronted with that situation. Lord Diplock accepted that youth has 'its effects on temperament as well as physique', and held that 'to require old heads upon young shoulders is inconsistent with the law's compassion to human infirmity, to which Sir Michael Foster ascribed the law of provocation more than two centuries ago'.[52] Thus, the *Camplin* decision implies that the state is not entitled to expect as much self-control from children as from adults,[53] and indeed that this applies at the age of 15, rather than being restricted to the 10 to 14 age group as the doctrine of *doli incapax* was. It requires an assessment not of the individual defendant but of the standard to be expected of a reasonable child of the defendant's age. On the other hand, provocation is only a partial defence: since it does not result in an acquittal, any adjustment to reflect culpability can be made at the sentencing stage. The subsequent modification and then restoration of the objective test of provocation in English law[54] left the concession for age undisturbed. The law is therefore that the only factor that may reduce the standard of self-control expected of a person is youth;[55] other factors such as mental disturbance do not affect society's expectations in this context, and in such cases diminished responsibility is the appropriate partial defence.

In Scots law the partial defence of provocation is much narrower: the above point appears not to have arisen for decision, and it was not specifically discussed by Sir Gerald Gordon.[56] However, in the case of *Drury v HM Advocate*[57] the appeal court applied the standard of what might be expected of an ordinary person; and, in their analysis of this and related cases (such as the coercion case of *Cochrane*),[58] James Chalmers and Fiona Leverick conclude that Scots law would most naturally adopt the test of 'the ordinary person of the sex and age of the accused',[59] similar to that developed in English law on this point, in the rare cases where it might be relevant.

(C) Diminished Responsibility

It appears that the current English law on diminished responsibility does not include any special reference to children. No reported cases appear to have discussed the point, and the re-worded section 2 of the Homicide Act 1957 suggests that few children could plead that their ability to understand the conduct,

---

[52] Ibid, 717.

[53] See J Gardner and T Macklem, 'Provocation and Pluralism' (2001) 64 *MLR* 815, at 826.

[54] In *R v Smith (Morgan)* [2001] 1 AC 146 and in *Attorney General for Jersey v Holley* [2005] 2 AC 580.

[55] Some statements of the law suggest that gender is another factor that should lead to a variation in the expected standard, but the implications of this appear not to have been worked through.

[56] Gordon, *Criminal Law* does not deal specifically with the relevance of age to the law on provocation (see Ch 25).

[57] 2001 SLT 1013.

[58] Discussed in n 47 above and accompanying text.

[59] Chalmers and Leverick, *Criminal Defences*, paras 10.18–10.19.

to form a rational judgment or to exercise self-control was substantially impaired by a 'recognised medical condition', since that phrase is only likely to include degrees of immaturity that are abnormal.[60] The Law Commission for England and Wales had recommended that 'developmental immaturity' should become a separate ground for diminished responsibility, where the offender was under 18 at the time of the killing. This would have ensured that children were not convicted of murder (but only of a lesser offence) where there was evidence of a developmental immaturity that substantially impaired the child's mental functioning, in terms of the capacity to understand conduct, form a rational judgment, or exercise control.[61] Thus, having earlier decided against a partial defence for all children that would reduce their offences from (first-degree) murder,[62] the Law Commission recommended a partial defence that would depend on evidence from psychiatrists or psychologists relating to the developmental immaturity of the particular child. This approach, flexible as to age and dependent on an assessment of each child, would be a significant step forward. It is rather alarming, however, to find the Law Commission stating that 'some ten-year-old killers may be sufficiently advanced in their judgement and understanding that such a conviction would be fair'.[63] This is extremely controversial, and there are certainly some in the United Kingdom and in wider Europe who would reject this proposition vigorously.[64] In the context of the reverse burden of proof – ie the defendant must satisfy the court that he or she was suffering from developmental immaturity of the required degree and effects[65] – the suggestion is even more controversial and inappropriate.

[60]   Homicide Act 1957 s 2 as substituted by s 52 of the Coroners and Justice Act 2009.

[61]   Law Commission, *Murder, Manslaughter and Infanticide* (n 42 above), paras 5.125–5.137; see also the arguments in Law Commission, *A new Homicide Act* (n 4 above), paras 6.75–6.76.

[62]   Law Commission, *A new Homicide Act* (n 4 above), paras 6.86–6.98; see n 44 above and accompanying text. It must be said, however, that the argument ultimately advanced by the Law Commission for that conclusion is weak and unpersuasive: 'suppose that anyone under the age of eighteen who intentionally kills is guilty of culpable homicide, not murder or manslaughter. Under this approach someone who kills intentionally on his or her eighteenth birthday can be convicted of first degree murder and will receive the mandatory life penalty, but had that person committed an identical killing on the day before, they could have been convicted only of culpable homicide. That seems wrong' (para 6.96). Similar consequences flow from all age limits recognised by the law, however. Different sentences are available for offenders when they attain certain ages; none of them was available the day before. A person is old enough to consent to sex at 16, but was not the day before, even though his wisdom has probably not increased materially overnight. And so on.

[63]   Law Commission, *Murder, Manslaughter and Infanticide* (n 42 above), para 5.130.

[64]   The Law Commission footnotes a contrary opinion (ibid, para 5.130, fn 91), but fails to scrutinise the reasoning of an assertion by the Police Federation on which its own statement appears to be based. When commenting on these matters in his *Report on Visit to United Kingdom* (CommDH(2005)6) at para 105, the European Commissioner for Human Rights did not hold back: 'I have extreme difficulty in accepting that a child of twelve or thirteen can be criminally culpable for his actions, in the same sense as an adult. I do not mean to deny that extreme measures may need to be taken, both to punish the act and to attempt to correct whatever it is that has clearly gone so drastically wrong. From this, however, to considering that a child of twelve can measure with the full consciousness of an adult the nature and consequences of their actions is, in my view, an excessive leap'.

[65]   For an assessment, see A Ashworth, 'Four threats to the presumption of innocence' (2006) 10 *International Journal of Evidence and Proof* 241.

In the case of *R v Wilson*,[66] no defence of diminished responsibility was raised and it seems to have been assumed on all sides that it was not viable. Some of the points made about the boy's behaviour and evidence, however, may have justified further exploration. Two examples of this are: (1) that much emphasis was placed on the fact that the boy lied repeatedly when questioned by the police – this was assumed to be evidence of malice and knowledge of wrongdoing, whereas it may have stemmed from a fear of his father or from an immature and distorted understanding of the situation; and (2) that, insofar as there was any substance in defence counsel's argument that the boy participated in the killing because he was swept along or carried away by his father's uncontrolled aggression, this can be linked to the three propositions about childhood development set out above – that children are less culpable than adults because of their under-developed cognitive abilities and emotional controls, and because they are easily led. Whether a partial defence of diminished responsibility could have been put forward on the basis of what was then 'arrested or retarded development of mind' is difficult to assess, but the boy in this case was only 13 and it seems manifestly wrong to judge him by the standards of an adult.

In Scots law there appears to have been little discussion of the specific problem of the diminished responsibility of children.[67] However, the re-statement of the test of diminished responsibility in *Galbraith v HM Advocate*,[68] in terms of an 'abnormality of mind which substantially impaired the ability of the accused, as compared with a normal person, to determine or control his acts',[69] leaves open the possibility that Scots law could encompass cases of developmental immaturity, particularly if Lord Rodger's reference to 'a normal person' were construed as a reference to 'a normal adult'. The Scottish Law Commission, reporting in 2004, appears not to have devoted separate consideration to the application of diminished responsibility to young accused persons, and there is no discussion of developmental immaturity as a ground for the verdict.[70]

(D) Ignorance of the Law

Knowledge of the criminal law is generally assumed in English law, and (save in special circumstances) there is no defence of *ignorantia juris*.[71] It is one thing to maintain, however, that all adults ought to be sufficiently aware of the criminal

---

[66] See n 37 above and accompanying text.

[67] The point is not mentioned in the relevant chapter of Gordon, *Criminal Law* (Ch 11).

[68] 2002 JC 1.

[69] Para 54.

[70] *Report on Insanity and Diminished responsibility* (Scot Law Com No 195, 2004), Part 3. At the time of writing, following the recommendations of the Scottish Law Commission, the defence of diminished responsibility was being put on a statutory footing, with the Criminal Justice and Licensing (Scotland) Act 2010 s 168 now inserting a new s 51B into the Criminal Procedure (Scotland) Act 1995. For the most part, however, this simply codifies the law as it stood in *Galbraith* and, as in the Commission's report, there is no mention specifically of the role of youth.

[71] See Chapter 3 above.

law to be able to conduct their lives without transgressing it; it is quite another thing to suggest that it is right to impose the same burden on children, and to make the same assumptions for them. It may be right to assume that they know that certain core wrongs are criminal – although it should be borne in mind that the doctrine of *doli incapax* presumed the opposite until the age of 14 unless the prosecution could establish that the child knew the act was seriously wrong. But many children, particularly younger children, may not know enough about the reach of the criminal law to be able to avoid conflict with it. Thus Brooke LJ held that a prohibition in an anti-social behaviour order that required a boy of 14 not to commit any criminal offences was not only too wide but also demanded too much of a child of that age, as he 'might well not know what was a criminal offence and what was not'.[72] Similarly, one might ask how many children of 14 and 15 know that any consensual kissing or intimate touching of each other is an offence, even if they know that sexual penetration is criminal. Thus it can be argued that the *ignorantia juris* principle should be modified in its application to children, by asking whether it may properly be expected that a reasonable child of the defendant's age should know that certain conduct is criminal. No English decision appears to have so held.

In Scots law the same general *ignorantia juris* principle is maintained, Gordon rationalising it on the basis of a general duty to know the law,[73] and Chalmers and Leverick discussing a number of supporting arguments, including the general expectation that people should know the law.[74] If it is justifiable for the state to expect citizens to know the law – and this is not to neglect the state's own duty to ensure due promulgation and fair notice of criminal laws – the question is whether this expectation properly extends to children. Fairness surely requires a variable level of expectation, which would, in effect, allow a defence if the ordinary 13-year-old or ordinary 15-year-old should not reasonably be expected to be aware of the particular legal prohibition. Even that concession might be insufficient if the particular child was conspicuously more or less mature than the average child of her or his age. It is suggested that there is nothing in Scots law or in English law to prevent a court from recognising a defence of ignorance of the law for a child in appropriate circumstances.

7.5 THE EFFECT OF CHILDHOOD ON CONSENT

We now broaden the discussion, extending beyond the criminal liability of children to consider the involvement of children in conduct to which they consent. When is such consent valid and effective, and when not? We focus here on offences against the person and sexual offences. The English law on offences against the person generally draws the line at common assault: a person can

[72] *R (on application of W) v Director of Public Prosecutions* [2005] EWHC Admin 1333, at para 8.
[73] Gordon, *Criminal Law*, para 9.20.
[74] Chalmers and Leverick, *Criminal Defences*, paras 13.03–13.08.

consent to acts against him or her that amount to common assault, but cannot validly consent to more serious violence, ie to an assault occasioning actual bodily harm, contrary to section 47 of the Offences Against the Person Act 1861, or to wounding or grievous bodily harm. The law is usually stated in relation to adults, which leaves open the extent to which children may validly consent to acts amounting to common assault. It was established in *Burrell v Harmer*[75] that the consent of boys aged 12 and 13 could not prevent the conviction of a tattooist for assault occasioning actual bodily harm, when the tattoos he had engraved on the boys' arms with their consent became inflamed and swollen. The Divisional Court appears to have held that 'if a child under the age of understanding was unable to appreciate the nature of an act, apparent consent to it was no consent at all'.[76] This way of putting the matter is unsatisfactory: the boys probably did appreciate the nature of what was being done when they were tattooed. If the argument is that they failed to realise the possible consequence that their arms would become inflamed and swollen, that might indicate that their consent would have been valid if no ill consequences had ensued. Surely a better approach is to focus on the particular child's ability to understand the possible consequences of certain treatment. In the event, the legislature went further and the Tattooing of Minors Act 1969 prohibits the application of tattoos to anyone under 18.

On a broader canvas, English law recognises various exceptions to its rule that consent can only negative conviction for common assault and not for more serious offences. These exceptions pertain to 'properly conducted games and sports . . . reasonable surgical interference, dangerous exhibitions, etc'.[77] Since that statement was made, a further exceptional category has been recognised which is relevant here. In the case of *R v Jones, Campbell et al*[78] the six defendants had seized another pupil from their school and tossed him into the air 'some 9 or 10 feet'[79] three times, allowing him to fall on to grass each time. He suffered a ruptured spleen, which had to be removed at hospital. They also seized another pupil and threw him into the air in a similar fashion, and his arm fractured on landing. The essence of their defence to charges of inflicting grievous bodily harm, contrary to section 20 of the Offences Against the Person Act 1861, was that 'the whole escapade was a joke and that they had no intention of causing their victims any serious harm, though they anticipated that they might get the odd bruise, as boys do in playground roughness'.[80] They also said that they thought their victims were consenting, even though they protested, because such protests were 'common form'.[81] The trial judge held that these claims, even if true, disclosed no defence. The Court of Appeal disagreed, finding authority for 'another exception to the

---

[75] [1967] *Crim LR* 169.
[76] Ibid, 169. It must be said that the report of this decision is extremely brief.
[77] *Attorney-General's Reference (No 6 of 1980)* [1981] QB 715, at 719.
[78] (1986) 83 Cr App R 375.
[79] Ibid, 377.
[80] Ibid, 377.
[81] Ibid, 377.

general rule' in 'cases of rough and undisciplined sport or play, where there is no anger and no intention to cause bodily harm'.[82] This exception has been applied to adults subsequently,[83] but what is of interest in the present context is that no point appears to have been taken in *Jones, Campbell et al* about the ages of the boys involved. Of the six defendants, one was aged 17, three were 16, one was 15 and one 14. More importantly, the two victims were aged 14. This ought to have implications for the validity of their apparent consent, and/or for the defendants' alleged belief in their consent. Can a boy of 14 validly consent to a risk of serious bodily harm? The answer must be in the affirmative if we are considering an organised sport such as rugby, soccer or hockey; but why should it be so for mere 'horseplay'? It is not clear on what ground this additional exception is founded. The justifications seem to stem from Sir Michael Foster's reference to 'manly diversions [intended] to give strength, skill and activity'[84] and to make people fit to fight for their country, but whether the dangerous and ill-disciplined events in this case can be brought within such a rationale must be doubted. True it may be that Foster and others who support this exception have always excluded cases where there is an intention to cause serious harm, thus confining the exception to cases where there is merely a risk of serious harm. However, it is one thing to question the sentence of six months' youth custody imposed by the trial judge on the first defendant, who was the oldest of the group; it is quite another to suggest that such a broad and poorly-defined exception to the 'no consent' rule should have a rightful place in English law.

It appears that Scots law finds no place for a 'horseplay' exception. Gordon's statement of the general rule that 'consent is a good defence, provided the accused did not act with intent to cause any bodily harm',[85] would allow the defence in cases like *Jones, Campbell et al* because there was no intent, only recklessness. Gordon goes on to state that 'where the prime intention is not to injure but to engage in a sporting contest with recognised rules, presumably for reward or prestige, there is no evil intent and so no assault'.[86] It therefore seems that 'horseplay' would not be included in this exception, since it is not a sport with recognised rules, even though such cases do not typically involve an intention to injure. Interestingly, the second edition of Gordon goes on to state that 'where the victim is incapable of giving true consent any apparent consent will be inoperative. The position of children and persons of weak intellect raises difficulties in this connection'.[87] This brings us back to the facts of *Jones, Campbell*

---

[82] Ibid, 378, quoting with approval from the judgment of Swift J in *R v Donovan* [1934] 2 KB 498, at 508.

[83] See particularly *R v Aitken* (1992) 95 Cr App R 304.

[84] M Foster, *Crown Law* (3rd edn, 1792, Dodson (ed), [1762]), 260. Foster's examples were 'cudgels, foils and wrestling' among friends.

[85] Gordon, *Criminal Law*, para 29.39.

[86] Gordon, *Criminal Law*, para 29.42, citing *Smart v HM Advocate* 1975 JC 30.

[87] Gordon, *Criminal Law* (2nd edn, 1978) (n 46 above), para 29.43. The passage is omitted from the third edition of Gordon, which cites the provisions of the mental incapacity Act 2005 (Gordon, *Criminal Law* (3rd edn, 2000), para 29.43).

et al, and to the questions (1) whether an ordinary boy of 14 should be able to consent to the risk of serious harm resulting from 'birthday bumps' or other rough play, not least when he cannot consent to being kissed or touched sexually; and (2) whether the older boys' belief in the consent of the boy of 14 was credible.

Turning to sexual activity, the age of consent is 16 and there are no exceptions to this. This was one of several controversial issues during the passage of the English legislation that became the Sexual Offences Act 2003.[88] The offences against children are broadly drafted, in consequence of which the government assured critics that the Crown Prosecution Service would not bring prosecutions for minor consensual touchings and so on between children. This reliance on prosecutorial discretion is unsatisfactory, as are various other features of the 2003 Act. One is the approach taken in cases where two children are involved: the law is aimed chiefly at adults who take advantage of children sexually, but section 13 of the Act provides only that where the defendant is under 18 the maximum penalty is lowered to five years' detention rather than the maximum of life imprisonment for adults. That provision announces a less severe view of sexual offences committed by young defendants. It is certainly true that some youths can bully other children into sexual activities that are not in their interests at all,[89] but the most difficult cases are those where two children of 14 or 15 have consensual intercourse.

The law clearly states that neither of them can validly consent to this conduct, and it does so for good reasons.[90] Children under 16 are assumed not to have sufficient awareness of the long-term significance of sexual acts, and so their actual consent is deemed to be insufficiently well informed to count.[91] Yet from another point of view the law assumes that the children are sufficiently responsible to be held criminally liable for the offence of sexual activity with a child – no worries here about their awareness of the significance of what they have done. Thus, in the recent leading case of *G*,[92] the House of Lords upheld the conviction of a boy of 15 for rape of a child under 13, even though the basis of his plea was that the girl had told him that she was also 15 and had consented. This case was complicated by the fact that the girl was actually 12, and the offence of rape of a child under 13 has strict liability as to age. More to the point is the fact that, had the girl been 15 (as she stated), both children would have committed the offence of sexual activity with a child. It is unlikely that

[88] Part 1 of the Act, which creates sexual offences, applies only to England and Wales.

[89] This is a possible analysis of the facts in *Jones, Campbell et al* (see n 78 above and the accompanying text): the older boys seemed to strike fear in the younger pupils.

[90] See Baroness Hale in *R v G* [2008] UKHL 37, [2009] 1 AC 92, at paras 48–54, esp at para 49: 'anyone who has practised in the family courts is only too well aware of the long term and serious harm, both physical and psychological, which premature sexual activity can do'.

[91] Home Office, *Setting the Boundaries: reforming the Law on Sexual Offences* (2000), para 3.5.7.

[92] *R v G* [2008] UKHL 37, [2009] 1 AC 92. The case should be distinguished from the House of Lords decision on recklessness of the same name (*R v G* [2004] 1 AC 1034) discussed in n 106 below and the accompanying text.

they would have been prosecuted (this discretionary element in the English system has already been criticised); but, if prosecuted, they would almost certainly have been convicted. Thus at the age of 15 a child cannot give valid consent to sexual activity but can be convicted of sexual activity with another child, a position that accepts the social wrongness of under-age sexual activity but regards the child as sufficiently responsible to be held guilty. The social condemnation of all sexual intercourse under the age of 16 is maintained, even if both parties are *Gillick*-competent and consent enthusiastically.

The only concession is the curious rule in *Tyrrell*,[93] which holds that, because the purpose of such legislation is to protect girls against themselves, it should not be possible to convict a girl under 16 of complicity in an offence of sexual activity with her, no matter how enthusiastic she was at the time. The Sexual Offences Act 2003 does not deal expressly with this point, but the Act makes the offence of sexual activity gender-neutral and so it is no longer accurate to refer to protecting girls against themselves. The purpose of the legislation is to protect children from adults and to protect children from children (including themselves). It may still be contrary to *R v Tyrrell* to convict a girl of 12 of aiding and abetting rape of a child by the boy of 15 whom she encouraged (to adapt the basis of plea in the case of *G*), but would it be contrary to *Tyrrell* to convict a 14-year-old who sexually penetrated another 14-year-old, both of them consenting in fact, of (1) sexual activity with a child or of (2) aiding, abetting, counselling or procuring sexual activity with a child? In the absence of evidence of exploitation or dominance, and assuming that the matter goes to court,[94] it seems inconsistent to convict one 14-year-old and excuse the other, when the basis for doing so lies in the same issues of age, understanding, discretion and self-control.

It appears that Scots law would take a similar approach to *Tyrrell* and would not render a consenting girl art and part guilty of a boy's sexual offence contrary to the Sexual Offences (Scotland) Act 2009.[95] However, the Scottish Law Commission's Discussion paper was astute to raise the question of whether children aged 13 need protection from other children under 16 where there is consent,[96] and in its report the Commission boldly recommended that, where both participants are aged 13, 14 or 15 and are consenting, sexual activity

---

[93] [1894] 1 QB 710. See M Bohlander, 'The Sexual Offences Act 2003 and the *Tyrrell* principle: criminalising the victims?' [2005] *Crim LR* 701.

[94] Baroness Hale in *G* accepted (at para 48) that many sexual activities between those under 16 should not be prosecuted at all, impliedly criticising the 2003 Act for over-breadth in this respect; but she seems to suggest that, where penetration takes place, even between two children of 14 or 15, this is such an important matter that criminal proceedings are appropriate (see para 49). Others would argue that, in the absence of evidence of actual exploitation, this is the wrong approach and will result in the needless criminalisation of many young people: see the Scottish Law Commission (n 96 below).

[95] Gordon, *Criminal Law*, para 5.05. Gordon was commenting on the law prior to its codification in the Sexual Offences (Scotland) Act 2009 but the same principle applies.

[96] Scottish Law Commission, *Discussion Paper on Rape and Other Sexual Offences* (Scot Law Com Discussion Paper No 131, 2004), para 5.40.

should not be an offence.[97] The Commission thus rejected the objectionable English compromise, whereby all sexual activity is criminalised and reliance is placed on prosecutors to ensure that there are no unfair prosecutions, saying that if conduct is not to be prosecuted it should not be an offence. This approach has now been enacted in section 39(3) of the Sexual Offences (Scotland) Act 2009, and it deserves further scrutiny south of the border. The Commission added that referral to a Children's Hearing should be possible where sexual activity between children gives rise to welfare concerns.

7.6 THE EFFECT OF CHILDHOOD ON *MENS REA*

How do the considerations discussed in the previous sections interact with the *mens rea* requirements of English criminal law? In part 3 above it was argued that there are two threshold tests that ought to be satisfied – a child should not be tried in court if an assessment shows insufficient understanding, and the age of criminal responsibility should be set so as to exclude those without a proper level of capacity.[98] Turning now to cases which overcome these thresholds, we begin with strict liability. Where an offence imposes strict liability, which requires no fault (unless there is a defence of due diligence), a young defendant is just as liable to conviction as an adult, even for a very serious offence. This was confirmed by the House of Lords in *G*,[99] holding that where the offence of rape of a child under 13 imposes strict liability as to age, that applies equally to young defendants.

The most serious criminal offences tend to require proof of intention to bring about the prohibited consequence. Intention is usually defined in terms of purpose (direct intention) or foresight of the virtual certainty that the prohibited consequence will ensue (oblique intent). The concept of intention is presented as value-independent, unrelated to the moral quality of what is intended.[100] Thus the defence argument in *Wilson*[101] to the effect that the boy of 13 was 'swept along' by his father's uncontrolled aggression does not necessarily negative intention. The first question is whether the boy acted with the purpose of causing really serious harm to the victim when striking her head with a metal pole: even if it is most unlikely that he would have behaved in that manner if his father had not been acting so aggressively, the fact is that he did so and that he was aware of what he was doing. The second question, if purpose is not found,

---

[97] Scottish Law Commission, *Report on Rape and Other Sexual Offences* (Scot Law Com No 209, 2007), para 4.55; it will be noted that this would not have altered the conclusion on the facts of *G* (n 92 above).

[98] See the detailed arguments of McDiarmid (n 6 above) particularly at 78.

[99] [2008] UKHL 37, [2009] 1 AC 92, discussed in the text at n 92 above.

[100] As Alan Norrie puts it, it is 'a particular legal model of responsibility that was devised to exclude or marginalise difficult or contested moral issues from the law and the courtroom': A Norrie, *Crime, Reason and History* (2nd edn, 2001), 58.

[101] Above (n 37) and accompanying text.

is whether the boy knew that it was virtually certain that the victim would suffer serious injury from his acts. The answer to this is probably yes. Yet one could argue that, in respect of both answers, a child of 13 would have only a hazy and under-developed notion of the social meaning of serious injury and of death. One might be tempted to say that a child of that age cannot really understand the significance of such acts and their consequences; but, as the earlier quotation from the Law Commission of England and Wales demonstrates,[102] this is a controversial assertion in England and Wales, particularly when combined with the possibility of trial in solemn proceedings. The prospects for arguing that a child lacks intention because of an inability to appreciate the social significance of acts and their consequences therefore seem poor in English law, and there appears to be nothing in Scots law to suggest a more accommodating approach.[103]

Turning to recklessness as a *mens rea* requirement, English law has changed its stance in recent years. For a while, the position was as stated in *Metropolitan Police Commissioner v Caldwell*,[104] where the House of Lords replaced the subjective test of awareness of risk with a test that included an additional objective element; that of failure to give thought to an obvious risk. In applying this test, no concessions were made to young defendants, and indeed one of the criticisms that led to the abrogation of the *Caldwell* doctrine was that it judged children by the same standards as an adult.[105] The House of Lords in *G*[106] could have chosen to create an exception for children, but instead overruled the whole *Caldwell* doctrine of objective recklessness. This means that, when a child is charged with an offence for which recklessness is sufficient, the question is now whether that child was aware of the risk of the prohibited consequence. However, as suggested in relation to intention above, this is a question of awareness of the risk, and not awareness of the social significance of the prohibited consequences. Lord Caplan's judgment in *HM Advocate v S*[107] suggests that Scots law's concept of wicked recklessness would be modified in its application to a child,[108] and this is one beneficial consequence of the doctrine's strong moral colouring.

The position of children charged with an offence of negligence or gross negligence is unclear. There are few offences of negligence that children might commit, but manslaughter by gross negligence should be considered briefly in

---

[102] Above (n 61) and accompanying text.
[103] Gordon, *Criminal Law*, Ch 7.
[104] [1982] AC 341.
[105] *Elliott v C* (1983) 77 Cr App R 136 (where a mentally handicapped girl of 14 was convicted of criminal damage by fire, having failed to understand the flammable properties of white spirit).
[106] [2004] 1 AC 1034 (where boys of 11 and 12 caused £1 million damage by fire, having failed to foresee the consequences of making a small fire with newspapers; their convictions for causing criminal damage by fire were quashed). For an instructive discussion and further references, see H Keating, 'Reckless Children' [2007] *Crim LR* 546.
[107] See n 17 above and accompanying text.
[108] Gordon, *Criminal Law*, paras 7.47–7.68.

this connection. In English law the prosecutor must prove (1) that the defendant was in breach of a duty of care towards the victim, (2) that the breach of duty caused the victim's death, and (3) that the breach of duty amounted to gross negligence.[109] The questions here are whether a child would have a duty and, if so, whether the standard of gross negligence is lowered for children. In principle, following the arguments above, the answer ought to be affirmative. This is generally the approach in tort law: the standard for breach of duty should be that of a child of roughly the same age and maturity as the defendant.[110] Although for the purposes of manslaughter by gross negligence the criminal law has gone beyond tort law in recognising duty situations,[111] the question of breach of duty should be answered on the same principles, recognising the developmental immaturity and therefore reduced expectations of children.

7.7 CONCLUSIONS

The aim of this study has been to explore the relationship between the doctrines of the criminal law and child defendants. The subject is one with wide-ranging implications, all of which could not be examined within the compass of this essay. Its importance is confirmed by international agreements such as the United Nations Convention on the Rights of the Child. Its significance for the legal systems of the United Kingdom is signalled by critical reports by international monitoring bodies, pointing to several respects in which the spirit and/or letter of the Convention is not being observed.[112]

The argument here is that the criminal law should recognise the developmental immaturity of children, outlined in part 1 above, and that fairness therefore demands the amendment of the doctrines of the criminal law so as to expect less of younger defendants. The state would be behaving unreasonably and oppressively if it were to apply the same standards to children as to adults. Instead, in doctrines relating to duress, provocation, diminished responsibility and ignorance of the law, it should aim to apply the standard of what may reasonably be expected of a child of the defendant's age and maturity.

This assumes that the criminal law will continue to be applied to children as young as 10 in England and Wales. International agencies have been critical of this relatively low age, and the recent raising of the age to 12 in Scots law – although still lower than many neighbouring jurisdictions – should lead to reconsideration of the equivalent English provision as a matter of urgency. However, any such re-appraisal should also examine the framework that would take the place of the criminal law if it were removed, for example, from all

---

[109]   *R v Adomako* [1995] 1 AC 171.

[110]   M Jones (ed), *Clerk and Lindsell on Torts* (20th edn, 2010), para 8.147.

[111]   Ashworth, *Principles of Criminal Law*, Ch 7.5; for discussion, see J Herring and E Palser, 'The duty of care in gross negligence manslaughter' [2007] *Crim LR* 24.

[112]   See n 21 above and accompanying text, and n 64.

children under 14. Compulsory measures would still be possible, under the powers of the children's services and social services (or a Children's Hearing in Scotland).[113] Their application and extent should be scrutinised, and there should be no naivety about the speed with which they would come to be regarded as punitive, in spite of whatever euphemistic label is applied to the confinement of the most difficult children within secure accommodation. Safeguards for the best interests of children must be incorporated, so as to avoid the kind of disastrous results (for some children) of the introduction of the anti-social behaviour order.[114]

One important but lingering issue is whether the 'age of criminal responsibility' should be altered to a set age (such as 14) or should vary according to the capacity of the individual child. There appear to be three leading possibilities – to adopt the standard of the 'ordinary child of 14' or whatever age the defendant is (as in defences such as duress, provocation, diminished responsibility and ignorance of the law); to require an assessment of each individual to determine the level of responsibility according to certain criteria; or to adopt the pragmatic approach of a fixed age.[115] The second approach is right in principle; the first approach may be a reasonable compromise; but the third approach is most likely to be adopted, on the ground that it is thought to be too resource-intensive to assess every child under 18 prosecuted in the courts. If this is the conclusion reached, despite the argument presented above, the most sensible approach would be to raise the age of criminal responsibility to 14 and to allow modifications of the defences in the ways proposed above.[116] This might also be sufficient to deal with the argument in part 6 above that the intention of a child of 12 or 13 is not the same kind of intention as that of an adult, since it lacks a broader understanding of social significance. That is a well-founded argument,[117] but if children under 14 could not be prosecuted in the criminal courts its main thrust would be blunted. This, however, lies some distance from the core of this study, which is to argue for flexible amendments to doctrines of the criminal law and for reconsideration of the implications of age limits, particularly in relation to consent to sexual activity between children.

---

[113] That would also be a preferable approach to dealing with children under 16 who engage in sexual relations, rather than criminalising all such contacts and relying on prosecutorial discretion. The English approach in the Sexual Offences Act 2003 is manifestly inferior to that recommended by the Scottish Law Commission: see n 97 above and accompanying text.

[114] See eg www.statewatch.org/asbo/AsBOwatch.html.

[115] It is certainly a weak argument to suggest that a fixed age is not sensible because someone a day older has different responsibilities from someone a day younger: that is inherent in all fixed limits, from the age of voting through the age of consent, and is a feature of many other social arrangements such as pensions, speed limits and so forth. See the unconvincing reasoning of the Law Commission for England and Wales (above, n 64).

[116] McDiarmid (above, n 6), 178–80 favours 12 as the relevant age, despite the strong arguments elsewhere in her book.

[117] J Fortin, *Children's Rights and the Developing Law* (2nd edn, 2003), 72–73 and 552, cited by Keating (n 106 above).

8

Human Rights and
Positive Obligations to Create
Particular Criminal Offences

THIS CHAPTER EXAMINES the positive obligations on states to ensure that they create criminal offences of certain kinds. The focus of the chapter is on those obligations that may arise from the European Convention on Human Rights, but it is important to recognise that there are other positive obligations arising from international law (for example, to criminalise genocide),[1] from the Council of Europe (for example, to create laws to prevent violence against the vulnerable, particularly domestic violence),[2] and most powerfully from EU law (for example, to criminalise various acts relating to child pornography).[3] All these positive obligations are significant, inasmuch as they require the state's law to include various types of offence (or to exclude certain forms of defence). In many instances the domestic law of a state will already penalise the relevant conduct and no particular adjustment of the criminal law will be necessary. But there may be other instances in which it becomes necessary to legislate, or to amend existing legislation, in order to ensure compliance with international obligations.

Before going further into those issues, we should note that international instruments such as the European Convention on Human Rights chiefly impose *negative* obligations on states in respect of their criminal laws, positive obligations being in a minority. For example, Article 8(1) of the Convention declares the right to respect for private life, and Article 8(2) states that there shall be no interference with the right except insofar as that interference is necessary in a democratic society for one of various reasons, including the prevention of disorder and crime. This means that states may create offences that abridge the Article 8 right, within the broad limits set out in Article 8(2). Thus the European

---

[1] The Convention on the Prevention and Punishment of the Crime of Genocide, applied in English law by the Genocide Act 1969 and now by s 51 of the International Court Act 2001.

[2] Council of Europe Convention on the Prevention and Combating of Violence against Women and Domestic Violence, CM(2011)49 final.

[3] For discussion, see S Peers, *EU Justice and Home Affairs* (3rd edn, 2011); P Asp, *The Substantive Criminal Law Competence of the EU* (2013); E Baker and C Harding, 'From Past Imperfect to Future Perfect: a Longitudinal Study of the Third Pillar' (2009) 34 *EL Rev* 25.

Court of Human Rights has consistently held, since 1982, that laws may not criminalise homosexual conduct between consenting adults:[4] such laws cannot be said to be 'necessary' interference with the right of respect for private life, not least because 'sexual orientation and activity concern an intimate aspect of private life'.[5] Another example of negative obligations is provided by Article 10(1), which declares the right to freedom of expression, subject (in Article 10(2)) to such restrictions as are necessary in a democratic society for various reasons including the prevention of disorder and crime. The English law on breach of the peace has been held to constitute a necessary restriction, at least in instances of clear disorder,[6] whereas binding over to be of good behaviour was held to be an insufficiently certain restriction.[7] The European Court has been equivocal about the necessity for laws penalising the insulting of public officials, upholding those laws in some instances but not in others.[8] Further examples of the impact on criminal laws may be found in the application of Article 9 (right to freedom of religion), Article 11 (right to freedom of assembly) and other Convention rights. The position in England and Wales, however, is that these negative obligations have impinged relatively little on the form and structure of the criminal law. This is not to suggest that the negative obligations are unimportant – there have been quite a few potential conflicts between the Convention and English criminal law for the courts to deal with[9] – but rather to conclude that this has not been a particularly significant source of challenge to the criminal law as a whole.

In numerical terms the same conclusion might be reached in relation to positive obligations, but their development by the European Court of Human Rights in particular has given fresh impetus to discussions of their scope and limits. This development and the potential for further growth will form the focal point of this chapter.

8.1 THE RANGE OF POSITIVE OBLIGATIONS UNDER THE EUROPEAN CONVENTION ON HUMAN RIGHTS

The ECHR was drawn up in 1950, and the UK – which had been heavily involved in the process of drafting – was one of the first countries to ratify it. From time

---

[4] *Dudgeon v United Kingdom* (1982) 4 EHRR 149; *Norris v Ireland* (1991) 13 EHRR 186; *Modinos v Cyprus* (1993) 16 EHRR 485; *Sutherland v United Kingdom* (1997) 24 EHRR CD 22; *ADT v United Kingdom* (2001) 31 EHRR 803.

[5] *Laskey v United Kingdom* (1997) 24 EHRR 39, para 26.

[6] *Steel v United Kingdom* (1999) 28 EHRR 603.

[7] *Hashman and Harrup v United Kingdom* (2000) 30 EHRR 241, applying *Chorherr v Austria* (1994) 17 EHRR 358.

[8] Cf *Janowski v Poland* (2000) 29 EHRR 705 with *Thomas v Luxembourg* (2003) 36 EHRR 359 and *Nikula v Finland* (2004) 38 EHRR 944.

[9] Even excluding certainty issues such as that raised successfully in *R v Rimmington and Goldstein* [2005] UKHL 63, there have been plenty of public order cases (notably *Percy v DPP* [2001] EWHC Admin 1125, and more recently *Abdul v DPP* [2011] EWHC Admin 247).

to time British politicians talk about the possibility of withdrawing from the Convention, but for so long as this country remains within the Council of Europe and subject to the jurisdiction of the European Court of Human Rights it will retain an interest in the Court's approach to the positive obligations arising from the ECHR.

One question, however, is whether it is the Convention or the Court that is responsible for the imposition of positive obligations. The Convention as drafted does not impose any positive obligations on states, and refers to the rights of individuals by repeatedly using words such as 'everyone' or 'no one' in the text of particular rights. But the wording of Article 1 is at least suggestive: by declaring that 'the High Contracting Parties shall secure to everyone within their jurisdiction the rights and freedoms defined in section 1 of this Convention', it may be said to impose a general obligation on states. Thus it is largely on this basis that in recent years the Court has developed a jurisprudence of positive obligations in relation to various articles of the Convention. That jurisprudence tends to support three forms of positive obligation in relation to each of the rights:

(i)   The duty to secure the right by putting in place effective criminal law provisions, backed up by law enforcement machinery for the prevention, suppression and sanctioning of breaches of such provisions;

(ii)   The duty, in certain well-defined circumstances, to take preventive operational measures to protect an individual whose right is at risk from the criminal acts of another individual;[10]

(iii) The duty to have in place effective machinery for investigating complaints of violations of Convention rights, combined with the duty to ensure that there is a thorough and effective investigation capable of leading to the identification and punishment of those responsible.[11]

Important as positive obligations ii) and iii) are in the Court's developing jurisprudence, the focus of this chapter will be on the first positive obligation, relating to the putting in place of effective criminal law provisions. In that context four of the Articles of the Convention will be discussed, in the following order: Article 8 (private life), Article 3 (inhuman or degrading treatment), Article 2 (right to life), and Article 4 (slavery and servitude).

8.2 DUTY TO SECURE ARTICLE 8 RIGHTS

It may seem strange to begin the discussion with Article 8, since this is a derogable right (unlike the other Articles to be considered below) and the Court has

---

[10] The formulation of obligations (i) and (ii) broadly follows the text of para 115 of the judgment in *Osman v United Kingdom* (2000) 29 EHRR 245, recently re-affirmed in *Van Colle v United Kingdom* (2013) 56 EHRR 839.

[11] The formulation of obligation (iii) follows closely the text of para 103 of the judgment in *Aydin v Turkey* (1998) 25 EHRR 251.

usually granted states a considerable margin of appreciation in complying with such rights. However, the decision to impose a positive obligation under Article 8 was one of the first, and it is all the more striking since the right is derogable and may (as Article 8(2)) states) be interfered with if it is 'necessary in a democratic society' to do so.

The facts of the leading case of *X and Y v Netherlands*[12] may be recited briefly. A young woman who was mentally handicapped was living in a residential home. Shortly after her 16th birthday a man who lived nearby forced her to have sex. At the time the law of the Netherlands required a formal complaint before a sex crime could be investigated: the law provided that a parent could make the complaint for a child under 16, but for persons aged 16 and over only the victim could make a complaint, and this victim was held to be too disturbed mentally to make a formal complaint. There was no special provision relating to mentally disturbed complainants. Both the victim and her father alleged that Netherlands law failed to respect her Article 8 rights.

Three issues arise in cases of this kind. The first question is whether the complaint falls within the ambit of Article 8, notably the concept of 'private life'. In *X and Y* the Court held that the concept of 'private life . . . covers the physical and moral integrity of the person, including his or her sexual life'.[13] There is ample authority that sexual activity and integrity are at the core of the right to private life.[14] The second question concerns the obligations of a state in relation to this right, and the Court held:

> '[A]lthough the object of Article 8 is essentially that of protecting the individual against arbitrary interference by the public authorities, it does not merely compel the State to abstain from such interference; in addition to this primarily negative undertaking, there may be positive obligations inherent in an effective respect for private or family life. These obligations may involve the adoption of measures designed to secure respect for private life even in the sphere of the relations of individuals between themselves'.[15]

This is one of the first assertions by the Court that positive obligations could arise in relation to particular rights. No specific reference was made to Article 1 or to any other authority,[16] but the die was cast. The third issue is, then, the criminalisation issue: does the existence of a positive obligation mean that the state must create particular criminal offences? In *X and Y* there was much discussion of the alternative ways of respecting the victim's right, including

---

[12] (1985) 8 EHRR 235. On the significance of this judgment, and more generally, see A Mowbray, *The Development of Positive Obligations under the European Convention on Human Rights by the European Court of Human Rights* (2004).

[13] Ibid, para 22.

[14] Eg *Dudgeon v United Kingdom* (1982) 4 EHRR 149, para 52.

[15] (1986) 8 EHRR 235, para 23.

[16] However, some members of the Court had made this link already: see the reasoning in *Marckx v Belgium* (1980) 2 EHRR 330, para 31, and in *Young, James and Webster v United Kingdom* (1982) 4 EHRR 38, especially para 49, although both discussions relate to the state's obligation to put in place civil laws respecting the applicants' Article 8 or Article 11 rights.

applying for an injunction to prevent further violations and an action for damages in respect of the violation that had already occurred. The Court recognised that there might be types of violation of Article 8 against which these would provide suitable protection, but held that they would not be a sufficient response to the wrongs to which this victim had been subjected:

> 'This is a case where fundamental values and essential aspects of private life are at stake. Effective deterrence is indispensable in this area and it can be achieved only by criminal-law provisions; indeed it is by such provisions that the matter is normally regulated'.[17]

The particular problem highlighted by this case was that, although the Netherlands had a range of sexual offences in place, it had failed to anticipate the need for a procedure to ensure that mentally handicapped victims were brought within the compass of those offences. But what the judgment stands for, more generally, is that when the issue concerns invasions of sexual integrity there is a very strong case for criminal offences to be in place, and that a state which does not have an appropriately full range of sexual offences will be failing in its positive obligation under Article 8.

No subsequent judgment of the Court has cast any doubt on the approach in *X and Y*. Indeed, in the leading case of recent years the Court followed the wording of *X and Y* very closely, summarising the position thus:

> 'While the choice of the means to secure compliance with Art. 8 in the sphere of protection against acts of individuals is in principle within the State's margin of appreciation, effective deterrence against grave acts such as rape, where fundamental values and essential aspects of private life are at stake, requires efficient criminal-law provisions. Children and other vulnerable individuals, in particular, are entitled to effective protection'.[18]

The nature of the positive obligation is that all states should have in place criminal laws that protect individuals against sexual violation by other individuals. It is not that the state is in any way responsible for the acts of those who violate the rights of others, but that the state is responsible for putting in place criminal laws that ensure appropriate protection for those rights. To what extent this indicates a criminal law with a particular content is discussed further in relation to Article 3 below.

8.3 DUTY TO SECURE ARTICLE 3 RIGHTS

Article 3 of the Convention states that 'no one shall be subjected to torture or to inhuman or degrading treatment or punishment'. It is elementary that torture

---

[17] (1986) 8 EHRR 235, para 27.

[18] *MC v Bulgaria* (2005) 40 EHRR 459, para 150. This case is discussed more fully in relation to Article 3, below.

must be prohibited by the criminal law. But what kinds of criminal laws does the prohibition on 'inhuman or degrading treatment' require a state to have in place? This issue arose in the context of a criminal law defence in *A v United Kingdom*.[19] English law has a range of offences against the person which penalise the use of force by one individual against another, as Article 3 would require it to have, but these offences are subject to various defences. One longstanding common law defence is lawful chastisement: a parent or person standing *in loco parentis* is entitled to use force on their child for disciplinary purposes so long as it amounted to no more than 'reasonable chastisement'. In the particular case a stepfather who used a garden cane to 'punish' a boy of nine was prosecuted for assault occasioning actual bodily harm. He relied on the defence of reasonable chastisement, and was acquitted by the jury. The applicant argued that the corporal punishment to which he had been subjected was 'degrading punishment' within Article 3, and that English law failed to provide adequate protection against this violation of his rights because of the breadth of the defence of 'lawful chastisement'.

Once again, three distinct issues in the Court's reasoning may be identified. First, was Article 3 engaged? The Court has always held that ill-treatment must reach a minimum standard if it is to be classified as 'degrading' within Article 3. But that minimum 'depends on all the circumstances of the case, such as the nature and context of the treatment, its duration, its physical and mental effects and, in some instances, the sex, age and state of health of the victim'.[20] In this case the Court concluded that the considerable force used on this nine-year-old boy, evident from the marks on his body when examined, reached the required level of severity. Secondly, was the state under a positive obligation? The Court's approach to this question was unambiguous:

'The Court considers that the obligation on the High Contracting Parties under Article 1 of the Convention to secure to everyone within their jurisdiction the rights and freedoms defined in the Convention, taken together with Article 3, requires States to take measures designed to ensure that individuals within their jurisdiction are not subjected to torture or inhuman or degrading treatment or punishment, including such ill-treatment administered by private individuals. Children and other vulnerable individuals, in particular, are entitled to State protection, in the form of effective deterrence, against such serious breaches of personal integrity'.[21]

Turning to the third issue, there was no discussion in this judgment about whether the protection of the criminal law was required. As is evident from the final sentence of the last quotation, the Court assumed that only the criminal law could provide 'effective deterrence'. What was unusual about this case was that the general criminal law did provide the requisite protection. The problem was a defence to liability which reduced the child's protection from ill-treatment

---

[19] (1999) 27 EHRR 611.
[20] Ibid, para 20.
[21] Ibid, para 22.

by parents. By the time the case had reached the Court the UK government had conceded that English law 'failed to provide adequate protection to children and should be amended'. In the event, the amendment was rather slow in coming, and the statutory provision – which allows the defence of reasonable chastisement (without further specification) on charges of common assault or battery, and not to more serious offences – may still be inadequate to comply fully with the positive obligation as laid down by the Strasbourg Court.[22]

Positive obligations under Article 3 have also been found in sexual cases. In *MC v Bulgaria*[23] the applicant was a girl of 14 who alleged that she had been raped by two men. The age of consent in Bulgaria is 14, and they alleged that she had consented. The prosecutor terminated the prosecution for rape on the ground that there was insufficient evidence of force or threats being used and of resistance from the victim. The applicant alleged that this showed that Bulgarian law failed to protect her rights under Article 3 and Article 8. The Court devoted relatively little discussion to the Article 8 claim, and focused on Article 3. In relation to the first issue of whether Article 3 was engaged, the Court assumed that the ill-treatment involved in rape amounted to 'inhuman or degrading treatment', but the point was neither analysed nor discussed.[24] On the second issue of whether the state was under a positive obligation to have in place a criminal law penalising non-consensual sex, the Court held that although Member States have a margin of appreciation there are limits to that, and states are expected to respond to any evolving convergence of standard practice. The Court recognised the diversity of legal definitions across Member States, but found that no state requires victims to have shown physical resistance and that, even though some states still have laws requiring the use of force or threats, the prevailing practice is to focus on the absence of consent.[25] Here the applicant claimed that Bulgarian law took an unduly narrow approach, pointing to the prosecutor's reasons for dropping the prosecution in this case, and the Court found a violation of the positive obligation under Article 3 on the ground that the Bulgarian government had failed to show that an unduly narrow approach was not followed.[26] Thus it was not so much that the Bulgarian law was unacceptably narrow (in fact, it was similar to the laws of some other Member States), but rather that it was applied in an unacceptably narrow way, as the various statements of prosecutors demonstrated. The Court concluded that:

[22] For discussion and references, see Ashworth's *Principles of Criminal Law* (7th edn, 2013 by A Ashworth and J Horder), Ch 4.7.

[23] (2005) 40 EHRR 459; for analysis, see P Londono, 'Positive Obligations, Criminal Procedure and Rape Cases' [2007] *European Human Rights Law Review* 158; C McGlynn, 'Rape, Torture and the European Convention on Human Rights' (2009) 58 *ICLQ* 565; L Lazarus, 'Annex A: Advice for the Stern Review' in Baroness Stern, *Independent Review into how Rape Complaints are handled by Public Authorities in England and Wales* (2010).

[24] Cf *Aydin v Turkey* (1998) 25 EHRR 251, paras 83–86, for a detailed discussion of whether rape during military detention amounted to torture, holding that in the circumstances of this case it did.

[25] It must be said that the comparative law survey on which this was based, at (2005) 40 EHRR 459, paras 88–108, is narrower and less compelling than it might have been.

[26] Ibid, para 174.

'any rigid approach to the prosecution of sexual offences, such as requiring proof of physical resistance in all circumstances, risks leaving certain types of rape unpunished and thus jeopardising the effective protection of the individual's sexual autonomy. In accordance with contemporary standards and trends in that area, the Member States' positive obligations under Articles 3 and 8 of the Convention must be seen as requiring the penalisation and effective prosecution of any non-consensual act, including in the absence of physical resistance by the victim'.[27]

The Court also found a violation of a further positive obligation; that of mounting a thorough and effective investigation into the allegations made.

8.4 DUTY TO SECURE ARTICLE 2 RIGHTS

Article 2 of the Convention declares that (1) 'everyone's right to life shall be protected by law', and (2) 'deprivation of life shall not be regarded as inflicted in contravention of this article when it results from the use of force which is no more than absolutely necessary (a) in defence of any person from unlawful violence, (b) in order to effect a lawful arrest or to prevent the escape of a person lawfully detained . . .'. This Article has been invoked many times in relation to killings by law enforcement officers,[28] although, as we shall see, its possible ambit is broader than that. At least three major issues arise from the Strasbourg jurisprudence on Article 2 – how the law's standards of conduct should be phrased and interpreted; whether the law should require reasonable grounds for believing that the use of lethal force is absolutely necessary; and whether the law should provide for the criminal liability of senior officers whose planning of an operation fails to minimise the risk to life.

In relation to the proper phraseology of the standard to be applied, Article 2(2) itself declares that the killing must be 'absolutely necessary' for the achievement of one of the purposes there stated. There is no requirement of proportionality on the face of Article 2, but there is a long line of judgments holding that a test of 'strict proportionality' should be regarded as an inherent element in Article 2.[29] This places a significant gloss on the otherwise broad wording of Article 2, and it is clear that the test of 'strict proportionality' is more demanding than the general proportionality principle applied to qualified rights such as those in Articles 8, 9, 10 and 11. Thus Article 2(2)(a) states that a killing may be justifiable for 'the defence of any person from unlawful violence', which could be taken to suggest that if killing were the only way to prevent a minor injury it would be permissible under this Article. The strict proportionality requirement

---

[27] Ibid, para 166.

[28] For detailed discussion of the relevant Strasbourg case law, see F Leverick, *Killing in Self-Defence* (2006), Ch 10; B Emmerson, A Ashworth and A Macdonald (eds), *Human Rights and Criminal Justice* (3rd edn, 2012), 794–803; D Harris, M O'Boyle and C Warbrick, *Law of the European Convention on Human Rights* (2nd edn, 2009), 61–69.

[29] Eg *McCann, Farrell and Savage v United Kingdom* (1996) 21 EHRR 97, para 149; *Giuliani and Gaggio v Italy* (2011) 52 EHRR 3, para 176.

remedies that potential defect. Similarly, Article 2(2)(b) permits killing for the purpose of arrest or preventing escape, but contains no reference to the relationship between the force used and the reason for the arrest. However, in *Nachova v Bulgaria*,[30] where law enforcement officers were chasing two soldiers who had deserted from the armed forces, the Grand Chamber placed great emphasis on the need for proportionality (though, strangely, it was couched in the language of necessity):

> 'the legitimate aim of effecting a lawful arrest can only justify putting human life at risk in circumstances of absolute necessity. The Court considers that in principle there can be no such necessity where it is known that the person poses no threat to life or limb and is not suspected of having committed a violent offence, even if the failure to use lethal force may result in the opportunity to arrest the fugitive being lost'.[31]

The Grand Chamber referred to the judgment in *Makaratzis v Greece*,[32] which held that states have a duty to put in place an appropriate legal and administrative framework defining the limited circumstances in which law enforcement officers may use force and firearms. That judgment quotes the UN Basic Principles on the Use of Force and Firearms by Law Enforcement Officials (1990), which is based on the principles of necessity and proportionality. Thus, to conclude the first issue under Article 2, there is a positive obligation to shape domestic law along these lines, even though Article 2 itself makes no reference to proportionality.

The second issue concerns the need for 'good reason' for the belief that lethal force is necessary. This point was made in the leading case of *McCann et al v United Kingdom*,[33] where the Grand Chamber controversially held, by 10 votes to 9, that the United Kingdom had violated Article 2 in the shooting by SAS soldiers of three IRA terrorist suspects in Gibraltar. The government's argument had been that the three suspects were believed to have a radio-controlled detonator which would activate a car bomb, and that it was necessary to kill them in order to prevent imminent detonation and loss of life. In the event, neither a radio-controlled device nor a car bomb was found. The Court held that the actions of the officers should be judged on the basis of 'an honest belief which is perceived, for good reasons, to be valid at the time but which subsequently turns out to be mistaken'.[34] This is an objective test, reflecting the high value placed on human life by requiring law enforcement officers to have reasonable grounds before they use lethal force. English law has, however, adopted a subjective test, and this was recently re-stated in section 76(4) of the Criminal Justice and Immigration Act 2008. In the one judgment in which the Strasbourg Court had an opportunity to scrutinise the English law on self-defence and

[30] (2006) 42 EHRR 933.
[31] Ibid, para 95.
[32] (2005) 41 EHRR 1092, endorsed by the Grand Chamber in *Giuliani and Gaggio v Italy* (2011) 52 EHRR 3, paras 208–10.
[33] (1996) 21 EHRR 97.
[34] Ibid, para 200.

justifiable force, it failed to deal convincingly with the discrepancy between English law and some Convention jurisprudence in relation to erroneous factual beliefs.

Thus in *Bubbins v United Kingdom*[35] a man appeared to be pointing a gun at police officers who were surrounding his flat, and so the police responded and shot him dead. The Court repeated the *McCann* formulation of the applicable law, with its objective standard of 'for good reasons'. Yet two paragraphs later, when summarising its decision on whether the officer who fired the fatal shot had violated Article 2, the Court held that the force was not disproportionate and 'did not exceed what was absolutely necessary to avert what was honestly perceived by Officer B to be a real and immediate risk to his life and the lives of his colleagues'.[36] This formulation suggests that a subjective test was applied, since there is no mention at this point of the 'for good reasons' requirement. The Court further stated that it would not 'substitute its own assessment of the situation for that of an officer who was required to react in the heat of the moment to an honestly perceived danger to his life', and some would say that if this 'heat of the moment' concession[37] is combined with the objective test, it would be indistinguishable in practice from the subjective test. Be that as it may, the conclusion must be that the Strasbourg Court has failed to deal convincingly with the distinction between the objective and subjective tests. The Grand Chamber's most recent examination of the issue follows the same pattern as that in *Bubbins*, failing to draw a clear distinction between objective and subjective tests.[38]

The third issue is whether the law should provide for the criminal liability of those officers whose direction of the operation fails to minimise the risk to life. The Grand Chamber's conclusion in the *McCann* case was that the control and organisation of the whole operation – including the decision to allow the three suspects to enter Gibraltar, and the failure to make allowances for the possibility that the intelligence on which they were acting might be erroneous in some respects – indicated that there had been a violation of the suspects' Article 2 rights, since the Court was not persuaded that the use of lethal force was absolutely necessary. It seems possible that such a finding might provide the basis for a prosecution for manslaughter by gross negligence. As Sir John Smith suggested, it would be necessary for the jury to be directed:

> 'to consider whether (i) in the actual circumstances the force used was unreasonable and, if it was, (ii) whether the defendant, in making the mistake, was guilty of gross negligence, so bad as in their judgment to amount to a crime. If they are sure that he was, then they should convict him of manslaughter'.[39]

[35] (2005) 41 EHRR 458.
[36] Ibid, para 140.
[37] Which is also part of the relevant English law: Criminal Justice and Immigration Act 2008, s 76(7)(b).
[38] *Giuliani and Gaggio v Italy* (2011) 52 EHRR 3, para 178.
[39] JC Smith, 'The Use of Force in Public or Private Defence and Article 2' [2002] *Crim LR* 958, at 961.

It seems that no prosecution has yet been launched in this country on that basis. It is not clear that the Court's positive obligations jurisprudence requires that, but it may already be part of English law, as Sir John Smith argued.

The discussion of Article 2 has so far focused on killings by law enforcement agents. However, as we saw when examining Article 3 above, the essence of the Convention is that it is intended to protect the right of every person. This means that the state has a positive obligation to put in place a law that recognises and protects that right, even if the potential violation comes from a private citizen rather from law enforcement officials. This was the reason why the English law on the use of force in parental chastisement was found to be in violation of the Convention. The same must surely apply to the English law relating to self-defence and force used for justifiable purposes: the law should be formulated so as to protect the Article 2 right of individuals from both state officials and private persons. This is another reason why the Strasbourg Court's vacillation, even confusion, about the objective and subjective tests is unfortunate. Without clarity on that issue, the content of the positive obligation remains uncertain.

8.5 DUTY TO SECURE ARTICLE 4 RIGHTS

Article 4 of the Convention declares that (1) 'no one shall be held in slavery or servitude', and (2) 'no one shall be required to perform forced or compulsory labour'. This Article was rarely invoked in the first 50 years of the Convention's existence, but the emergence of various forms of human trafficking has revived interest in the ambit of Article 4. It is one of the Articles which is regarded as so important that it is declared by Article 15 to be non-derogable (alongside Articles 2, 3 and 7). There have been two major judgments of the Court relating to Article 4. The facts of the first, *Siliadin v France*,[40] concerned a girl of 15 who was brought to France from Togo on a tourist visa, with a promise that her immigration status would be regularised, she would be educated, and she would be able to earn her return fare by working for the woman who brought her in. In the event the woman took her passport from her and she was loaned to another family, where she was forced to work some 15 hours a day without payment or education. Eventually her case was taken up and her employers were prosecuted; but convictions for the serious offence of subjecting a person to living conditions incompatible with human dignity were quashed, and all that remained was a technical employment offence and a civil judgment for damages. The applicant claimed that her Article 4 rights had therefore been violated. The facts of the second case, *Rantsev v Cyprus and Russia*,[41] were that a young Russian woman went to Cyprus to work as an 'artiste' and did so, but soon left her

---

[40] (2006) 43 EHRR 287.
[41] (2010) 51 EHRR 1.

employment and stated that she wanted to return to Russia. Her employer found her, took her to the police as an illegal immigrant (they expressed no interest in her), and then took her to a second-floor apartment. Soon afterwards she was found dead in the street below. The applicant (the father of the young woman) alleged, *inter alia*, that Cyprus had failed to protect her against trafficking and that Russia had also failed to take operational measures to prevent trafficking.

Examining the reasoning in terms of three issues, the first question is whether Article 4 was engaged. This depends, in turn, on the meaning of the key terms in Article 4, which the Strasbourg Court had not previously sought to define. The Court in *Siliadin* held that the three prohibited forms of conduct are in descending order of seriousness. Thus the most serious is slavery, defined by the Slavery Convention 1927 as 'the status or condition of a person over whom any or all of the powers attaching to the right of ownership are exercised'. Applying that definition to the facts of the case, the Court held that the question was whether the applicant's employer exercised legal ownership over her and treated her as an object.[42] Turning to servitude, the Court again followed the Slavery Convention by defining it in terms of the use of coercion to require the victim to provide services for another and to live on the premises of that other, combined with the victim's inability to change status.[43] Forced or compulsory labour was held to refer to work exacted from a person 'under menace of any penalty' or exacted from a person who had not offered to do it voluntarily and who was under some 'physical or mental restraint', following the formulations of the Forced Labour Convention 1930.[44] On the facts of *Siliadin* the Court concluded that the applicant had not only been subjected to forced labour but had also been held in servitude (though not slavery).

The Court in *Rantsev* went much further, emphasising that the Convention is 'an instrument for the protection of individual human beings' and that 'its provisions [must] be interpreted and applied so as to make its safeguards practical and effective'.[45] The Court found that human trafficking, 'by its very nature and aim of exploitation', involved the exercise of powers of ownership, treating human beings as commodities, subjecting their activities to close surveillance, and involving the use or threat of violence against people who live and work in poor conditions. Thus, the Court concluded:

'There can be no doubt that trafficking threatens the human dignity and fundamental freedoms of its victims and cannot be considered compatible with a democratic society and the values expounded in the Convention. In view of its obligation to interpret the Convention in light of present-day conditions, the Court considers it unnecessary to identify whether the treatment about which the applicant complains constitutes slavery, servitude or forced and compulsory labour. Instead, the Court concludes that

---

[42] (2006) 43 EHRR 287, para 122.
[43] Ibid, para 123.
[44] Ibid, para 116.
[45] (2010) 51 EHRR 1, para 275.

trafficking itself, within the meaning of art. 3(a) of the Palermo Protocol and art. 4(a) of the Anti-Trafficking Convention, falls within the scope of art. 4 of the Convenion'.[46]

In this way the Court has implied a further right into Article 4, that no one shall be subjected to human trafficking. This was a bold step, and one taken without an explanation of the relationship between the definition of human trafficking and the definitions of the key terms already expressed on the face of Article 4. The tripartite Palermo definition of human trafficking refers to a certain activity ('recruitment, transportation, transfer, harbouring or receipt of persons'), a certain means (including force, fraud, and the making of payments for the purpose of securing consent to a controlling relationship), and the intent to exploit another for the purpose of sex, labour, or the removal of organs.[47]

On the second issue of whether the state was under a positive obligation in relation to Article 4, the Court in *Siliadin* started from the obligation imposed on all Member States by Article 1. Specifically in relation to Article 4 it noted that the other relevant international instruments placed positive obligations on states, particularly in relation to the protection of children and other vulnerable people. On this basis, the Court held that 'governments have positive obligations . . . to adopt criminal law provisions which penalise the practices referred to in Article 4 and to apply them in practice'.[48] In line with its general approach, the Court in *Rantsev* developed the nature of the positive obligations more fully:

> 'The Court considers that the spectrum of safeguards set out in national legislation must be adequate to ensure practical and effective protection of the rights of victims or potential victims of trafficking. Accordingly, in addition to criminal law measures to punish traffickers, art. 4 requires Member States to put in place adequate measures regulating businesses often used as a cover for human trafficking. Furthermore, a state's immigration rules must address relevant concerns relating to encouragement, facilitation or tolerance of trafficking'.[49]

The Court went on to spell out other positive obligations, such as that of taking operational measures to protect persons in immediate danger, that of investigating claims of trafficking thoroughly, and that of co-operating with international efforts to combat human trafficking.

Turning to the third issue, in *Siliadin* the Court found that French law at the relevant time did not have offences of slavery or servitude, and concluded that

---

[46] Ibid, para 282. In para 283 the Court stated that there can be no derogation from Article 4, according to Article 15(2) of the Convention, but this is inaccurate. Article 15(2) exempts only 'Article 4 (paragraph 1)'. This means that it is crucial to know whether the Court was implying the prohibition of human trafficking into Article 4(1) or Article 4(2), at least for the purposes of assessing any derogation.

[47] Protocol to Prevent, Suppress and Punish Trafficking in Persons, especially Women and Children (the Palermo Protocol, 2000), Art 3(a), cited in *Rantsev*, ibid, para 150; see also Directive 2011/36/EU, on preventing and combating trafficking in human beings, and protecting its victims, in the European Union.

[48] (2006) 43 EHRR 287, para 89.

[49] (2010) 51 EHRR 1, para 284.

its much more limited offence of the exploitation of labour in conditions incompatible with human dignity was not adequate to assure Article 4 rights.[50] In *Rantsev* the Court did not find fault with the criminal laws of Cyprus or Russia, but found that both states had failed to investigate alleged human trafficking when relevant information had been given to them.

8.6 CONCLUSIONS

The development of positive obligations by the Strasbourg Court, based on a fair view of the implications of Article 1 of the Convention, has brought some welcome minimum standards for the criminal laws of Member States. Recognition of a positive obligation does not always require an extension of the criminal law: in *X and Y v Netherlands*[51] the Court considered whether civil liability would be sufficient, and in *Rantsev v Cyprus and Russia*[52] the Court indicated that regulatory measures and new immigration rules were necessary, as well as criminal prohibitions.[53] But when it comes to criminal legislation, any extension of the law in one or more Member States needs to be carefully and convincingly argued. As John Stuart Mill warned in the mid-nineteenth century,[54] and as Liora Lazarus has argued effectively in recent times,[55] it is relatively easy to claim that laws are necessary to prevent harm or to protect people from harm. These are criminalisation decisions which require principled debate: behind the rhetoric of prevention lie various coercive powers which should be argued over in detail and not short-circuited by the finding of a positive obligation. In conclusion, we may explore three aspects of the positive obligations mentioned above: first, the correct phraseology of the justification for a positive obligation; secondly, the problem of conflicting rights; and thirdly, the future scope and impact of positive obligations.

The classic formulation in the *Osman* judgment is that, where a positive obligation relating to criminal law provisions is found, it amounts to a 'duty to secure the right by putting in place effective criminal law provisions to deter the commission of offences involving the violation of that right . . .'.[56] Care should

---

[50] (2006) 43 EHRR 287, para 148.

[51] Above, n 12.

[52] Above, n 45.

[53] For another area where the Court has held that civil law remedies are sufficient, at least in the absence of the consensus needed to support a criminal prohibition see *Vo v France* (2005) 40 EHRR 259.

[54] Mill wrote that, although the preventive function of government is undisputed, it is 'far more liable to be abused, to the prejudice of liberty, than the punitory function; for there is hardly any part of the legitimate freedom of action of a human being that would not admit of being represented, and fairly too, as increasing the facilities for some form or other of delinquency': JS Mill, *On Liberty* (1859), 106.

[55] Most notably in L Lazarus, 'Positive Obligations and Criminal Justice: Duties to Protect or Coerce?' in L Zedner and J Roberts (eds), *Principles and Values in Criminal Law and Criminal Justice: Essays in Honour of Andrew Ashworth* (2012).

[56] *Osman v United Kingdom* (2000) 29 EHRR 245, para 115.

be taken in this use of the deterrent rationale. It is surely right to say that the existence of a criminal law against certain conduct conduces to deterrence; but it is far more doubtful to suggest that higher penalties for offences result in lower rates of offending. Indeed, there is plenty of criminological evidence to show that the latter proposition is far from inevitable.[57] It would be preferable to avoid any potential confusion by re-phrasing the positive obligation so as to emphasise the importance of censuring people for committing certain wrongs and imposing proportionate punishment on them (as distinct from, or in addition to, merely rendering them civilly liable). While an underlying element of deterrence should not be denied,[58] it would be preferable for the *Osman* formulation to be amended so as to refer to 'putting in place effective criminal law provisions to censure and punish persons who violate that right'.

The problem of conflicting rights emerges vividly from the Article 8 case law, in particular the positive duty to have in place laws that protect the sexual integrity of the young. The House of Lords failed to confront two conflicting duties in *R v G*,[59] and the European Court of Human Rights fell into the same error.[60] G had been convicted of rape of a child, because he had sex with a consenting girl of 12 believing that she was 15. The defence was that conviction for this very serious offence amounted to a violation of the defendant's Article 8 right, and that a lesser conviction would have been more appropriate. Baroness Hale's speech is heavy on the social and psychological importance of preventing premature sexual intercourse, but devotes little attention to the age of the defendant. He was 15 years old, and therefore unable to consent to sexual activity himself. This case is therefore a strong example of the pitfalls of positive obligations. Of course there is a positive obligation on states to have in place a criminal law that provides for censure and proportionate punishment for sexual wrongs against the young. But it makes little sense to apply that law unremittingly to someone who is supposed to be within its protection: an adjustment needs to be made, so that the boy's rights are recognised too. Convicting G of rape of a child under 13 ought to have been recognised as a breach of his Article 8 rights, a conclusion that could stand with the substance of Baroness Hale's speech.

Finally, what is likely to be the future impact on English criminal law of positive obligations under the European Convention? There is no easy answer to this. Few would have predicted, a decade ago, that Article 4 would suddenly spring into life and give rise to positive obligations in respect of human trafficking (although, in terms of impact on English law, the relevant legislation was

---

[57] Eg A von Hirsch et al, *Criminal Deterrence and Sentence Severity* (1999), and A Doob and C Webster, 'Sentence Severity and Crime: Accepting the Null Hypothesis', *Crime and Justice: A Review of Research*, vol 30 (2003), 143.

[58] For elaboration, see A von Hirsch and A Ashworth, *Proportionate Sentencing* (2005), 23–24.

[59] [2008] UKHL 37, discussed critically at [2008] *Crim LR* 818 and by Lazarus (above, n 55), 148–49. See also ch 7 above, especially 7.6.

[60] *G v United Kingdom* (2011) 53 EHRR SE25.

already in place). Article 8 is of particular interest, since it gives rise to both negative obligations (eg no criminalisation of homosexual acts over the age of consent) and positive obligations (to have in place sexual offences that penalise non-consensual sexual assaults). Along similar lines there may be some scope for the development of positive obligations in relation to Article 9 (freedom of thought and religion), Article 10 (freedom of expression) and Article 11 (freedom of assembly and association), although at this stage one cannot be sure what form they would take. What Article 5 refers to as the right to security of the person may also give rise to positive obligations of some kind, and the Court may further develop the ambit of positive obligations arising from Article 3. Moreover, one possibility is that the Court may give more detailed specifications of the positive obligations in relation to, say, sexual offences under Articles 3 and 8, in a similar way to the level of detail on the use of firearms in relation to the right to life in the *Makaratzis* judgment.[61] However, as argued above, it is important that new criminal offences or narrower defences are not required by the Court without proper examination of the arguments for and against using the criminal law to reinforce the state's obligations.

---

[61] Above, n 32.

9

Epilogue: Emphasising the Positive

IT IS EVIDENT from the eight chapters above that, while some obligations can be identified unambiguously as 'positive' (in the sense that they require action, rather than abstinence), there are many contexts in which obligations have positive and negative aspects intertwined. For example, some offences have elements that criminalise acts and other elements that criminalise failures to act: rape and other sexual offences may provide an example, insofar as they specify both an intentional act and the absence of a reasonable belief based on the taking of steps to ascertain whether the other party consents. For the purposes of this volume such offences have been treated as offences of omission, on the reasoning that liability for such offences can only be established if the failure to fulfil a duty (in sexual offences, to ascertain whether the other party consents) is proved. Insofar as an omission is an essential part of an offence, that offence requires a special set of justifications, according to the arguments set out in Chapter 2. A similar intertwining is evident when we consider the obligations of the state. Indeed, as we shall see, there is an inevitable tension between the state's obligation to provide its subjects with security and the state's obligation of justice, and within the obligation to provide security there can be overlaps between duties to create prohibitions and duties to criminalise omissions.

The relevant obligations of the liberal state include the duty to provide security and the duty of justice, and more needs to be said about them both. As argued in Chapter 2.2 and Chapter 3.4, the state ought to develop structures and institutions capable of minimising threats to security of the person. In most theories of political obligation, this duty of the state is presented as the corollary of the subject's undertaking to obey the law: the subject yields some of her or his freedom to the state in return for the promise of reasonable efforts being made to minimise threats to personal security. The citizen's duty to pay taxes can be rationalised on a similar model, as the corollary of the expectation that certain public services will be provided. More generally, the state's duty to provide security requires it, among other things, to ensure that it maintains emergency services capable of responding when a person is in physical danger (see Chapter 2), to afford special protection to the rights of children (see Chapter 7), to ensure that there are criminal laws in place to protect people from violations of their rights, and to ensure the due enforcement of those laws (see Chapter 8).

All of these three elements in the duty to provide security amount to positive obligations in their own right – in the sense that they require the state to take certain actions – but our focus here is on the second and third of these duties. In terms of political theory the state must have a duty to enact laws prohibiting murder, violence, sexual attacks and so forth. Such laws are justifiable both as censuring those who commit such egregious wrongs and as a form of deterrence to minimise the occurrence of those wrongs. We saw in Chapter 8 that European human rights law and other international human rights documents support the view that states have a positive obligation to have such laws in place, for the protection of the rights of (potential) victims. We also saw, in Chapter 8.2 particularly, that there are some rights that yield both a positive obligation (to have in place laws that protect sexual integrity) and a negative obligation (to ensure that any such laws do not trespass on the liberty of adults to follow their sexual choices).

Persuasive though the argument for the state's duty to provide security undoubtedly is, the problem is to be able to know where it ends. If we continue to confine the argument to offences that criminalise conduct against personal security, the question of limits on criminalisation seems difficult to answer. There may be a political irresistibility in claims of the need to enhance security, public safety, social defence, public protection – a vocabulary that sometimes seems to make an unanswerable case. Attempts to answer the case can be made by, for example, mobilising empirical evidence to cast doubt on claims of the effectiveness of a law in providing protection, or by drawing attention to arguments of principle against criminalisation (on which see Chapter 1 above), or by insisting on the limitations stemming from the State's duty of justice (to be reviewed below). It is important to bear in mind the starting-point – that criminal laws are necessary to minimise the deprivation of citizens' fundamental rights, and to censure those who attack or endanger those rights – and to reflect that the citizen's right to be free from unwarranted coercion and unjustified conviction should also be maintained. Thus within the state's duty to provide security, properly elaborated, there should be found a constraint in the form of the security of individuals from unjustified state intrusions on their liberty.[1] Put bluntly, security should not be seen as a one-way street in which greater state powers for 'public protection' are regarded as unqualified goods.

More tellingly, the state's duty of justice should also be a source of significant limits on pursuit of the duty to provide security. The two principles operate in tension with one another, although there are certainly respects in which (in practice) the tension is too slight or entirely absent, as with the serious strict liability offences discussed in Chapter 4. To the extent that the duty of justice is taken seriously, however, it operates as a constraint on legislative endeavours put forward as necessary for greater security. The foundations of the duty of justice lie in the obligation of the liberal state to respect its subjects as responsible

---

[1] See further L Zedner, *Security*, Key Ideas in Criminology Series (2009), 157–58.

moral agents within a political community. The state should respect the individual worth of each person, rather than regarding them as mere numbers. Treating individuals as responsible moral agents means at least four things:

i) Requiring the state to abide by rule-of-law values, which prescribe that the law be clear, certain, stable and set out in advance (see Chapters 4, 5 and 6 above), so that individuals are able to decide how to conduct themselves in full knowledge of the consequences;

ii) Recognising the state's duty to publicise its criminal laws, so as to ensure that the law can operate as a guide to conduct and so that individuals can, without undue effort, find out what the law is (see Chapters 2 and 3);

iii) Requiring advertence as a precondition of criminal liability, which means that, in principle, offences should require proof of intention, recklessness or knowledge as to the prohibited consequence or circumstance (see Chapters 4, 5 and 6 above), so that individuals are not open to criminal conviction for accidental or unknown events unless a strong case has been made out for punishing (gross) negligence;

iv) Requiring the state to take due account of the reduced capacity of some subjects, particularly children, so that they are not open to criminal conviction when their capacities are not sufficiently developed (see Chapter 7).

These positive obligations flow from the state's duty of justice which, in turn stems not so much from the European Convention on Human Rights or other international obligations as from a relationship between the state and its subjects that insists on respect for individuals as responsible agents. It is plain from Chapters 4 and 6, on strict liability and on possession offences respectively, that what is here termed a positive state obligation has often been entirely ignored by the government and the legislature in this country. Strict liability offences and possession offences may be created without even a mention, let alone any open consideration, of the principles set out above. Similarly, in relation to Chapter 3, offences are often created or extended without adequate publicity (adequate in the sense of being designed to reach those who might be thought likely to fall foul of the new law). Further, we noted in Chapter 7 that in the UK there has been variable recognition of the special rights of children in the criminal process: even if we pass over the vexed but fundamental issue of the age of criminal responsibility, there are several respects in which the law appears to hold children to the same standards of expected behaviour as adults. It was argued in Chapter 7 that this is wrong, and that it stems partly from a failure to recognise the problem and partly from a political reluctance to be seen to 'soften' the law for the young.

The eight chapters are not entirely about the positive obligations of the state in respect of criminal law, however. Chapter 3 argues that individuals should accept a positive obligation to make reasonable efforts to know the criminal law: the thrust of that chapter is that the state has an obligation to take steps to make it easier for individuals to fulfil their duty, but that individuals have the duty nonetheless. This argument was taken further in Chapter 2, where a whole range of positive obligations on individuals to take action in particular situations was sketched out. The strongest case presented in favour of positive obligations on individuals was at the confluence of three streams of argument – the priority of life, the principle of urgency, and the principles of opportunity and capacity. Beyond that, there was detailed discussion of the boundaries of other positive obligations arising from the family or household, from voluntarily incurred obligations, from situations of causal responsibility, and from civic responsibilities. The argument for positive obligations stemming from civil responsibilities required several steps of contentious reasoning, and led to proposals for an offence of failure to report serious crimes, which some would oppose on the grounds that it might usher in a society dominated by suspicion, betrayal, intimidation and worse. However, these issues have been discussed too little by criminal lawyers as well as by governments and their law reform agencies. Chapter 2 shows that the traditional common law reluctance to impose criminal liability for omissions is supported by some good reasons and some less good reasons. Let us hope that the chapter acts as a stimulus for re-appraisal of the shape of the criminal law, particularly in respect of positive obligations on individuals.

It is evident that the chapters in this volume represent, not a description of existing Anglo-American criminal law and its supporting doctrines, but rather a set of normative arguments in favour of the state recognising the importance of respecting individuals as responsible agents when shaping its criminal laws (or, where they are not fully responsible agents, as with children, shaping its criminal laws to make due allowance for that fact), and correspondingly a set of normative arguments in favour of imposing clearer and, indeed, further positive duties on individuals which may result in criminal conviction for failure to carry them out.

Index